FROM STAGE TO PULPIT

AN AUTOBIOGRAPHY

Rev'd Lawrie Adam

A poem composed and given to me by a dear friend
Margaret Mills

God's last gift is remembrance.
He gave us memories that we might have
Roses in December.

To Paul:
With Best Wishes
& God's Blessings
Lawrie Adam
27·7·18

Published by BookLocker.com, Inc., St. Petersburg, Florida.

Printed on acid-free paper.

BookLocker.com, Inc.
2018

First Edition

Dedicated

To all the highly skilled professional performers I have had the pleasure of working with during my twenty-five magical years in show business.

With grateful thanks

To my loving wife Wendy who, for 54 years has been unswerving in her devotion. To our two daughters Tracey and Fiona, their husbands Stu and Jay for their encouragement and support through the hard times, sad times and happy times. Not forgetting, our adorable grandchildren, Benjamin, Mollie, Harry, Tilly, Dani and Matt who all keep us on our toes, especially with technology.

A special thank you

To my Editor, my dear cousin Janet Steemson who has been invaluable for her encouragement in the writing of this book.

To John Berry for his patience in checking all was correct.

Finally, to my friend Sir Ken Dodd who looked me in the eye and said, "You have to write a book Lawrie, your story must be told."
Well, here it is Ken.

This book was written by four inputs: Almighty God for the inspiration, Jesus for the love and compassion and the Holy Spirit as my conscience and my guide.

I merely held the pen.

Table of Contents

Introduction
CURTAIN UP!

"Okay people; get into a line two by two please. In a few minutes we will enter the ark!" The chattering stopped. A hush fell on the waiting nervous men about to be ordained as Church of England Deacons in the huge Blackburn Cathedral.

A woman pushed past the queue saying in an urgent tone, "Is there a Lawrie Adam here please?"

What now? "Yes that's me," I said. She paused and thrust into my arms a large bouquet of flowers.

"These are for you, sir!"

I heard a few sniggers as I glanced at the gift card.

'Best wishes Lawrie from your pal Colin Crompton. P.S. Couldn't for the life of me think of what else to give you.'

Colin, a well-known television star, had worked with me at many venues. This was a reminder that my 25-year show business career was ending. That part of my life was changing forever.

"Okay lads, green light, let's go." Handing the flowers to someone to look after, I started the sedate walk into the body of the cathedral to the uplifting singing of the hymn 'Crown Him with Many Crowns'.

How did a Scottish coal miner's son from Lochgelly Fife come to be here?

It is an intriguing story. Let me take you back to the beginning of my adventure.

One
Family Life

On Monday 24 January 1938 in the mining town of Lochgelly, Fife. A newborn baby, held up by the ankles, was given a smack across the bottom, and war was declared. I was that baby.

Mum, Dad and brothers, Ronnie and Bill, not forgetting Flossy our wee fat golden Labrador lived in what Mum called a 'coonsilhoose': a two bed-room upper-half of a semi-detached council house.

Beyond our lounge window was a field and beyond that, a view of rolling hills stretched unbroken as far as the eye could see. A fence enclosed the large unkempt field, which provided my pals and me in later years a place to re-enact the latest Errol Flynn, or John Wayne movie. Crawling on our bellies, we were the cowboys, soldiers, or sailors surprising the Indians, Germans, Japanese, or even the pirates. Goodness knows what we were scraping over buried there deep in the grass, but there was sometimes the strong smell of doggie-poo greeting the nostrils of our parents when we went back to our warm homes. Sadly, the welcome was not, "Hi son, had an enjoyable day?" More often than not it was, "Oh! Bloody hell! Whit's that awful stink?"

We played out of sight of adults exploring a world that seemed completely safe. The Braes were our jungle with many trees for adventurous little boys to climb. We ended up soaked in the small stream catching the odd unsuspecting minnow in an empty jam jar.

While the view from the lounge window was appreciated in spring and summer, winter dulled the view with rain, hail and snow propelled against the glass by the full blast of any wind or gale. As the storm battered against the glass, we huddled round the crackling glowing coal fire. Facing the fire was lovely and warm, but our backs were frozen!

There were moquette–covered armchairs for Mum and Dad, one each side of the fireplace, vacated by anyone else when they entered the room. A homemade brown and cream patterned rag rug lay on the floor between them. Mum always sat down the same way - a slight hover poised above the seat and then a controlled sinking movement accompanied by a sighing moan "Aaaaah!" Everyone shared the relief with her as she safely landed.

Dad ritually grasped his well-worn old pipe from the mantelpiece, opened a small pocketknife, and began performing his 'smokers juggling act'. With his knife, he sliced small portions of his 'Thick Black twist, Bogie-roll' tobacco into the palm of his hand, (and here I inhaled deeply, as I loved the pungent aroma) placing one large palm on top of the other, he rolled them in a circular movement, opened them and Voila! All broken down. Somehow, he managed to empty out all the old dead tobacco and ash, into his palm, but kept this pile separate from the new. Carefully, using a light pressure he tamped the new tobacco into his pipe. Lovingly, he lit the pipe with a match until it glowed red. He puffed like a steam train getting ready for the off. Finally, he sank back with a look of pure ecstasy smiling through thick billowing clouds of smoke. The whole ritual fascinated me. When the opportunity presented itself, secretly, I picked up one of his pipes, tasted it, and posed in front of the mirror above the fireplace. In my twenties, I smoked a pipe hoping to impress my girlfriend.

Our square folding-leaf table dominated the centre of the room. The table usually had a thick rust coloured chenille cover on it, which hung down almost to the floor. Underneath it, I was the captain of a submarine in the depths of the ocean, or a king in a corner of my huge castle. The only intruder was Flossie who insisted on sharing which was not a pleasant experience if she had been out in the rain or shared a horrible fart.

In one corner, a low radiogram replaced a wind-up gramophone. The whole family sat around the fire listening to our favourite radio programmes 'Life with the Lions', Jimmy Clitheroe in 'Call-Boy', or the 'Jimmy Clitheroe Show'.

God bless harmonious family life. I was a millionaire then and did not realise it!

On the ground floor lived a quiet elderly grey-haired couple called Johnstone. Mr. Johnstone was seldom seen without his flat cap. When he was admitted to hospital, I asked Bill why. He said, "For an operation to remove his cap!"

Unfortunately, they did not like music. My mother had been a first violinist in a Dundee orchestra and liked to keep up her standard. Ronnie fancied himself as an exponent of the mouth organ and father did his best to murder a second-hand mandolin. Bill, a drummer in the Dundonald Pipe band, was learning to play the bagpipes. My paper-wrapped comb produced a sort of strangulated buzzing bee sound. Flossie raised up her little snout and issued a low wolf-like moan. Even the Johnston's in the flat below joined in the musical extravaganzas by thumping on their ceiling with the end of a brush-shaft, but sadly out of rhythm. However, we encouraged them to join in by playing louder!

One of the main industries within the Kingdom of Fife was coal mining, and my dad William, (Wull), was a 'Lochgelly coal miner'. This was never a chosen career but more lack of choice with few opportunities for advancement. Dad was a hard-working, sincere and honest man. He had a lovely sense of humour and an infectious laugh. He was tall, well-proportioned and carried himself with dignity, until mother shouted at him. Then he developed a stoop and slunk away. He was blind in his left eye, which had a bad squint. He wore wire-framed glasses for reading and bought them from Woolworths, chosen from a mound on the counter, trying each pair until they felt comfortable. When the glasses broke, he mended them with sticking plaster. Never a big wage earner it must have been very difficult bringing up a family. However, there was always enough food on the table and clothes on our backs and shoes on our feet. Mother knitted sweaters and cardigans all shapes and colours. Years later, not until I had a family of my own, did it occur to me that many loving sacrifices had been made for my brothers and me.

Our car was an old Hillman Minx 4 seater, which was very unreliable. I think we probably pushed it nearly as often as we rode in it. The front window had mottled around the edges and that together with Dad's defective eye, made for some terrifying moments.

My mother's name was Euphemia, (Greek for well-spoken) but most folk called her Phemie. She was much shorter than dad was and smartly turned out. In the house she wore the working-class housewife's uniform of the times: a cotton brightly coloured floral wrap around apron only removed if mum was off-duty or being 'posh'.

Mother hailed from the city of Dundee and was a fund of never ending stories about her young days. She had the ability to hold her audience spellbound having you laughing fit to burst one minute, and the next feel as if your heart would break with compassion. She knew poverty. Like many from her generation, she was part of a sizeable family and as the eldest took responsibility for her three young brothers and sister. Her father was by all accounts an accomplished flautist and died from tuberculosis when she was quite young. She would plead with the market street traders for a bag of spoilt fruit or a bag of broken biscuits for pennies that she could share with her brothers and sisters.

Once, she related, there she was with her charges, sharing out the rotten fruit when a carriage drew up in front of the Palace Theatre. Inside were two children dressed in lovely blue velvet outfits and sharing a huge box of chocolates.

"They teased us with each one they popped into their mouths. As I looked at those two little girls and looked at my brothers in their threadbare hand-me-down clothes, I was reminded," she continued, "that there were those who had, and those like us who, for one reason or another, had not."

Brother Ronald (Ronnie) was 12 years older than I was and sadly, we never had much in common. William (Bill) who was 10 years my senior shared a room and a double bed with me. He was the quiet one who seemed to think a lot and kept his feelings very much to himself. He worked for the Co-operative Society as a Painter and Decorator and seemed content with his life. He played in the Dundonald Pipe Band. He looked very dashing in his highland uniform. I persuaded him to take me to his band practice and started learning to play the bagpipes. When I was proficient enough, they gave me a set of bagpipes and a uniform.

I was fine until the first engagement. During the parade, the heavens opened, and it poured down soaking me to the skin! The glamour and illusion rapidly disappeared, and I made a sudden decision. Goodbye to being a Bandsman! However, there is an upside to everything. I could now read basic music.

Two
Relatives

Mum's younger sister Helen, (Nellie) was a favourite aunt. Auntie Nellie's husband was Alec, (Eck). They had two children Alec and Jenny. Uncle Eck would take me out for walks around the city giving me his full attention and time: a precious commodity treasured and remembered by small children.

Mother's brother Bobby lived in Bournemouth, but I saw a lot of Uncle Tommy who was always going to break into show business. Finally, the youngest of Mum's brothers was Uncle Eddie. He had been an acrobat working with a famous act called 'The Three Royce's'. He did stand-in stunt work doubling for various film stars. I caught a glimpse of him once falling down a staircase replacing Stewart Granger in the film 'Waterloo'.

I loved Dundee, the quaint accents and the trams (trolleys). Visits to Dundee were an adventure. We caught a double-decker bus to 'Newport'. Catching sight of the River Tay made me gasp. "Oh! Jings, will you just look at that!"

The tangy smell of the sea caught my nostrils as we queued for the ferry to take us across the water. I stared in wonder at the huge poster advertising the shows at the Dundee Palace Theatre. This would be the first theatre I would play as a paid theatrical artiste, and one day my name would grace a similar poster.

I thrilled to the feel of the throbbing underfoot as the ferry's engines started up the huge revolving paddles on the sides of the ferry. Leaning over the rail like two old sea mariners, dad related the story of the collapse of the Tay rail bridge. I could well imagine the groaning of the railway girders as they buckled and tumbled into the sea accompanied by the screams of the poor folk crashing to their death in the wild tossing icy cold River Tay.

Aunty Nellie's family lived at the top of a steep cobbled street high up in a tenement block. I liked to shout and hear the echoes of the 'close' or stairway up to the flat. There were no lifts and the stairwells were very clean with no rubbish or graffiti as the occupants took a pride in their surroundings.

The Fife Lot

Although my father came from a large family of ten, few of the Fifeshire relatives were familiar to me. I think there were petty jealousies, squabbles and fallings out. The ones I knew I grew to love dearly.

We often met up with my father's brother Bob, his wife, Chris, daughter, Janet and a son who was born much later called Robert They lived in Dundonald. I always remember a huge roaring fire in a large black-enamelled grate and a lovely smell of baking. The kettle was forever on the boil and Aunty Chris made my favourite delicious raspberry jam.

Uncle Bob would produce his 'Long-necked Banjo' lifting everyone's spirits as they listened to him.

Three
Memories of a War Baby

My parents lived like everyone else wondering into what sort of world they had brought their children. Military Police wearing red caps checked identity cards in cinema queues. Mother pointed out men to me who wore bright blue suits with white shirts and red ties, telling me to they were very ill and wounded in the war.

Once we joined a group of neighbours standing at the garden gate, pointing out distant flashes in the sky as someone said, "Jings! They're bombing Glasgow: it'll be the Clyde shipyard."

I felt the ground give a sort of 'wump' underfoot and Glasgow was miles away. If we could feel the earth move here, what must it have been like to be right in the middle?

"Poor souls!" someone murmured. Everyone walked quietly away not saying another word.

Schools were named after the points of the compass in Lochgelly. In 1942, I started at the 'West School', which was a five-minute walk from home.

We children had never seen fresh fruit. So, it was a big event when a little lass of Italian descent, whose father owned an ice cream shop on Main Street, brought some lovely red apples into the classroom and presented them to the teacher. They were shared out and consumed very quickly!

One morning, the teacher passed around a funny looking green thing called a 'Banana'. The teacher said, "And now children I am going to place it here on the window sill where it will ripen to a lovely golden colour."

Mysteriously, it vanished the next day and was never mentioned or seen again!

As a young lad, I was very thin and consequently the school bully made me miserable. He was a big stocky lad. Every time we went out for a break, he picked on me. It came to a head one morning when, encircled by a cheering group of his supporters, he bumped me on the nose and it bled. In retrospect, I believe my character building started from that moment.

I ran home up the stairs to our flat shouting, "Maw...Maw!" (Scottish for Mum).

She came running out of the kitchen wiping her hands on her apron and looked at me but said nothing. When I explained what had happened, I was shocked to hear her say something that I have never forgotten. She stood in front of me, took me by the shoulders, and said, "Listen son, you have to go back to this bully right now. Walk up to him. Hold his eyes wi' yours. Say nothin' at all to him. Then give him a punch right on the nose wi' yer full weight behind it, and just walk away. Not only will he never bother you again, but also very likely neither will anyone else. Noo go, and dinna bother coming hame unless you dae it."

In a state of terror and shock, I walked back to school. That my lovely mother had actually asked me to do this awful deed. However, I had complete faith in her and did exactly as asked. He went down with a great whump. How his nose bled! Brought before the headmaster, he gave us both a severe telling off. I marvelled at how my mother was quite correct. He avoided me like the plague, and no one ever bothered me again. In fact, I even collected a few admirers!

Every summer the school attended a Gala in the South Park. We all marched behind the exciting sounds of the local Brass Band, competing fiercely with the local Pipe Band, at the head of the procession. Folk lined the streets waving and cheering us on.

As we entered the gates, each child received a large paper bag containing various goodies to eat. Each school class ran various races to the encouraging cheers of pals and parents. To me it was an exciting event and I was always sad when it was time to walk home.

When the war ended in 1945, we were staying with aunty Nellie. There was singing in the streets below and I was aware of a lot of excitement. The adults explained that they were all going out but assured me they would not be long. I could not go, as there was a chance I would get lost in the huge crowds. I looked out of the window and listen to the wireless. However, the end of the war for me was when sweets were no longer rationed.

Family Holidays

We had few family holidays. I presume we simply could not afford them. On one occasion we travelled by steam train to Oban on the North West coast of Scotland. Ron and Bill, being so much older, were not with us.

When the train arrived like a huge steaming, hissing monster, I was entranced. The guard blew his whistle and waved his flag. The acrid steam belched out of the train chimney as we climbed into the cosy carriage. Dad hoisted our cases onto the luggage rack while I wriggled into a window seat. After more whistle blowing and doors slamming, we were off with a squealing, clanking lurch. On the wall, there were pictures of our destination. A fascinating sliding door on the carriage led into a corridor where we could walk up and down. I gazed in wonder as we passed moors, bubbling streams, mysterious looking lochs and heather covered mountains.

One warm morning we arrived at the quayside and I could smell seaweed while the screaming gulls dived and soared in the cloudless blue sky. We embarked on an open boat to sail to the island of Iona. As we pulled away, we had a beautiful view of Oban from a different perspective. I asked my Dad what the large circular monument was on the hill and he explained it was called the 'Oban Folly' He thought that a rich man had started to build it, but for some reason abandoned it and there it stood ever after.

He added, "And by the way Lawrence, dinna move, there is a large wasp on the back of yer neck."

I froze. My mother looked near to panic.

Dad continued in a level soothing voice, "If you just keep still, son, it will simply flee awa'."

It did not! It must have thought, "Oh! Yea?" and promptly stung me. Poor old dad got it in the neck from my mother.

Another year we stayed in a bed and breakfast for two weeks in Ayr, a seaside town on the west coast of Scotland. Once we travelled by coach and ferry to Northern Ireland. We arrived at a large hotel called the 'Laharna' in a place called Larne. I had never been in a huge hotel before, nor had I ever seen police walking about town wearing big revolvers strapped to their side.

Four
Life Threatening Breathing Problems

In 1944, I started suffering from chest problems diagnosed as bronchitis. This plagued me until I was 22 years old. As a result, I missed many days of important schooling.

I do not know how my poor brother Bill managed to sleep in the same bed with me coughing and wheezing the night away. My mother was worried sick as she took me to clinics and doctors.

On one occasion, in a room with a strong smell of disinfectant, I was asked to strip to the waist and sit on a small wooden chair alongside about eight other children. Someone handed me a pair of dark glass goggles to wear. A very bright light was switched on in front of us after being warned not to remove our goggles otherwise we could harm our eyes. I think this was 'infrared light treatment', which was believed to have good healing properties.

At some point, a doctor told my mother "If your son had his tonsils and adenoids removed that might do the trick." Soon after, I sat sitting shivering dressed in a white cotton affair in a corridor in the Dunfermline Infirmary. The scene that unfolded beggared belief! Each child was led into a doorway presumably leading to a surgery. Next, a nurse would emerge carrying a galvanised bucket with something floating in blood. The nurse wore a green top and a large orange coloured rubber apron with huge glistening wet bloodstains on the front of it. This routine carried on five or six times. However, when it got to my turn, my mother grabbed my little quivering hand and said in a loud voice, "Richt, that's it. Come on son I'm no givin' you up tae this slaughter hoose!"

A few days later, following the operation to remove my tonsils, I was tucked up in bed in the Edinburgh Infirmary finding it tricky to speak or to swallow.

In 1947, my bronchial problems seemed to worsen. One night struggling to breathe, I managed with difficulty to get from my bedroom into the hall. Everyone was in the lounge listening to the radio. Suddenly they became aware of me stumbling about in the hallway. They ran out of the room by which time my face and lips were a horrible bluish colour as I slowly sank to my knees. They thought I was dying...and so did I!

The doctor decided that I would benefit from a stay away from the coal dust in the atmosphere where we lived. He suggested a convalescent children's home at Ovenstone, near Pittenweem by the seaside in East Fife.

This huge convalescent home was also an orphanage to about ten other children. My mother tearfully kissed me goodbye, it was too far to be able to visit me but they would come and pick me up when it was time to go home.

I was there for seven long weeks, which felt like an eternity to me at aged 8 years. It was a very cold, snowy December. I spent most of my days in the large warm hall. At one end was a blazing log fire with a large black wire safety fireguard round it. All the staff were very kind, and the gardener found me a job gathering up wood for the fire.

At last my mother and father arrived to take me home remarking how much better I looked. I did feel better. I did not have a single bronchial attack all the time I was there.

Five
From Primary to Secondary School

I have a vague memory of sitting an exam (11 plus) and my mother and teachers telling the class that this was very important and that we should do our very best. I did not make it to Beath High School (2 miles by bus). Instead, I found myself relegated to the Lochgelly Junior Secondary School, which was about a ten-minute walk for me.

My first impression, as I walked through the school gates was far from exciting. It looked dark, grey and foreboding. Inside was no more cheerful.

At assembly, we were informed that we would have a variety of teachers and that we would follow a timetable to which must be adhered to strictly. We were reminded that the school practised 'corporal punishment' administered by cane or tawse.

Many Scottish schools used tawse at that time produced in Lochgelly by a leather company called Dickenson's. This was a leather strap about two feet long, by an inch and a half wide by approximately an eighth of an inch thick. However, the sadistic part of the design was that the strap had a split down the middle, running for about a foot. These items were displayed menacingly to us. All the teachers, without exception, plus the headmaster used them frequently and I had the distinct impression that they derived much perverted pleasure from the exercise. To my knowledge, not a single teacher enjoyed even a modicum of admiration or liking by any of the pupils.

It felt like a jail sentence and indeed, it was the most miserable time of my life. The only commendable thing I can say about the experience was like living through a cold dark miserable winter, to appreciate a bright warm summer!

Problems at school

I was still troubled by bronchial problems and alas, missing school lessons. At the start of a new term, the classes lined up in the gym hall. The headmaster, a small sour faced stocky little man, stood at the front and shouted to us all.

"If you hear your 'class name' called out, take three paces forward. However, if your 'name' is not called out stay where you are as you will be repeating a year."

What a humiliation and this happened to me twice whilst I attended this penitentiary.

One day, we endured a science class under the tuition of the teacher we nicknamed 'Savanah Junior' after a weekly comic figure of a mad scientist. This day he threw down the chalk and said, "Why am I bothering really, you'll all just end up down the pits like your fathers...huh! Coal miners!"

Drawing and sketching seemed to be in the genes. A locum teacher recognised my abilities in art. This skill gave me a ray of hope that I could qualify for a more enlightened school. Sadly, grammar schools were not about the arts, but about mathematics, science, English and foreign languages. In retrospect, I was not ready for such a move.

Christmas Pantomime

In no time at all, it was Christmas. Mum and dad took me in a coach party to my very first pantomime at the Kings Theatre in Edinburgh. The star was Harry Gordon, well known to Scottish audiences. He was playing the Dame. I would never forget my first experiences of that evening. Walking into the brightly lit foyer festooned with pictures of the pantomime. We walked up some marble steps, through glass doors and into the stalls. There was a lovely aroma.

I nearly fell down the stairs leading to our seats as mum warned. "Oh! Watch where you're going Lawrence!"

I gazed all around me at the safety curtain with all its adverts, the dress circle behind me and the upper circle or as I was later to learn 'The Gods'. We sat on red plush seats. The lights dimmed, and the music played. I realised that there was a sizeable orchestra in the 'Orchestra Pit'.

Mum nudged me and whispered,

"Look, there's the conductor noo, and they are playing the Overture."

I said to her, "Was the orchestra you played in as big as this one?"

She smiled, "Oh no, son, ours was much bigger than this one."

I felt very proud of her and wished I could have seen her play.

Gradually the safety curtain went up. Seconds later huge green velvet drapes festooned with gold braiding and large gold tassels gracefully rose revealing a stage full of dancers and singers in brightly coloured costumes. One day I would walk on that very stage. God moves in mysterious ways, his miracles to perform.

Christmas and New Year in Scotland

Scots did not make such a big event of Christmas as the English did. We put up some homemade decorations such as a coloured loops round the lounge. There were the usual Nativity plays at school and a choir. I recall assisting my Dad to put a glass of Mum's ginger wine (strong and lethal!) together with a slice of homemade cake for Santa on his journey. I would awaken in the morning and be thrilled to bits when my feet caused parcels (wrapped in brown paper; no fancy stuff and no Sellotape either, just string) to make exciting rustling noises.

Bill bought me presents one of which was a Magic Set. I loved that magic set and it whetted my appetite to learn more. I saved up my pocket money and managed to buy myself a few tricks. I was thrilled to bits at the "oos" and "aaahs" uttered by mystified folk. In a few short years, people would offer to pay me to perform magic. Thus, my philosophy was born.

'Do what you enjoy doing. You will become good at it and eventually people will want to pay you to do it.'

Celebrating the New Year was a much bigger event than Christmas in Scotland. In those days, everyone visiting received a warm welcome and a drink or two. Anyone who played an instrument, or could sing or tell a humorous story, was called upon to do so. The first person through the door was the 'First Foot'. Superstition had it, that if the person was male, tall and dark and came bearing a lump of coal then you were assured of good luck throughout the year.

A Boxer I Will Be

Dana Andrews played a boxer in a film and that influenced me to want to be one. Uncle Bob had been a Bantamweight Amateur Champion, so I asked him to help. He talked it over with mum and dad and agreed to take me to a boxing trainer he knew with a good reputation.

Dad said, "Well it won't do any harm I suppose if he learns how to defend himself."

Mum was petrified at the thought saying, "What if he gets a broken nose or something?"

After a year of lessons, Uncle Bob reckoned I was light on my feet, a quick thinker, always willing to attack and good enough to take part in an amateur fight in Glasgow. Uncle Bob and dad accompanied me.

There were two doors in a small room with about five chairs. One door was an entrance/exit door to a passageway the other led to the boxing ring in the main hall. I was not very warm dressed in just a pair of shorts and a white singlet vest. Uncle Bob bandaged my hands and told me to keep moving around 'shadow boxing' like the two lads in the room.

All at once, the hall door opened and one of the lads was called through to the sound of a round of cheers followed by the bell for the start of the bout.

In a very short time, two men burst into the room carrying the lad on an old door. Blood was pouring from his nose.

Another lad was called in...same procedure. Once again, the door burst open and back HE came carried on the door!

"Lawrence Adam?" It was my turn! He left the door ajar and I could see the brightly lit ring where a rough looking, well built, wee Glasgow lad bounced around the ring punching the air. That did it! I grabbed my clothes and shouted over my shoulder, "Sorry Uncle Bob I'm aff hame noo," and bolted!

To my mother's relief that was the end of my boxing career. On the plus side, it did teach me confidence. I was never afraid of a confrontation again. I knew I could handle myself should the occasion ever arise, and it nearly did as when I worked in some very dodgy places in the company of some very dodgy people (even some London professional gangsters)!

Pocket Money

The idea of earning some pocket money appealed to me. Early one morning, following a tip-off, I waited down a side street for the milkmen to come out of the dairy gates to start on their rounds. Two other scruffy lads joined me, elbowing to get to the front but I stood my ground. The clip clopping of a horse's hooves heralded the milk cart coming into view pulled by a huge brown horse. A smallish stocky built man aged in his forties, dressed in a fawn coloured stiff heavy-duty raincoat, checked scarf and flat cap drove the cart. He wore shiny brown leather leggings up to his knees.

He smiled down at me and said, "Want a job lad?"

I shouted back "Aye, I do Mister." He put out his hand, which I grabbed, and he hoisted me up beside him onto his milk cart.

"Ma name's Bob," he said.

I replied, "An ma name's Lawrence."

He stared at me, "Michty me," he said, "That's an awful big moothfi...What if I just call ye Law?"

"Aye fine," I replied. We chatted getting to know each other in no time. I liked Bob and I think he took a shine to me. He loved his horse called Nobby, and his job. He told me the pay rates and that I could have four bread rolls every morning. All I had to do was, when the horse stopped, (Nobby knew where and when) nip down off the cart and grab the allocated amount of milk bottles from the grey metal crates, plus any bread rolls ordered and deliver them to the doorstep of the houses he pointed out to me. I was to memorise the quantities and the houses. I soon got the hang of it and enjoyed the work. I even got on friendly terms with Nobby. I was sure he nodded to me each morning. One problematic moment was when Nobby stopped outside our house refusing to budge until a familiar figure came out with a slice of bread and jam accompanied by a loving stroke. Bob murmured to me out the side of his mouth, "Bloody woman always does that. When she's away I've the devil of a job getting Nobby to bloody move on."

I replied, "Have you met my mum Bob?"

Bob offered me work on Saturdays. It was extra money plus some free cakes. I agreed. This was a surprisingly high bread cart: shiny bottle green with gold leaf writing emblazoned on the side and rested upon a bright red carriage with red wheels. I realised why it was a high box shaped vehicle because when you opened the double louvered doors at the back, inside there were many wooden shelves each with different types of cakes and buns on them. I felt like a cowboy sitting on a stagecoach. We sat side by side at the front on top of the box. There was a definite knack in getting up there with my wee legs. The start was at a more civilised time.

School Days End

At the end of 1952, as my miserable school days ended, the Headmaster handed me a final appalling report. He said in his usual gruff manner, "Here you are Adam (the staff called us by our surname) give this to your employer, assuming anyone ever gives you a job!"

I looked at it and it was full of zeros. I then looked at his mocking podgy face. I knew there was nothing he could do or say to me now, so I tore the card in half and said, "Thanks for nothing!" turned on my heel and walked out with a smile on my face. I am pleased to say I have never seen or heard of any the staff from the Lochgelly Junior Secondary School from that day to this. In fact, the actual school is now gone. Good riddance too.

At home, I announced that I was finished with school.

Dad said to me, "Well Lawrence when you look back on your time at school, you will say to yourself, 'They were the happiest days of my life'." I think not!

Dad then said that he was taking me down the pit with him in the morning. I should put on some old clothes.

Six
A New Era Begins

It was still dark outside as it was only 5.30 am and I was wide-awake and feeling mixed emotions about the day ahead of me. Bill was still in deep slumber. I heard some quiet movement and the clink of crockery noises coming from the direction of the kitchen. That would be Dad getting ready for work and preparing some breakfast.

It was January and the year was 1953. I was 14 years of age and wondering what the future held for me. I did not have a clue about what sort of job I might do. I was fully aware that I had lost a lot of education and so anything academic would be denied me. Neither did I feel that I was cut out for heavy manual work.

Slowly, the bedroom door opened, and Dad whispered, "Lawrence, come and have some breakfast son." He had made some porridge and my favourite, French toast: bread cut into fingers, dipped in eggs and fried until golden brown. He was already dressed in his navy-blue overalls. After we ate, and Dad had his brew of a steaming mug of tea, on went his heavy steel capped boots, his coat, scarf and flat cap. I wrapped up warmly and off we set on my latest adventure.

I had never been near Dad's place of work before and as we walked through the gates, I was far from impressed with what I saw. Underfoot the ground was a mixture of mud, sludge and grit. The Coal Miners looked like robots displaying sad blank expressions on their faces, reluctantly dragging their feet towards 'The Cage'. I realised that it was still dark. When these miners finished their shift at the end of their working day, they would go home in the dark. They must have seen daylight only at the weekends!

My father's voice broke into my deep thoughts "Okay now son, just do everything I tell you and nothing more. Keep your wits about you and do not allow yourself to panic should anything unusual happen. You'll spend the morning here with me and see what it's like to be a coal miner."

One of the men crammed into the cage looked at me and said, "This yer son Wull, is he goin' to be joinin' us then?"

Dad replied, "Aye weel, we'll see whit he thinks o' it by denner time."

With a sly smile the man replied, "Aye, mebbie no so much if he's any sense. Ma lad started twa weeks ago."

It was very quiet apart from the sounds of the miners shuffling their heavy leather boots and the clearing of dry throats. The cage gate clanged shut, the light dimmed and flickered on and off, there was a whirring sound and then my stomach rose up to meet my mouth as we descended the lift shaft until eventually we thumped to a stop.

The gate opened again. It was very dark. It smelled musty and I heard the dripping of water echoing in the gloom. I wore a pit helmet held just above my eyes thanks to my ears. Dad turned on the small lamp fixed on the front of the helmet. The lights on the miners' helmets was pretty much the only illumination. Dad placed his large hand on my skinny little shoulder and said, "We've quite a way to walk now to the pit face. As you get nearer you'll notice that the roof gets lower and lower so be prepared to stoop a wee bit."

Wooden poles like small tree trunks reached from the floor to the ceiling. I asked what they were for.

Dad said, "They are called 'pit-props' because that's what they do: prop up the roof and keep it from falling down on us."

There was a sudden loud rumbling noise growing louder and louder and someone shouted "Bogie!"

I shouted to dad, "Bogie, what the heck's a bogie?"

He grabbed me and roughly pulled me aside, "Look doon. Di ye see these narrow railway tracks?" I nodded. "Well they are whit the small wagons or bogies run on." Just then, a wooden carriage piled high with lumps of coal came in sight, went past at a fair speed, and disappeared into the gloom. Gently pushing my shoulder and urging me ahead, he said, "Aye they've caused many a nasty accident doon here, ye really have to be a bit alert."

I said, "Here, anything else I should know about that's threatening?"

There was a short silence, he took a deep breath then replied,

"I dinna really want to frighten ye son, but there has been the odd pit prop that for no obvious reason gives way and then there's a fall that can be a bit nasty and has sometimes caused some deaths."

I gulped, "Anything else?"

Another silence. A miner walked past us carrying what looked like a small yellow bird in a cage. I said, "Ah! That's nice Dad. You can bring your pets down here with you then?" He gave a chuckle,

"No, that's no' a pet son, that's oor early warnin' system. See if that wee burd falls off its perch, we git the hell oot o' here as quick as our legs will carry us, it means there's gas aboot and it could kill ye, or if there's a spark we all git blawn tae hell!"

I was speechless. I went very quiet and did not speak for ages.

Dad said, "Gets a bit low here son watch yer heed on the roof noo."

After about 10 minutes walking with a bent posture my back was already starting to ache. I was not enjoying this experience one little bit and would be very glad when he said we were going out!

"Whit's all that banging and clanking Dad?" It was deafening.

"We are nearly at the coalface son where the miners hack at a wall of coal with their picks, shovel the loose coal onto a bogie then start again. It's back-breakin' work and not fer the faint-hearted. Ye ken how when a git hame all I want is to sink into ma comfy armchair, fill my old pipe wi' thick twist baccy then usually fall asleep until Mum shouts that the tea's nearly ready."

"Right son, I think ye've seen enough noo to get the hang o' things."

He took me by the shoulders, looked me in the eye and said, "Just say the word an' ye'll be working doon here wi' me next week. What do ye think, is it an aye or is it a no?"

I did not take too long to reply. "It's a great big 'NO' Dad!"

He smiled and patted me on the shoulder and said, "Whit a relief to hear ye say that. That is what I was hopin' fer. Come on let's get oot o' here and make sure you never ever come back." His plan worked a treat. I never did.

The magnetic lure of the piano accordion

Any time we were near a dance band or on a coach trip where they had an accordionist playing for sing-alongs, I sat as near to the accordionist as was humanly possible with my eyes glued to his fingers in absolute wonder and amazement.

Dad said to me one day, "Lawrence you and I are taking a bus ride and I think you might get a very pleasant surprise at the end of it."

"What now?" I thought.

I found myself inside a small terraced house with a roaring coal fire crackling away, whereupon this large man appeared and produced a small 8-bass piano accordion. (The number of buttons on the bass side governs accordion sizes).

He handed it to me and said, "There yar ma boy, see what ye kin do wi' this." I slipped the straps over my shoulders and just started to play tunes! I quite surprised myself how many tunes I could play.

My Dad was beaming at me. He exclaimed, "Okay, I'll tack it, a poond ye said?"

"Aye that's right Wull, I think he's a natural. I coudna mak it speak like that mysel' an' I've had it for a while!"

I was desperate to play it and as soon as were we in our own house, I was playing it again. This tiny instrument my kind Dad bought for a humble £1 would eventually change my whole future. (God's mysterious ways again?)

The lure of magic

One of my pals, a smallish tubby lad called Billy Richardson asked me to go with him to an English Church on Sunday. I had never attended church before and so agreed. That Sunday morning, he called for me and off we ran to a church called St. Finnian's Episcopal Church right on the boundary of Lochgelly. The vicar was very friendly and welcoming and so was his wife. I must have gone for about three weeks although nothing theological pierced the gloom. I did a few magic tricks for the vicar's wife who said, "I'm going to write to a good friend of mine who is the President of the Kirkcaldy Magic Circle to see if he will invite you to be a member. I certainly think you are good enough."

About two weeks later, a letter arrived inviting me to come to Kirkcaldy and perform a short audition for the consideration of membership. Thinking of something special, I made a scarlet velvet cushion with gold braid trimmings and golden tassels at the corners. Raiding mum's remnants drawer, I found a piece of purple velvet. I fixed some gold ribbon round the edge. The idea was to create a golden orb with a jewel cross on it. This meant dismantling the cistern ball from the toilet and polishing it up until it gleamed beautifully. A bit of tin cutting for the cross was required and sticking some of mum's paste jewellery on it, then I soldered to my orb. I was able to get it to float around without any means of support. (The secret cannot be revealed to the reader) but it looked great. When the family saw the trick, they were in awe and completely baffled. Until that is, someone tried to flush our toilet!

The President welcomed me warmly and introduced me to about thirty magicians. I performed an audition on a small raised platform. After some card tricks, I lifted the purple velvet cover revealing my orb and described it as 'The Floating Orb' illusion. I was happy to note that some of them leaned forward in their seats displaying a keen expression on their faces. Feeling nervous, I entered the realms of 'risk'. The orb slowly rose up in the air from its crimson velvet cushion and appeared to float along the purple velvet cloth and become airborne, finally coming back down to rest gently upon the cushion. For a few seconds there was complete silence, which I found deafening, but then they erupted into spontaneous applause (thank goodness!) They thought it was brilliant. They made me a full member there and then. One of the members came up to congratulate me, his name was Sam Nardone, saying "I'll be in touch with you, we can do great things together kid."

Carefree days of youth.

Almost every weekend I would be away on an adventure with my best pal Billy Meikle to a Youth Hostel. We were both proud members of the 'Scottish Youth Hostel Association.' They had affordable hostels all over Scotland. In the main, they were very large houses, usually situated in the country. One was a large castle. I loved the experience of arriving at a hostel after a long cycling haul. At the approach to the building, the smell of bacon cooking on portable paraffin stoves reached the nostrils. The odd whiff of toast and other appetising aromas reached out temptingly as earlier arrivals busily prepared their evening meals. Billy and I could not wait to get booked in and do likewise!

My place of birth.
8 Dewar Street,
Lochgelly.
Kingdom of Fife
Scotland

A Family Camping
Holiday.
My Dad, Me and
Brother Bill.
They couldn't afford
posh hotels...but they
were always happy.

My Mum, Brother Ron
Me, Brother Bill.
All taken I think on our
Brownie Box Camera.
I'm the wee bauld one
yawning!

My Mum and Dad.
Mum lived in Dundee
Dad travelled a long way
from Lochgelly to see her.
A strange match really,
Mum was a 1st Violinist
in an orchestra and Dad
was a coal-miner.
They were in love right to
end of their lives.

On the left,
my Uncle Eddie who was
a professional acrobat.
On the right,
my Uncle Tommie
who could play many
musical intruments but
never really mastered
any of them.

My Mum and Dad with
my Uncle Eck and
Auntie Nellie.

1947. My neighbourhood kids. How they got us to sit still is a wonder.
I am 5th from the right on the 3rd row.

1948. Aboard the Dundee ferry

On holiday in Ayr with my Mum.

Brothers Bill and Ron

My Dad.

Me, Mum and Dad and our old Hillman Minx

The Floating Orb Trick

My Dance Band. Bill,drums. Sandy,violin. Dave,bass. Me.Cathy,piano.

Seven
The Working Man

Looking through the 'Jobs Available' section in the local Lochgelly Times newspaper with my mother, she said, "They are looking for a Butcher's Boy at the Co-op."

"No, I don't fancy galloping about on a heavy iron butcher's bike handling cold sausages," I replied.

"Well, they want an Apprentice Jiner (joiner) at the Co-op."

I shook my head. "Anything else?" I asked.

"Oh aye, this would suit ye down to the ground Lawrence. They want an Apprentice Draper's Assistant, at the Co-op" she replied,

I took my mother's advice without any thought and applied. The information sent in reply said, "All applicants are required to sit a short examination."

At the main offices of the Co-operative building, I was shown into a large Board Room. Seated round a long highly polished table were thirty boys. The Secretary in charge of the proceedings was a tall serious looking woman in her forties. She escorted me to an empty chair and ticked my name of the list on her clipboard. To each of us she handed a sharpened yellow pencil together with a white form to complete immediately. When we finished, she collected the forms and disappeared through a large heavy oak door.

I recognised some of the other applicants and knew many of them were from

Beath High School. I seemed to be the only one from the Secondary School. No one spoke. When our eyes connected, they immediately looked away again. I was growing more nervous by the second.

The secretary appeared again, walked quickly round the table placing a white sheet of paper, printed side down, in front of each boy.

She said, "These are the test papers please do not turn them over until I say so, otherwise you will be asked to leave the room immediately."

She took a seat holding a stopwatch in front of her, and the very room itself seemed to hold its breath.

"Go!" she said.

There was a loud rustle of paper as we turned over the exam papers, pencils poised. Some sat and scanned their sheet, while others started scribbling right away.

I looked at mine. "Oh, my God!" The questions required us to use decimal points, vulgar fractions, centimetres, inches, yards and weights. My palms were very sweaty, but I did my best to wade through the exam paper.

I put down my pencil, sat back in my chair and looked around the room. Most were still writing furiously, some chewing at their pencils, all looked worried, especially as I appeared to be the first one finished.

The secretary collected the papers and disappeared through the large oak door. I was sure I would be at the bottom of the pile with no chance of getting the job.

Once more, the secretary came back, adjusted her glasses as she looked round the room,

"Who is Lawrence Adam, please?"

My heart gave a leap. I must have been the worst of the lot and now singled out for a speedy departure.

"Follow me please Lawrence."

In the next room, a very smartly dressed slim man sat behind a large desk,

"Mr. Adam," he said, "we have decided to award you the job. The wages are to be forty-five shillings per week. Can you start on Wednesday?"

"W-w-why yes, sir," I stammered.

The plaque on his desk read 'Mr. Charles McEwin, Managing Director'. He continued, "You will require a white shirt, tie and a dark suit. Oh! And a pair of black lace up shoes, please. Welcome to the Lochgelly Co-operative Mr. Adam. I hope you enjoy many happy years with us."

The secretary gently manoeuvred me towards the door.

I hesitated, and said, "May I ask you a question, sir?"

"Why certainly Mr. Adam."

"I've just got to ask. I know many of these boys out there and they are all quite brainy. How is that I have got the job?"

"They are here for the joiner's job. You were the only one who ticked the box for the draper's job," he replied with a large smile.

As I made my way down the large concrete stairs heading for the pavement, I paused.

"Good grief, I start on Wednesday and I don't even know what a draper is!"

The adventures of an Apprentice Draper 1953

On the morning of 4 February 1953, I was up at 7 am and freezing cold. The bedroom window had a coating of ice round the edges. I washed, got dressed in my new navy-blue suit mum and dad bought for me, a brand new white shirt with separate collars, brass collar-studs and cuff links and a tie. I had trouble fitting the brass studs in the back and front because the collar was stiff with starch. Then I fiddled with the new cuff links, knotted my new tie and felt ready to go.

It was blowing a blizzard outside and the snow looked very deep.

"Come and get some breakfast doon ye son. A've made some porridge, braw and hot," Mum shouted.

Most days, we ate our breakfast and lunch in our warm kitchen. The table was in the centre of the room covered with a brightly coloured waxed-cloth.

Mum exclaimed, "My goodness, jist look at you. Yer mare like the manager then an apprentice. We are all very proud of you son, passin' that exam."

I decided to keep quiet about the ticking the box episode.

I put on my new lovat-green overcoat and started out on a journey that was to last for 6 years. "Thank goodness the weather had calmed down a bit." I thought, as I walked up North Street towards

Lochgelly's main shopping centre. I had no idea what to expect. I realised that my feet were getting damp and already my poor new shoes were looking a bit sad covered in wet snow.

There were small groups of people standing outside the door to the main Co-operative store, so I joined the queue of young girls outside the drapery. A smallish built woman wearing a fawn overcoat arrived jangling keys and unlocked the large wrought iron double gates to the entrance.

"Good Morning Miss Allen." The waiting girls said in a chorus, to which she murmured "Good morning."

When she unlocked the large glass doors, everyone walked in and I followed nervously. No one had spoken a word to me. I felt invisible!

The first thing I noticed was the warmth and a faintly perfumed smell. The best way to describe it would be to remind readers of the TV series 'Are you Being Served?' It had a large rectangular area with glass counters on both sides displaying various colourful goods. Behind the counters were shelves packed with neatly stacked items.

At the far end of the area was a raised wooden panelled box with large glass panels on three sides. Cables with tiny wooden cups dangling from them entered this area from all the counters. For the life of me, I could not figure out what they were for.

I was jolted from of my thoughts by Miss Allen. She was slightly shorter than I was, with very neat tightly permed grey hair. She smelled of perfume and face powder. She wore dark red lipstick very sparingly applied, and pink framed spectacles. She had changed into a dark, maroon-coloured overall coat.

"Mr. Adam is it?" she said smiling at me.

"Yes," I replied.

"Come with me Mr. Adam. I'll show you where to hang your coat and introduce you to our senior apprentice."

I followed her to the bottom end of the store, behind a large pine wooden counter with some bales of coloured curtain material piled neatly upon it. She continued down three wooden steps, opened a metal door on her right and ushered me through. It was a large packing area, dark, grey and cold. There was a young man there busy tearing up a pile of cardboard boxes and aggressively ramming them into a large rubbish bin.

He looked up in surprise as Miss Allen said, "This is George, and now that you are here, he is promoted to our Senior Apprentice." I noticed George draw himself up a few inches and square his shoulders and a proud smug expression appeared on his face.

"This is Mr. Adam George. Please show him the ropes. This is his first day and in fact your first job. Mr. Adam, is that correct?"

I nodded. With that, she swept out.

George said, "Hi, what's your first name?"

"Lawrence," I replied.

He sniggered. "I'll call you Lall."

I cannot say I warmed to George who seemed a bit cocky and superior. He was about 18 years old, dressed in a dark grey double-breasted suit, blue shirt and tie.

He said, "First job every morning, carry the gates from the front of the store right through to the back and place them against that wall. Let's go and get the gates." He walked smartly back the way I had come in.

There were two heavy looking black wrought-iron gates at the entrance.

"Easy! First get you shoulder under the gate, lift it up, place one hand in front of you carefully raise the gate off its hinges and walk it through the store. OK go for it."

I got my shoulder underneath, felt it bite into my thin bony shoulder, raised it off the hinges, then it smacked down behind me with a loud bang.

He had a good laugh and said, "Oh! I forgot to tell you that you must find the balance point. Try again."

This time I managed it and then staggered through the store. Within seconds, I thumped into the large rear of a little fat woman who gave a loud shriek then fell on her backside in a perfect sitting position! I immediately offered profound apologies. Two girls helped her up and into a chair.

Miss Allen appeared and said, "Oh dear! We are so sorry, the boy only started today."

I glanced round at George who was having a good laugh. I managed the other one and suffered no further mishaps throughout the years I was in that department. Next, I was relegated to finish tearing up the boxes left by George. It took ages and my hands were getting sore. This was to be a regular morning chore.

George appeared and said, "When you've finished that Lall, Mr. Given the big boss wants you in his office."

Back in the store, I was grateful to feel the warmth once more. Miss Allen was sitting behind a large desk sorting invoices.

She looked up. "Ah! Mr. Adam, the Departmental Manager would like a quick word with you."

"Could I ask you," I said, "what's in there please?" pointing to the little wooden cups whizzing along the wires from all directions and smacking into a collection terminal. A hand appeared and with a quick twist tore the cup from its socket.

"Ah!" Miss Allen said, "That's the 'Cashier' removing the payments for goods sold and putting in the required change. You'll learn all about that later. This way please, Mr. Adam."

At the end of the passage, we reached a frosted glass door. She knocked.

A deep voice shouted, "Come!"

Miss Allen timidly opened the door a little way, poked her head round and said, "I have Mr. Adam for you, Mr. Given."

"Send him in," the voice boomed. "Send him in."

I entered the medium sized office to see by a man in his early sixties, immaculately dressed in a very expensive looking navy-blue suit with a pale blue silk handkerchief tucked in to his breast pocket, crisp white shirt and a blue patterned silk tie. He sat at a large roll-top desk and spun round in his executive black leather chair to face me with a beaming smile. I liked him immediately.

He broke the silence by saying, "Well Mr. Adam, you seem to be settling in okay. Do you think you are going to enjoy working here?"

"Oh yes!" I said. "I didn't really know what to expect, in fact I didn't even know what a 'Draper' was."

He chuckled and explained what drapery involved. As he spoke in his soft but authoritarian educated Scottish accent, I must have gazed at him in rapture. I had never had a conversation with anyone quite like Mr. Given in my life. My eyes were wandering from his silk handkerchief to the half an inch of shirt cuff protruding from each sleeve displaying an expensive looking gold cuff link. I also caught a peek of a chunky looking gold watch on a leather strap. His hands were those of someone who worked with their head rather than with hard manual labour. I thought of my poor dad's palms, which were always rough, and course with 'blue scar' cuts that filled with coal dust.

I was jolted back when he stood up and said "But now Mr. Adam, I want to see how you might shape up as a salesman. "Follow me." He was a tall man who towered above me. He walked with complete confidence but not arrogance. He had a 'presence'. As he strode through the store, I noticed how everyone he passed looked at him with respect.

Customers almost bowed before him saying "Good morning Mr. Given." He smiled, nodded and even paused here and there for a quick word. Sometimes he placed a well-manicured hand on an elderly lady's shoulder.

As he walked, he murmured to me, "Remember Mr. Adam the customer is our very life-blood and they are 'always right'. Never forget that that."

We arrived at a large mahogany glass-fronted counter with a tall girl behind it in a smart black linen overall coat. She had long black hair, was pretty with a sense of humour playing around the corners of her mouth.

She broke into a grin as we approached her. "Good morning Mr. Given."

"Good morning May, this is Mr. Adam. I want you to introduce him to the stock. Give him the advantage of your wide experience and advice. Let him serve customers right away to see how he gets on."

"Here is some advice to start you off Mr. Adam. Present yourself to the customer showing that you are very interested in them. Stand erect and smart, give them a smile, rest your fingertips on the counter and balance yourself on the balls of your feet. Feel like a sleek black panther ready to spring into action. When you leave the customer to fetch the goods, do not just turn and walk away. Rather, sweep away to the side displaying graceful, controlled energy. Finally, Mr.

Adam, if the required goods are packaged then please remember to open the package before displaying to the customer. When you do display the goods, make sure you do this with a certain panache. Do not just lay them on the counter before the awaiting purchaser but display them to their best advantage." With that, he swept away.

I glimpsed George in the background sniggering. With a shake of his head, he turned and walked away. It was an angry walk introducing me to the human ingredient of jealousy. I met this many times in my life. Thank goodness, I can place hand over heart and say I have never experienced this destructive emotion. I have admired many people and their talent but have never begrudged them their gifts.

May looked me up and down and was not over friendly. I noticed a sign hanging over the counter, which I could hardly pronounce.

"What is 'Lingerie'?" I asked her

She gave a snort and said, "Och, jist underwear but dearer!"

The shop door opened and in walked two very large rotund Nuns in traditional black habits. For a minute, I thought it was an eclipse! They walked towards me stopping directly in front of me. I decided it was time to go into the 'panther routine'.

Smiling broadly, I swayed on the balls of my feet, lightly rested the tips of my fingers on the counter, arms spread apart, then said, "Good morning ladies, how may I help you?"

They did not look pleased to see me. The larger one of the two (bearing in mind they were both quite enormous) cleared her throat and muttered in an Irish brogue,

"No offence sone, bot could we please have a lady to serve ozz?"

"I am quite capable I assure you, what is it you require?" I replied,

There was a longish silence then she said, "We want combinations."

I thought for a moment then jocularly replied, "Combinations? That's a motorbike and side-car isn't it?"

The only sound breaking the silence was a sort of muffled, choking noise, coming from May who was by this time bending down out of sight apparently tidying the contents of a counter drawer and seemed to have a handkerchief rammed in her mouth.

"Please excuse me a moment," I said to the nuns.

I remembered Mr. Given's advice not to just walk away so I swept away to the side, still displaying a big smile. However, as I swept away my trouser flies caught on the shop counter brass knobs and ripped all the buttons open displaying white baggy drawers and contents! I grabbed a large book with 'On Approbation' stamped upon it and clutching it to my draughty crotch headed for Miss Allen for advice. I nearly fell over a helpless hysterical red-faced May lying on the floor. I walked right passed Miss Allen's desk into the back passage and very quickly buttoned up my flies. Squaring up my little shoulders, I mustered as much confidence as I could and marched back to Miss Allen.

She looked up from the piles of invoices covering her desk, adjusted her pink rimmed glasses on her nose and asked, "Well Mr. Adam, what is it? I am really very busy you know."

"Very sorry to bother you Miss Allen but you did say you would be on hand to offer any advice if needed. I have two nuns up there and they want combinations?"

She bent backwards and glimpsed the two nuns waiting at the far end of the store looking at her with pleading eyes. She gave a slight smile, but then again, it could have been flatulence, and replied with a nod in the direction of the shelves behind me, "On that shelf there, Mr. Adam. First you will have to ask them what size they require."

"Oh!" I said. "Right thank you."

I then committed a cardinal sin and shouted up to the other end of the store,

"What size do you require ladies, small, medium large, extra-large or extra-extra- large?"

In that instant, the whole store seemed to go quiet.

Looking very cross, Miss Allen said, "Mr. Adam, do not shout at customers, approach them and quietly ask them what size."

Immediately, I did as requested. Their faces were by this time beetroot red.

They glared at me and muttered, "Extra-extra-large, if you please."

I hurried away back to the shelves, took a package marked in their size and recalled Mr. Given's instructions about displaying the goods to the customer with a flourishing panache. As I walked, I undid the package. Upon reaching the counter, I threw the goods up in the air with a large theatrical flourish. The huge billowing shape seemed to take an age to float then gently come to rest on the counter.

"Good grief, you could go camping in these!" I said.

I was aware of poor May getting on her hands and knees and crawling away. The nuns just grabbed the combinations rolled them up and stuffed them into their shopping bag, "Tank you very moch sone, here's the roit money, good mornin'." With that they were off.

I put the cash into the wooden cup, clicked it into the receptacle on the overhead wire, pulled the chain and it went flying off at 100 miles an hour towards the grumpy faced little cashier who immediately beckoned me to come to her desk.

I climbed the few steps to the cashier's box and opened the gate-like door to enter. The cashier glared at me - a twentyish aged woman, very primly dressed in a blouse buttoned to the neck, with a rather severe hairstyle for someone so young.

"You are not allowed to enter here. Get out! "

"Certainly," I said, "Very sorry."

She continued, "I know you are new here but surely you must have been told to make out a counter slip in duplicate. Place the top copy in the cup with the customer's cash and then send it down the wire to me."

I replied, "No. No one told me that and anyway the customer paid the correct amount then left."

"Well, don't do it again do you hear?"

I felt a little bit flushed at being told off in such a brisk manner and replied,

"Certainly, Madam, and thank you for the advice, even if it was delivered to me in a most rude tone." I left and made my way back to the counter.

No sooner was I back behind the counter, about to question May about the cash slip routine, when the door opened again. Standing before me was a large woman whom I had known all my life. She owned the corner sweetie shop.

"Good morning Mrs. Suttie. What can I get you please?"

She looked at me and then replied, "You can get a lady to serve me thank you very much!"

I looked at May who was once more fiddling about out of sight in a counter drawer.

"I am quite capable of seeing to your needs Mrs. Suttie I assure you."

There was a pause. She took a deep breath and said, "Very well, I want towels, for our Ella."

Ella, I knew was her daughter. She was over six feet tall and every time I went to see an amateur dramatics musical production at the Carnegie Hall in Dunfermline, there was Ella, towering above everyone else in the chorus. This time I was on the ball.

I smiled confidently and asked, "Now is that face towels, hand towels, bath towels or tea towels Mrs. Suttie."

Another long pause, "No," she said, "Sanitary towels, please."

The panther routine once more, I said to myself, but being careful of my fly buttons on the counter this time. "Certainly, please excuse me one moment," I said as I swept away. I noticed that May was trying to stifle a giggle as she continued to shuffle around in the drawer. I arrived in front of Miss Allen's desk again.

"Really Mr. Adam you just cannot keep interrupting my work like this. What now?"

I paused a beat, "A lady requesting sanitary towels." Once more, she leaned back in her chair to glance up the length of the store noting the woman standing all alone at the counter.

"On that shelf Mr. Adam but ask her what size first."

I did it again, I shouted up the store "What size sanitary towels Mrs. Suttie, small, large, extra-large or extra-extra-large?"

Miss Allen looked near to a fainting fit, "Mr. Adam, not again. What did I tell you before?"

"Oh! Very sorry," I stammered.

Quickly, I made my way back to Mrs. Suttie who muttered "Large, please." I hurried off to obtain her request.

I reached for the packet, glanced at Miss Allen who glared at me shaking her head in disbelief. Again, I remembered Mr. Given's instructions about panache and started to undo the package as I walked. As I opened it and removed the object a strange sight met my innocent eyes. I held the goods up by the attached strings and remarked,

"Well, I've never seen anything like this before!"

Mrs. Suttie turned and ran out of the store with a hand up to her mouth. May was apparently having a convulsion on the floor and Mr. Given appeared, waving me to follow him. As I walked past Miss Allen I noticed she was standing up, her mouth open wide with a bewildered expression on her tiny pink rouged face. The only movement from her were her saucer like eyes following me as I passed by. I entered Mr. Given's office. He motioned me to sit down. "Perhaps I threw you in at the deep end Mr. Adam and to my mind you coped very well indeed with some difficult situations. I am going to hand you over to Mr. Malone now and a change of counter experience. Mr. Malone is our Window Dresser and is widely experienced in serving at any counter in the store. I am going to suggest you assist him in the art of display for a few days and then you can go on the Curtain and Fabrics counter.

Eight
Learning Curves

My life seemed to consist of going to work, washing the store windows armed with a pair of heavy wooden stepladders, a bucket of water and a chamois leather, then polishing with newspapers. This was no quick task as there were about 10 large display shop windows. It took me a whole morning to perform this task.

I was greatly relieved when a new apprentice started, and I had the pleasure of showing him the ropes. His name was Wee Danny. Strange thing about us Scots. If you were tall, the adjective Big was added to your name. For example, Big Jimmy, Big Geordie or Big Mary. If you were on the small side, it was Wee Nellie, Wee Ronnie etc. No boy wanted to be called Richard as this was automatically abbreviated to Dick!

Evenings were spent mainly going to the cinema twice a week, (no TV yet) Country Dance classes every Wednesday with my brother Bill and then occasionally going to a Country Dance and Social on a Saturday to a live Scottish Dance Band. Most of the men wore kilts. The women dressed in long white dresses, their clan tartan sash across their shoulders...all very colourful. I loved Scottish music and most of the time I sat in wonder watching the accordion players' fingers. Understanding the dances proved to be a big help to me in a couple of years down the road.

One weekend we had a visit from two of our Dundee relatives. One was Uncle Tommy, my mother's younger brother. He always had a musical instrument of some description on the go, such as a guitar, an accordion, a steel guitar or a banjo. He managed a tune on them all but never really mastered any. He got bored and switch to another. The other visitor was Aunty Nellie's son Alec. He was an excellent player of the violin and excelled in classical music.

As I walked into our lounge, they all went quiet. "They have been talking about me," I thought. Then their eyes swivelled in the direction of what looked like a large accordion case in front of our table.

"Uncle Tommy, have you brought your accordion to play to us?" I said.

"Open it Lawrence and see what you think of it."

I knelt down, laid the case flat and opened the lid. It was a lovely deep rich red colour and had the words Frontalini written down the front in white lettering with diamanté stones set in the writing.

I just stared at it and said, "Wow!"

"Take it out Lawrence and try it on. It's got a lovely rich Italian tone."

I did not need to be asked twice. I strapped it onto my shoulders in seconds. I started to play it and was in heaven. It was much bigger than my tiny eight bass accordion that my Dad had bought for me for a pound and had tone changing couplers attached to the grill.

Uncle Tommy said, "It's a 48-bass model but a very good serious starter instrument. It looks very good on you Lawrence. Which is just as well, because it is all yours now."

My jaw dropped open. I was speechless.

My mother said, "Okay, take it off now son and put it back in its box." I reluctantly started to obey.

"Surely, he can play us some music a bit longer, I'm really enjoying this," Dad said, "No!" she said. Put it in its box son."

Dad came in again saying, "Hang on, I want to hear him play my favourite. Just play 'Endearing Young Charms' for me son, then you had better put it away in its box."

Enthusiastically, I played his request for him. I noted Dad closing his eyes, resting back in his big comfortable armchair puffing on his pipe with a lovely smile on his face.

"What did that piece of music mean to him?" I wondered. I came to the end of the music then I gently laid this beautiful-sounding accordion to rest in its case. I closed the lid and Mum stepped over and put a small key in the locks. Click click!

"Now," she said looking at me and holding the key up to my eyes, "Dad has just paid £14 which is more than a week's wages for this accordion. The case stays shut until you agree to start music lessons and learn it properly. No more busking tunes."

"But I don't know any accordion teachers," I said pleadingly.

"Well, I do," she replied, "and here is his address. He's expecting you tonight at six o' clock. Get the bus to Crossgates and here is the money for your first lesson. If you drop out of lessons, the accordion will be sold. Remember son, you dinna get anythin' fer nothin' in this life. There's always a price tag, but the profits could be more than ye've ever dreamed o'. An' dinna forget son, I've been doon that road before ye, so I ken all aboot having to practise. I ken fine ye can do it. Now, have yer tea an' get yersel off to yer first lesson."

I made my way up a short hill from the bus stop into a council housing estate. I was sweating with carrying the heavy case and very nervous about meeting the accordion teacher. As I walked up the path leading to the house, I heard an accordion being played followed by a man's voice shouting, "Naw! Naw! Naw! Dae it again!"

"Oh dear!" I thought, "I don't like the sound of him very much."

I rang the doorbell and held my breath. A middle-aged woman opened the door and said, "Come in son, he's nearly ready for you. Are you the lad from Lochgelly?"

"Aye," I murmured.

"Jist you tak yer coat aff an sit oor there. He'll call ye in in a minute son."

I sat on a kitchen chair. Soon, the door opened and a tall, bald-headed, well-built man, in a well-worn green knitted sweater came in and glared at me.

"Richt, in ye come son and bring yer box wi ye."

I followed him into a smallish lounge where a lively coal fire burned and crackled in the fireplace. In the middle of the room was a metal music stand. I was aware of the heat in the room after the cool air outside. A stout girl, who was about 16 years old, put on her fawn coloured coat, followed by carefully wrapping a heavy, knitted, black, woollen scarf round her neck.

She picked up her accordion case and said, "See ye next week then Mr. Anderson."

"Aye hen," he said, "an mak share ye learn that 'My Florence' better than ye did this time eh? I ken ye kin do it if ye try. Ye need to practise though. And try no tae greet when I shout at ye."

She gave him a shy smile, wiped a tear from her eye and quietly went out the door. I felt sorry for her.

He turned to me. "Okay, son, let's see ye wi that box on noo."

Very proudly, I strapped on my new accordion. He looked at it and said, "Oh! A Frontalini, 48-bass.

He started to adjust the shoulder straps. "There that's better eh? Ye'll be needin' a bigger one than this soon enough son. Never mind we'll just hiv tae mak do wi' whit we've got the noo. Can ye play anything at a'?"

"Oh aye." I said, "I ken quite a lot o' tunes but no by music."

He raised his eyebrows and said, "A busker eh? Well dinna bother, am no interested in buskers. Tak it aff."

He sat me down and wrote on a pad some books he wanted me to bring next time. He took a sheet of manuscript paper and wrote down various music guides he wanted me to memorise. I looked at them and realised that I knew all of them from my early pipe band days. I decided not to say anything, as I did not think it would help my cause at that point. He told me how much the lessons were and that they were of a half hour duration.

He stood up and said finally, "If I think yer no good son I won't waste yer time or yer money or more important, my precious time. See ye next week son." I left the house not exactly uplifted or enthusiastic.

I went for lessons until I was 17 years of age and although he was quite tough and rough to deal with he did teach me how to play and to read music. I still had a long, long way to go I realised. After each lesson, when I got home, the first thing I did was to practise what he had taught me. Every lunchtime I would dash home, gulp down my lunch, then go straight on my accordion. By the time I went for my next lesson, I was note perfect.

He often talked about his dance band and that he might ask me to come along to gain experience. "Yer a very fast learner son." Coming from him, who never usually gave any praise at all, this was praise indeed and spurred me on. He did open my eyes and ears to the sounds of other types of music other than Scottish music for which I will always be grateful. More importantly, I realised that playing alongside other music-reading musicians would have been impossible unless I could also read music.

Back at work, Mr. Given introduced me to a small balding, quietly spoken man in his 40's. He wore a dark green suit, checked shirt and maroon coloured tie, which looked all right but did not quite go with his plumb coloured hand-knitted pullover.

"This is Mr. Malone, Mr. Adam. Mr. Malone is going to train you in the art of window dressing. He does all our windows and he will take you under his wing for a week."

We shook hands and he seemed very likeable. "Okay, follow me to the stockroom and we'll make a start."

I followed him out of the store, and then we made a left turn and climbed the same stone stairs I climbed on my journey to sit the entrance exam. We went along a passageway to a large wooden door leading into a very big room containing floor to ceiling shelves crammed with various lines of stock. Mr. Malone made for the far end where I noticed many display stands of every shape and size.

He drew up a chair and invited me to do likewise. We sat facing one another. He took out a packet of cigarettes, offered one to me, which I declined, then started to light his. He inhaled deeply, blew out the smoke and had a look of relaxed pleasure on his small wrinkled face.

"You can call me John, Lawrence. We Window Dressers are a cut above the sales people you know. You are very privileged to have Mr. Given take such an interest in you. He must like you."

The door flew open and in entered George looking tense. He approached us and stood glaring at me. "Here, what is he doing getting trained in window dressing John? I've been here longer than him and I've never been asked once!"

John gave a quiet smile and said, "Perhaps the boss doesn't recognise that you have any leaning for artistic work George. I'm sure you are better suited to the shop floor really. You want to be a branch manager one day, don't you?"

"Aye, that's true enough. I suppose he doesn't want me wasting my time muckin' aboot with all this rubbish anyway." With that, he turned on his heel and did a quick exit, slamming the door as he went.

John gave a snort and said, "Huh, he's not even a really good salesman either poor bugger. Too full of himself. You can't tell him anything, you know, he knows it all. Right, let's make a start then. I'll call out what I want. You collect it all and pile them up here."

By the time we finished, there were display stands of glass shelves and unclothed mannequins. He started to stroke a well-endowed mannequin with a leery expression on his face saying, "We can't forget my wee favourite. This is Marilyn."

I felt my naive cheeks go red.

"Ah hah!" He giggled, "Nae experience wi the opposite sex eh son? Ok, I'm going down. You follow on and start carrying all this lot down to the store and line it up just outside the main left-hand shop window door."

After staggering up the stairs for about the fourth time, and sweating profusely, a small door opened on my right and out came a very pretty, fair-haired girl. I guessed she was about 18 years old. She was dressed, in a black overall, red high-heeled shoes with lipstick to match, large dangling earrings and well-mascara-ed eyes.

She smiled engagingly and said, "Who are you and what's all this noise? I can't concentrate on my work in there. How much longer are you going to be clanging and banging up and down these stairs, please?"

"Oh!" I gasped, "I'm very sorry but I've got to get all this stuff down in order to dress the drapery shop windows."

"Aw! Take a break for goodness sake. Come in and have a cup of tea, come on, in you come." She stood aside and waved me into her room.

Glad of the distraction I entered the small room situated at the front of the store with a good view of the main street below from a window.

Motioning me to a seat, she explained what she was doing. She worked on her own using a heat-embossing machine. It printed coloured words and prices on show cards of different shades, to be used in all the departments and branches of the Co-op stores.

We enjoyed a good chat, became good friends and subsequently she printed many cards for my personal use. She agreed to become my magical assistant when required. There was never any romance between us as she had a steady supply of boyfriends, but she often asked my advice and shared her problems. Her room was my personal 'bolt-hole'.

I must have been about an hour humping all the display materials down the stairs. John was in the window when I finished, and the navy-blue blinds were down with the lights on to enable us to see. "Close the door and come and sit down." He said, producing a Thermos flask with two small plastic cups.

"In this game you've got to learn to pace yourself." Unknown to John this was my second cup of tea and I had already been learning to pace myself.

He sat comfortably on a display box and said, "Now, this window could be finished in a day, but we are going to make it last until Wednesday. Then we'll start the other one and that should take us up to Saturday. Here, have a hot cup of tea and here's a cake from the bakery to go with it."

I was enjoying this. It was very cosy and peaceful. I could hear the front door opening and closing as customers came and went. I picked up the sounds of the little cash cups flying at great speed along their wires and smacking into the cashier's box. "Little wonder," I thought, "she's always got a sour face with those cups smashing into her box all day. It must be very jarring." I would be a bit nicer to her. Wednesday came and it was 'curtain up' time. John went outside, tapped on the window, and I pulled on the cord and up went the large blue blinds. A small group of women gathered and looked at all the goods l displayed. Some were offering comments to John who seemed to be enjoying his moment of glory. Then Mr. Given appeared alongside me and asked if I had enjoyed my new learning curve.

"Oh yes indeed!" I replied.

"Good. At the end of the month, I have booked you on a window dressing course in Glasgow. You can follow the big professionals around and see how they do it in the city.

I will expect you to come back here and show us all a thing or two. You'll be on you own because Mr. Malone will be on holiday."

He went outside, looked at the window, gave John some comments then walked off up the street. John came back in not looking too pleased.

"You do your best and what does he say?" 'It's far too busy again John, too much in. It lacks class. Try more planning next time.'

We had almost finished the second of the front large store windows on Saturday when Miss Allen opened the side door of the window.

"The store is very busy today gentlemen and so I need you to leave this and come on the fabrics counter please," she said.

"Very well Miss Allen," said John, "I suppose we have finished now anyway."

"Okay, Mr. Adam, raise the blinds then we will go and relieve the beleaguered troops," John said with a hint of irritation.

The fabrics counter was very large, made of wood and had a brass-measuring rule sunk in to it.

"This is the trickiest counter of all Lawrence and the best way to learn is to just do it. I'll be here keeping an eye on you so don't worry. You can do this," John said.

A woman approached the counter and asked to see curtain material. I handed down some heavy bales of cloth and displayed them to her.

She made a choice, produced a scrap of paper from her bag and said, "These are the measurements, and can I have it matching, please."

John said, "Carefully measure the cloth on the measuring rule and then make a nick on the edge." I did as instructed.

"Now, comes the first tricky bit," he continued. "Get a thread and gently pull it all the way out across the material and that will give you your line to cut straight. I'll explain all about 'warp' and 'weft' later."

Again, I did as he told me and was quite amazed at the perfectly straight line across the material.

He handed me a huge pair of scissors and I started cutting. "Now, slide the material up and down to match up the pattern, nick it again and same procedure. You're doing really well."

I did this another twice and ended up with four curtains and some spare pieces.

John said, "Well done, Mr. Adam, you are now skilled in the art of cutting and matching. I'll leave you to do the arithmetic and present the customer with her bill. I'm going to pop to the toilet."

I was left to work out what was a most complicated bill for the customer. Everything seemed to end up with a something and so many eighths at four shillings and eleven pence per yard! It must have been obvious that I was struggling.

Mr. Given materialised at my side to complete the equation for me. He parcelled up the goods, saw the customer off and then motioned for me to follow him into his office.

"Take a seat please Mr. Adam." He swung his chair round until he was sitting opposite me. "You had great difficulties in calculating that bill, Mr. Adam?"

I felt very hot and very embarrassed and must have been squirming in my seat.

"I'm so sorry, Mr. Given. You see, I suffered from bronchitis all my school life and as a result missed important lessons on decimal points and fractions and such like."

He looked sympathetic then asked," Do you like working here, Mr. Adam?"

I must have looked quite anxious as I replied, "Mr. Given, I love it here. I'm learning something new every day."

He replied, "But it is a retail business Mr. Adam, and a knowledge of mathematics is quite vital, so here is what I suggest. I can enrol you on a Day School three times a week at a technical college in Cowdenbeath. I suggest you start right at the very beginning. In addition, you will be offered courses on bookkeeping, accountancy and a whole range of subjects, which you are welcome to take should you feel inclined and we will pay for it all. What do you say?"

"Well I am very grateful, Mr. Given, and assure you I will be trying my very absolute best not to let you down."

He gave an encouraging smile, "I am so pleased you said that, Mr. Adam, otherwise, I would have had no alternative but to 'let you go'. I know you will try very hard, Mr. Adam. I have noticed you are very fast on the pick-up. In fact, I have a feeling you will do very well indeed. We will start you after you come back from Glasgow. Now, off you go then. Finish those store windows with Mr. Malone."

George was hovering outside the door. He sniggered and said, "I saw you having a bit of trouble with your counting Lall. Well, remember the old saying…nearer the boss, nearer the door." He walked away chuckling to himself.

Nine
1954 A Very Busy Year

Most Saturdays I was up with the lark and on the road cycling to some far places either with my pal Billy or with my brother Bill and his friends. It mattered not what the weather was like. We cycled in rain, howling gales, even snow. My bike was a Hercules Kestrel, heavy, no gears, and drooped handlebars. In wet weather, we wore yellow wax cloth capes, which covered the cyclist and his bike to just over the handlebars. The headgear for wet weather was a yellow sou'wester, the same as worn by the anglers. It was very hard work peddling in that lot against a strong headwind, which billowed out our capes like yacht sales. After a bracing happy weekend cycling I arrived at work fully refreshed and ready for action.

Music and Magic

My accordion lessons were progressing. I was playing marches and learning bass solos. Not easy on an accordion as it is all done by touch because you cannot see the buttons.

I was also busy practising my magic tricks and performed at the odd function for which I received a small fee.

One night whilst attending the Magic Circle in Kirkcaldy, Sam Nardone asked me to rehearse with him for a booking he had at a Church Hall in a place called Ballingry. His fee was three shillings and six pence. My fee was two shillings and six pence. I knew a lass called Jean from the Millinery Department could play a piano, so I booked her, and she too received a small fee.

Sam particularly wanted to do his fantastic 'Magic Cylinders Illusion'.

We fixed a rehearsal date at his house. I had devised some illusions of my own. He said he saw me as his straight man and himself as the comedian. I did not think he looked particularly funny. He was smallish, which can be a good start for a comic because lack of height can sometimes evoke pathos. However, Sam was of Italian extract and so had a darkish coloured skin, black thinning hair, a large nose (again the nose could be an added comedy feature) but somehow, he just did not look a funny man.

We arrived at the said venue on 16 November. Ballingry was a depressing place. Most of the small population either worked down the pits or were unemployed. There was only one main road through the town with about half a dozen small shops drastically in need of a coat of paint, including the proverbial Co-op.

"Imagine being the Branch Manager of that poky hole," I thought to myself'.

The hall we were to play was small and more than a bit dowdy. It was teaming with elderly women dressed up in their Sunday best frocks complete with an assortment of felt and straw type hats placed on top of their recently permed bonces.

There was a stage, but no piano.

When I enquired, they said, "We just manage with the organ. You use the large pedal to pump air into the bellows and the tone is still wonderful although no one is sure how old it is." The keys were well worn and a dirty shade of yellow. Jean looked a bit disappointed but said she would manage fine and that one keyboard is pretty much like the next and for me not to worry Feeling quite confident. I told her to play whatever she felt fitted the act, as it was not a patter act, so it needed music throughout.

The women had finished their meal and were tidying things away. Some were folding up long wooden trestle tables and stacking them down the side of the hall. Two women were sweeping up all the old buns, wrappings, and general muck into a pile in front of the stage.

Sam said, "Right Lawrence, the last thing we both pull out of the small cylinder is that huge Union Jack flag you have (it was about 6 feet long and 5 feet wide), so load that in first then we will both reach in, grab a corner each and with a grand flourish pull it out."

My mum had sewn a brass curtain ring on the two corners for easy handling.

"It will be our 'Big Finish' and should go an absolute bomb, can't fail," said Sam with confidence.

The trick consisted of a large cylinder and a smaller one. Each stood about 3 feet tall and measured about half a yard wide. On the outside, they were a rich polished chrome, and, on the inside, they were painted matt black. They did look very smart. The idea was to first show the cylinders one at a time as empty. Then start producing at a fast pace, lots of coloured large silks, bunches of flowers, parasols and such like finally both reaching in and pulling out the Union Jack in a very patriotic finish.

We went into a dressing room at the side of the stage to start preparing ourselves for the show. I was already dressed in my black blazer with a white shirt and a black silk bow tie. All topped off with a pair of light grey trousers and shiny black shoes. As a draper, at least I knew how to look the part.

Sam wore a down at the heel outfit such as a vagrant would wear. A flat cap pulled down onto his ears, a ragged shirt with an old tie knotted of centre, a baggy pair of old trousers too small for him and a pair of old lace up boots.

An old woman with very thick lenses on her glasses appeared at the door with a huge shovel full of rubbish collected from the floor.

"Here Mabel, where's that rubbish bin hen?" She said to another woman rushing past.

"It's over there look. Come on hurry up dear we're almost ready to start the show noo." They both left quickly.

Meanwhile, I headed for the stage with the suitcase full of the production stuff and started loading into the cylinder trick. I was ready and eager to go.

Sam went quietly down into the audience and stood unnoticed at the back of the darkened hall waiting for his cue from me.

Madam Chairperson introduced me to the audience, saying,

"You are in for a rare treat. So, without any more ado, here he is, the fantastic Magic Circle Magician Mr. Lawrence Adam."

I nodded to Jean seated at the organ. I could hear her working her feet on the bellows then it burst in life with a rendering of 'Poor Old Joe'. Not the music I was expecting but I had given her carte blanche.

With a big grin, I walked on twirling a shiny black cane, which disappeared and became two silk squares. Instant applause!

"Oh goodie!" I thought, "This sounds like a great audience." I spotted a woman in the front row with a gold chain and medallion round her neck and realised she was the Mayoress.

I did a few quick tricks then said, "And now ladies and gentlemen, oops sorry, no gentlemen only ladies, I need the services of a volunteer. Is there someone who might oblige?"

There was a loud shuffling sound from the back of the hall and

'Enter Sam'. "Aye, I'll be your volunteer."

He got on to the stage acting a little drunk. The audience looked a bit concerned. I did a trick involving a trick-candle that burst into flames (with the help of a wet paraffin wick). This got some mirth. I then handed Sam a silver tray with a bottle of

Guinness on it. It was made of rubber and very light but a perfect replica.

Sam exclaimed, "Oh! Great! I could jist dae wi anither wee drink, thank you."

"No no," I said, "I'm going to perform an experiment of anti-gravity." He held the tray with the bottle in front of him. I picked up a fan and started to fan the bottle, which started to rise in the air. The secret was a black thread running from the fan, through the neck of the bottle to a small plastic cork, which Sam had placed in his mouth.

Just as the applause started, he suddenly went, "Arghhh," and opened his mouth causing his set of false teeth to land on the tray with a loud clang.

The women laughed loud with tears streaming down their cheeks. I must say I did enjoy hearing and seeing folk laugh at something we had done...an introduction to the intoxicating experience of comedy.

Spurred on and greatly encouraged I then went into the cylinder trick, showing first the large one as empty, then the smaller one, placing the smaller one inside the larger one. Meanwhile Jean played Poor Old Joe repeatedly and continued to play it. I walked over and remarked to her, "Jean, is that the only tune you know?"

She looked up and replied with a smile, "Aye, it's good isn't it?" The audience laughed loudly again thinking it was all part of the act.

Sam and I reached into the bin and produced loads of the previously loaded items, which drew loud gasps and applause.

Then our big finish we both reached in together, grabbed a corner ring, and with a big flourish flicked the large Union Jack into the air. Unknown to us, the old woman previously wandering around with the shovel, had mistaken our trick cylinder for the dustbin, and emptied all the rubbish on top of our flag. It flew everywhere! There were half-eaten mutton pies, bits of sandwiches, sticky cakes wrappers, old buns, paper cups and plates, screwed up napkins. I just have the memory of women standing up and dusting the rubbish off their frocks. Trying to get the sticky buns out of their new hairdo not forgetting the Lady Mayoress with a large sticky jam doughnut on her chest not looking happy!

Jean was in absolute hysterics and wiping the tears from her eyes.

"Och! Michty me," she giggled. "Well 'ave never seen the likes o' that before. Whit a right laugh that was. You guys are great, yer goin' to be stars I kin tell. When's our next bookin'? I canna wait."

The word soon went around all the departments of the Lochgelly stores thanks to Jean, that we were apparently fantastic. Bookings started to come in for various small functions. I decided to do these on my own however. Not only did I get a bigger fee, but also I knew there would be no surprises. I introduced the accordion to the act, which led to even more bookings. I became a "very busy wee lad," my mother remarked.

The fair sex

About this time, I developed an interest in the female sex. I did not know much at all about anything. There was a wee lass who had been in the same class as me at school and her name was Jean.

I thought she was lovely. Every time I went into the Grocery Department, where she worked, I would go bright red and very hot under the collar if she even said "Hullo Lawrence" to me.

This carried on for some time until the annual Store Dance. The venue was called the 'Palais De Dance' (known by the locals as 'The Pally') some two miles away in the small town of Cowdenbeath.

My first experience there was one of amazement. As I walked in, I was astounded at the sound of 'Ken MacIntosh and his dance band' on the stage. They were a well-known broadcasting band at that time.

Around the edges of the large dance area were seats arranged at tables covered with red cloths. There was a bar and a buffet.

I sat at a table with the lads from the drapery and the Gents Outfitters department. The men sat down one side and all the girls down the other. It took great courage to cross the great divide and ask a girl to dance.

Eventually I plucked up courage to ask Jean for a dance. I was astounded when she agreed. It was a modern waltz to the music of a hit at that time by Ruby Murray called 'Softly Softly,' (little did I think that one day I would work with Ruby), I was in heaven. Jean's perfume smelled lovely. I made up my mind there and then to ask if I could see her home.

All was going well until she raised her arm to place it on my shoulder that something dark caught my eye. When I looked more closely, I was horrified. She had very hairy armpits! My fascination ended there and then!

Ten
Out of the Large Goldfish Bowl and into a Smaller One

It was very early in the morning as I walked out of my hotel right in the heart of the city of Glasgow. As I made my way to the main Glasgow Co-operative Store to spend a week with their top Window Dressers and hopefully gain new skills for the store in Lochgelly. I marvelled at the sounds and smells of the big city coming to life and preparing for a new day. The sun was already shining brightly in a clear blue sky and it was showing signs of being a lovely warm day without even the hint of a breeze. I passed an Italian cafe where they were placing tables and chairs on the pavement and I could already smell the delicious aroma of fresh coffee. I smiled to myself as I passed by and thought, "In Lochgelly, when the tables and chairs were placed on the pavement, it meant 'the Bailiffs had arrived'." There were the smells of last night's beer from the pub doors, a variety of food smells already drifting out from restaurants and a lovely perfumed aroma as a florist arranged her flower displays outside her shop windows placing colourful bunches in tubs and boxes.

I liked the feel of a city I decided. I probably got it from my mother who used to tell me many stories of her childhood memories in the city of Dundee. I arrived at the huge store and was directed to the Art Department. I was welcomed and introduced to a young man with wild blonde hair and dressed in a colourful shirt open at the neck. He was busy packing various display items into a hamper.

He looked up brushed his mop of hair from his eyes, reached out his hand and said, "Hi Lawrence, the name's Peter, welcome aboard. We are off to dress some branch shop windows around the city. Just hang in there with me. Let's go, I'm ready."

The week went in very quickly and in no time at all it seemed I was saying my farewells.

Still, I did pick up many useful tips that were new to me:

how to pin shirts, blouses and suits skilfully to make them very attractive,

the use of focal points,

the blending of colours

how to use invisible fishing line to make things appear to float in mid-air. This especially appealed to my magical leanings and I could not wait to get back home and try this out but above all, to plan the general idea of a display and work out the details. This was not how John Malone worked. He just started at the front and worked backwards until he had no more room for any more items.

Upon my return, Mr. Given asked if I felt the trip had been worthwhile.

"Most definitely," I replied, "Thank you so much for sending me Mr. Given."

He patted me on the shoulder and said, "Right Mr. Adam, the front main windows await your newly acquired Glasgow knowledge and skills, go to it."

I had sketched out a window plan on the way home in the train and started collecting everything I needed.

My first window was very different from that which had gone before. I worked at it all day and most of the following day as well. When I decided there was really nothing more I could do, I took a large breath, walked up to Mr. Given's office door, gave it a little nervous tap, then I told Mr. Given that it was ready for viewing.

He rose from his desk and I followed him out onto the pavement where he took up his position in front of the main large window. I walked forward and gave a sharp tap on the windowpane, which was a signal to wee Danny to raise the large navy-blue blinds. I felt nervous and anxious, but all mingled with a touch of excitement. I felt this same emotion many times again some years in the future, when a theatre curtain went up on one of my shows,

Mr. Given gave a gasp! "Goodness me Mr. Adam!" He looked at me and said, "Well, this is more than I had bargained for, this is the sort of thing I have wanted for this store for years but never got it, until now."

I had managed to present a display, which also incorporated a bit of illusionary magic. Using fishing gut, suspending a large old brown wooden cabin trunk with its lid partially open, which appeared to be slowly sinking towards a seabed of sand. Spilling out of it were various fabrics, colourful tartans, shimmering silks and tapestries apparently slowly waving about. Other items could be seen slightly buried in the sand others floating down like the results of a shipwreck. An old fishing net was the backdrop with some lobster and starfish caught in it and items from various departments within the store floating downwards. Some artificial fish were waving about suspended on fishing gut.

"Well done. Well done." He patted me on the back and went back into the store positively beaming. Within minutes, a small crowd of shoppers had gathered alongside me.

I heard one woman say to her friend, "Hey! Wull ye look at this Maggie, the store's gone posh!"

Her friend gave a nod and replied, "Aye it is that right enough,'ave never seen the likes o' this afore."

Mr. Given had said something to the staff because when I walked back in and I got the whiff of good old jealousy again. I encountered this all my life and just had to deal with it. I have always considered it a very negative emotion. I was saddened however, when John Malone returned from his holiday and seemed a bit cool towards me. It took a while before he thawed out, but he was never quite the same with me again.

The faceless ones

The weekly visits to the Technical College were showing signs of paying off as I found the girls from the various departments were bringing their sales pads to me, when they had completed a large order requesting I check their sums. They reckoned I was the fastest 'adder-upper' on the floor. Not bad, considering what I was like when I started!

Exam time arrived. Arithmetic, Single Entry Bookkeeping and Co-operative History. After these were finished, I was summoned into Mr. Given's office.

"Sit down Mr. Adam. It seems you have caught the attention of the faceless ones. I have been asked to give you time off to allow you to attend a course in Rothesay which is for one week. All travelling expenses will be met so it will cost you nothing at all. Are you agreeable to that?"

I was very surprised. "Why me?" I asked.

He smiled. "Well, every so often one candidate from each county in Scotland is chosen to attend this gathering. You are being considered for suitability for promotion in the future. You are this year's candidate for the Kingdom of Fife and I am very proud that you are one of mine. So, what do you say? It's quite an honour you know."

Rothesey

Rothesay is a very beautiful place situated near the bottom of Loch Long at the top of the River Clyde just further down than Dunoon on the West coast of Scotland. The ferry took me from Greenock, and the first thing I noticed was how clean and fresh the air was.

I boarded a bus which took me up Canada Hill and minutes later I arrived at a group of cream and green painted wooden shack styled buildings. 'Probably some sort of holiday camp' I thought. There was a 'Registration' sign so I entered the hut to stand in front of a high counter with a young man behind it.

"Good day tae ye, sir, and yer name is?" He said smiling broadly at me.

"Lawrence Adam," I replied.

He handed me a white card badge with a pin attached to the back of it. My name was printed on it. "Please pin this tae yer jacket so others may know who ye are. Hope ye enjoy yer stay, sir."

Standing by a blackboard, was a man in a summery, open necked red and green short-sleeved checked, shirt. He smiled and motioned us to take a seat. There were about another ten lads already seated, who turned around giving me a welcoming nod and smile.

"In a way," he said, "this is a little reward to you all for your noted extra efforts in your various societies. During your stay, you will be asked to perform a variety of tasks that will be assessed. A report will be sent to the head office in Glasgow."

The time spent at Rothesay went all too quickly and in no time at all we were having our last chat together and preparing to leave and head for home. Jim, a salesman from Glasgow, said his boss had told him to do his very best as most lads who had been on this course had gone on to be managers.

The parting shot of the course leader was to join our Co-op Youth Club and try to be voted onto the committee. We went our various ways promising to write to each other, however, we never did.

Eleven
1954 Entertainment Beckons.

The year was 1954 and I was aged 17. I organised a concert party, at various Tuberculosis Sanatoriums within our region to try to cheer up the patients. Each hospital was so grateful for our visit that they sent little press notices to local papers thanking us for our excellent shows. A semi-professional concert party noticed the credits, invited me to join them and paid me more than I had received in payment so far. Their usual venues ranged from special functions in hotels to a dinner-suited audience with their suitably attired wives. Adding four shows a month to my own Magic show bookings and Accordion gigs where I played for dancing paid me nearly as much as my day-job. It was about then that someone asked if I could supply a drummer. I talked it over with Bill. "You play the drums in the Pipe Band," I said. "I'm sure you could also manage to play dance band music."

He thought about it then said, "Aye, right enough I'm sure I could manage it."

"Well," I replied, "Why don't you treat yourself to a second-hand drum kit, we'll form a duo and I'll split the money with you." He agreed.

Of course, the next thing we needed was a vehicle to carry everything. Bill was the only one who had any money. We borrowed from him if we were a bit short. An ex-army mini-bus arrived which he said he bought cheaply.

We had our first booking the following Saturday in Cowdenbeath and it went so well we gained another two bookings that same night. We were off!

One of the bookers said, "If you can include a pianist I can pay you a bit extra."

Eventually we found a lass and booked her.

The Youth Club

Our Society had a Youth Club, so I went along to the Co-operative Hall where the meeting had just started. The Chairman rose to his feet, a very well-spoken tallish slim lad in blazer and grey flannels.

"Good evening to you all, my name is John Soutar, I work in the Furniture Department. On my left is our Secretary Mr. Jimmy Logan from the Radio & Television Department, and on my right is Miss Christine Marshall, who incidentally is resigning tonight as our Treasurer and so I am asking for any nominations, please."

"Well, this seems a good opportunity," I thought. My hand was no sooner in the air than I was proposed, seconded and invited to step up to the table and take my place. That was the beginning of a friendship with John Soutar, which lasted until he died 59 years later.

John mentioned a conference in Galashiels, which Jimmy and he hoped that as the new Treasurer, I might feel that I could join them. It would not cost me any money and they were usually very enjoyable. I agreed to attend the conference of members from Co-op Youth Club Committees from all over Scotland.

On the second evening, volunteers were requested who might contribute to an evening's show.

John said to me, "Lawrence I enquired about you from my sources and was told that you were a good magician. So, what about it?"

"Well I would but I don't have any props with me," I said, "Oh dear!" said John, "I'm afraid I took the liberty of putting your name in and they were delighted."

"Okay," I replied. "But you will have to assist me and do everything I ask you to do, it that a deal?"

He seemed a bit taken aback, laughed and said, "Och aye why not, ask away."

During that evening, I explained to the large expectant audience that it was a surprise for me to be asked and that I had nothing prepared. However, if a gentleman will come up to assist me I will try to do something entertaining.

Up came John. I conducted a sort of interview, did a card trick with him (managed to borrow an old dog-eared pack of cards) then thanked him very much. As he left the stage to a warm round of applause, I asked him if he had the correct time.

He rolled back his sleeve and exclaimed, "My watch, it's gone…"

"Does this look like yours?" I said, holding up a watch.

"Why aye it does," he said taking it and placing it on his wrist. The applause got louder. He walked away.

"You'd better check your wallet as well," I said, winking at the audience.

He put his hand in his inside jacket pocket and said, "My wallet, where's my wallet gone?"

"Don't worry," I said, here it is safe enough." The applause was now louder with some cheers as well.

Just as he got off the stage, I shouted to him,

"Careful how you move John, you'll need these." I held up a pair of trouser braces. The audience applauded loudly. Just then, as he turned around his trousers slipped down to his knees which he grabbed and shouted "Hoy!" The audience were ecstatic, roars of laughter and shouts for more!

For the remainder of the weekend we were famous, and the Lochgelly Co-operative was on the map!

Music

My music teacher told me it was time I moved up to a full size 120-bass accordion as I had shown much improvement and this present one was now cramping my style.

He said, "Make it as soon as you can."

His wife said as I left, "I shouldna say it son, but you are his star pupil. You're nearly as good as the teacher already."

I mentioned it to my Mum and Dad who said, "We can't really afford another one but if you sell your present one the money can be a healthy deposit for another on hire purchase, and we'll stand as your guarantors"

I ended up with a full-size accordion called a 'Scandali' another Italian make with a beautiful mellow tone.

I was making extra money now from my gigs, which were coming in thick and fast. Bill seemed to enjoy playing for the dances.

Twelve
Decisions

Mr. Given asked if I could pop in to his office and see him before I went home after work. As I walked into his office, I noted he looked very serious. He said, "I won't beat about the bush." He then asked me if I was willing to sit an entrance examination in Edinburgh for the Co-operative College in Loughborough. If I passed, he said I would then have to go to Glasgow to sit another exam for a Scholarship.

"I did tell you that you had been noticed by the faceless ones before you went to Rothesay. Well, in their opinion you will probably pass both exams and gain a place at the college."

"I don't think I could be bright enough for a college Mr. Given, but bearing in mind all you have done for me I can't really say no."

"Good. After attending the college for about three years, likely you will be offered a Departmental Manager's situation."

"What! Surely at best it would be a Branch Manager job first?"

He smiled and shook his head, "No son, armed with college qualifications it would be straight to a job just like the one I am doing now." I must have shown some hesitation. He went on,

"You see, I am retiring this year Lawrence (he had never used my first name before) and please keep this to yourself, it would give me great pleasure to see one of mine go to the college. I have watched you grow very quickly from humble beginnings to a possible top-drawer job. I know you can do it."

I heard myself saying, "Yes, okay I will then."

"Good lad, good lad," he exclaimed.

Loughborough College 1956

On 25 April 1956, I travelled to Edinburgh to sit an Entry Exam for the Co-operative College in Loughborough. A few days later and to my surprise, I learned I had passed and was to be interviewed by the Principal later.

On the 2 May, I sat a scholarship exam in Glasgow and again was surprised I passed that one also.

On 19 May, Mum and Dad took me to the Kings Theatre in Edinburgh: a wee treat for passing all my exams and making them proud. The stars of the show were comedian, Alex Finlay, Rikki Fulton and well-known singer Kenneth McKellar. It was a first class show in a beautiful theatre. Life is strange: you just do not know what lies ahead. I appeared in that theatre again in but on that occasion, I would be on the stage.

Thirteen
Mr. Given Retires

One morning Miss Allen came to me and asked if I would like to give a donation towards a retirement present for Mr. Given who was retiring at the end of that week. I was shocked and very saddened to hear it. He had mentioned it to me earlier but to be told it was now a reality was a bit stunning. He had been my mentor since I had joined the firm and was supportive and encouraging. I would miss him. The day arrived and we all sadly said our goodbyes.

He shook my hand, and said, "I'll be keeping an eye on your progress Lawrence. Good luck to you." He made a short farewell speech, then with a tear in his eye, but still displaying the same familiar dignity, walked out the door for the last time. The place felt empty.

Dance Band Progress

I was very busy mainly with the dance band, which now consisted of Bill on drums and our pianist in her twenties called Anna. Bookings came in thick and fast for our trio. Soon we were able to add a violinist and a double bass player.

We were so busy with engagements that the van would screech to a halt at the shop door and honk the horn. That was my queue to dash out, climb in and get into a dinner suit as Bill drove like a demon to some village hall or other for a function.

I thought the time was right to suggest we adopt white Dress Stuart tartan dinner jackets with a black silk shawl lapel, with black dinner suit trousers, white shirts and black bow ties. Everyone agreed. Sandy our violinist said, "Aye, that soonds great Lawrence, but who's goin' to pay fer them, eh?"

I replied, "They will be your own property, so we pay for our own. I can get a special deal from our Co-op Gents' Department. I have the price here for you." They all agreed and said they would present themselves to be measured during that week.

Things were moving along at a good pace. I thought it the appropriate time to inform them that I had booked a recording studio in Edinburgh to make a record. That astounded them!

Arrangements were made to present ourselves at 'Jeffrey's Recording Studios' on George Street in two weeks' time.

Fourteen
Noticeable Changes

I opened the brown square shaped envelope which contained my weekly pay and noted, that I had a pay rise taking me to £4.6.8d. Considering I started with a wage of £2.5.0d it was not a fast-track rise. I was very fortunate to be making quite a bit more with my entertainment engagements. I had just received a letter inviting my dance band to play every Wednesday evening at the George Hotel in Pitlessie, not far from Lochgelly.

The hotel had a decent sized ballroom and I know we looked the part with our white Dress Stuart tartan dinner jackets and our smart colourful music stands. I was very proud of my musicians. I could tell at the end of the evening when the owner paid me the fee, that she was very pleased with our performance. Soon we were playing every Wednesday, and many Saturday evenings for special functions and she paid us well.

Banishment

Life in general seemed to be going very well until one Wednesday night I turned up as usual for my accordion lesson. The tutor's wife opened the door and ushered me in.

However, as I entered the lounge, my music teacher glared at me, placed his huge hands on his hips, and said in a very angry voice, "Oh! It's you!

Well, dinna bother to tak yer coat aff, yer no stoppin'. In fact, I think ye have a right bloody cheek comin' here at all."

I felt a bit shaken by his sudden outburst and asked what was wrong.

"Whit's wrong?" His voice getting louder, and spittle flying everywhere, "Whit's wrong he asks. Oh! I'll tell ye whit's wrong sonny. Ma Band has been losin' bookin's, and I finally found oot who it is that's takin' them frae us...it's you ya wee bugger!" Lawrence Adam and his bloody Thistle Dance Band!"

I was shocked, "I'm very sorry, I didn't realise we were competing with anybody else," I said.

He took a step towards me, and for a second, I thought he was going to strike a blow. "Git oot o' ma hoose this very minute and dinna dare come back!" I did as he requested and never saw or heard of him ever again.

Loughborough again

The letter arrived inviting me to go to the Co-operative College, Stanford Hall, Loughborough. I was able to stay for a long weekend to meet with the college Principal to discuss the possibility of becoming a residential student.

When I showed the letter to my parents, my Dad beamed and said, "Take this offer son and you'll never look back."

My mother looked at me long and hard and said, "How do you feel about this son?"

I replied that I somehow did not feel motivated at the prospect but would give it serious thought. "I will go to Loughborough and test the water."

A new brush sweeps clean

Mr. Given was replaced with a completely different style of person. We never saw eye to eye from the very start. He had a portly figure, wore steel wire-rimmed glasses and was squeezed into a black jacket, white shirt with starched collar and pinstripe trousers. He was the nearest thing to an impression of a penguin I had ever seen. He walked briskly, taking short aggressive noisy steps, which included a side-to-side waddle. What hair he had left covering his balding pate, flew about in all directions as he moved. He had a habit of standing directly in front of you, glaring at you for a few minutes, before eventually speaking sounding gruff and impatient.

He did not appreciate my style of window dressing.

"I really cannot stand your arty farty window displays," he said.

I asked him what style he did like, and he replied,

"I used to come here as a branch manager, before you started here Mr. Adam. I believe a Mr. Malone used to do the windows then. I liked the way he did them."

"Mr. Given liked them," I replied.

He gave a sneery scoff and said, "Huh! Mr. Given, aye, I can well imagine he did. Well I am definitely not Mr. Given."

I said with a smile, "No that's true, you certainly are not, sir."

He went a deep pinkish colour and said, "Mr. Malone's windows were full of merchandise. That is how a shop window should be. I have asked Mr. Malone to take over from you forthwith. So, what do you say to that?"

"Well, as we are having this conversation, I have no objections to handing over the window displays back to Mr. Malone, and I intended having a chat with you regarding the need to have a have a few days off, to go down to Loughborough College," I replied.

He glared at me, looked down at his highly polished shoes, then slowly up again at me with a snigger playing upon his lips.

"I never went to any fancy college Mr. Adam. I came up the hard way, worked my way up from the bottom. I suppose that means you may be leaving us soon then eh?"

"I really don't know. I'm still considering the offer, but I'll let you know when I have decided." I turned and walked away, thinking to myself, "You would certainly be one good reason to accept any offer."

Band Recording

Early one misty morning, my dance band headed in the direction of the ferry at North Queensberry on our way to Edinburgh to make a record at Jeffrey's Recording Studios. There were two prominent lights above the gallery window: one was red and the other green. The recording engineer proceeded to place microphones near our positions. We were all very quiet and subdued. We had rehearsed our programme carefully.

This experience was to prove invaluable to me in later years. The studio manager informed us that we were recording live onto a wax disc and so we could not stop. We did not have the luxury of recording tapes, which could be edited. We had to be perfect. It was a very tense session and at the end of it, we were all very exhausted and sweaty! The green light came on.

There was a long silence then the studio manager came in. "That was brilliant folks. I'm going to make another copy of your record for a colleague of mine who produces the weekly Scottish County Dance programme on BBC radio. I'll be surprised if he doesn't ask you to come again and do an audition."

I thought, "Goodness me, if we get a regular BBC radio booking we are made." I decided not to say too much to the band at this point.

A new venture with the band

One day, still in my teens and quite amazed that I had become an employer, I entered the realms of risk. I booked the Town Hall in the small town of Milnathort, had some posters printed and advertised a dance. Youth Club friend John Soutar agreed to manage the door admissions for me. I knew I would have to pay my dance band whether or not I made a profit, but I thought it was worth a try. Fortunately, I broke even.

The buzz I got out about the venture spurred me on to a repeat at the Town Hall in Kinross. Once again, I broke even. I realised I was a risk taker.

Experimenting further, as it approached summer I arranged a week's tour of one-nighters in the Scottish Highlands. Delighted by the prospect, the band arranged their holidays to coincide with the week booked even though I explained that I could not guarantee wages but would cover accommodation costs. Attractive posters went up and the local newsagents sold tickets for the events. These were the first of many more ventures repeated in Scotland and elsewhere. John Soutar agreed to join us as our touring manager being responsible for the door takings.

Loughborough College decision

The day arrived when I found myself face to face with the head of the Co-operative College

Loughborough. He was a slim youngish looking man, whereas I had expected someone with grey hair, or perhaps even bald and elderly. In front of him, on his desk, sat a buff coloured folder, which I surmised contained my details.

After some pleasantries, he said in a gentle, educated, cultured voice,

"Now then Mr. Adam, I have followed your progress with great interest and have already decided to offer you a place here in our college. However, first, I must make sure that you feel you could be at home here with us, and that you are keen to advance your knowledge. What are your feelings about this?"

I stared at him. I could not quite frame the words that were in my head.

He smiled and continued. "Oh, I fully appreciate it all feels a bit daunting for you, and it's quite a decision to have to make, but I really must be sure as your education costs us valuable time and the society...money."

I decided to be completely honest and explained that in a way I was keen and very flattered to be offered a place, but in my heart of hearts felt that this was not what I really wanted at this time. My head was saying yes, but my heart did not agree. I apologised very much for having to refuse this opportunity but felt I would regret it if I did not. We talked more, and he seemed to understand my feelings and was sympathetic. I had expected him to be impatient and angry for wasting people's time, but the opposite was the case. We shook hands, he wished me well, and I took my leave. I felt I had made the correct decision and experienced a sense of great relief that this part of my life had concluded satisfactory.

However, when I returned home my father was very disappointed when I related all that had happened and felt that I had regrettably thrown away a once in a lifetime opportunity. I felt very guilty about my last conversation with Mr. Given. However, I consoled myself with the thought that we are each responsible for our own life and the decisions we feel called upon to make.

Fifteen
A Huge 'Pivotal' Decision

I had the impression that I was on an aeroplane, poised on the runway, engines revving up, preparing for a thrusting take off! Sometimes in control, but again, sometimes not. All the halls were booked. All seemed ready for our tour of the Scottish Highlands, with my Dance Band.

Sandy, our violinist, said he felt he could not leave his wife on her own and so declined to come with us on the tour or to the recording session. The BBC Producer for a weekly Scottish Country Dance programme contacted me. The programme featured all the top bands in Scotland, most of whom were professional. He had invited us back to Edinburgh for an audition. Without a violin, we just did not sound the same, and I was not surprised when the producer said that we did not produce the same sound he had heard when we first recorded.

I was arriving at the conclusion that the band did not feel the need to rehearse every week any more. I told them without rehearsals, standards would drop. I suspected sadly, they were now riding upon their laurels, and searching for excuses.

First Band Tour

Our first dance band date was to take place in the picturesque fishing town of Ullapool. Situated on the North West of Scotland. The first time I saw Ullapool was during a cycling holiday with Billy Meikle. It was a very hot sunny day and we just turned a corner, and there, far below us, was the lovely harbour view of Ullapool. I stopped, walked to the edge and just stared at the beauty laid out before me and drank it all in. Fishing boats unloaded their catch, gulls screamed, ducking and diving, like attacking enemy planes, hoping to pick up any visible fish. The sea was a shimmering blue and silver as it lapped upon the shores. The deep blue sky was cloudless. I would have stayed longer but for my friend giving me a nudge saying, "Hey, come on pal. Let's get going on down there. I'm tired and hungry." I came to recognise times like these as 'Golden Moments'. A moment, which you do not want to end, but know sadly, and reluctantly, it must but will never be repeated.

It took us all of Monday to reach Ullapool. We were booked in at the Caledonian Hotel, the biggest hotel in town. To a lad born in a council flat, who holidayed every year in Youth Hostels, it was quite awe-inspiring to stay in this large posh hotel. My feet sank into the carpeting. So different from our linoleum covered floors at home with homemade rag rugs. Once booked in and luggage deposited, John Soutar and I walked to the hall where we would be playing. It was a thrill seeing our posters displayed outside.

A man dressed in fisherman's clothing stood alongside me.

"Well, that looks great," he said. "Pity no one will be there though eh?"

I swung round and stared at him, "What do you mean?" I exclaimed.

"Well, no one goes tae a dance roond here that finishes at 10 o clock. That's when it should be starting!"

He explained why, and I looked at John and said

"Quick get a pen and we'll start changing all these posters right away, let's go!"

That night when we opened the doors they poured in. Poor John could hardly get the money from them fast enough. What an experience. We played until the early hours of the morning. The dancers had brought their own liquid refreshments with them. I will never forget the eight-some reel as long as I live. Eight people in a ring, galloping round with such enthusiasm, that the women's feet left the floor, and they were almost horizontal! I remember thinking, 'If one of these lassies loses their grip, they will fly like rockets, and at least two bodies will be coming in our direction.' They were well-built girls. Not only would it hurt, but it could be lethal! Eventually in the early hours of the morning, we played the last waltz and as they staggered out. John was jubilant and said, "They certainly had a ball. Best dance they have been to for ages, they said. When is this band coming back again?"

I asked if he thought we had made much money. John replied,

"More than you could even guess Lawrence."

The following morning, we were up early, had a lovely full Scottish cooked breakfast and the conversation was full of last night's success. The next stop was the small town of Aviemore. We enjoyed another very successful night. As we were driving off a man walked up to Bill's van window, tapped on the glass and shouted,

"Hi son, yer big ends goin' ye ken?" then he swayed away into the darkness.

I looked at Bill, "What's a 'Big End'?"

He shook his head as he put the bus into first gear and muttered,

"Oh! I haven't a clue. Anyway, look at him he's as drunk as a skunk, what does he know?"

The next venue was in the Boys Brigade Hall Wick. We even had the time to stop at a few beauty spots and take some photographs for the album. Once more, we had a very successful evening.

The next morning, it looked like it was going to be a lovely warm day. Davy tied his double bass to the roof rack and off we headed, for the town of Bonnybridge. When we were on the outskirts of the town, the bus gave a bang and a cough and ground to a halt. Fortunately, there was a garage in sight. Bill and I called in and explained we were a dance band and to where we had to reach. The mechanic conducted a brief examination of our vehicle. He announced to us that our big end had gone! He added, that he had seen our posters in the town and had intended coming to the dance with his wife that night.

"Let me phone a pal," he said. "He'll get you into the town with your instruments, so that you can still play tonight. A lot of people would be sorely disappointed ye ken, should the dance be cancelled. I'll get your bus fixed by the morning." We thanked him very much indeed and waited for his friend. We stood outside the garage and tried to see the humorous side of things. At last, we heard a rumbling of an engine and a dustcart pulled up in front of us. A man in a flat cap looked out of his window and said, "Hi! You'll be the bond eh? Well this is yer lift folks. Yer instruments kin go in the rubbish section, and I kin git ye awe in the front wi' me." So, we made our magnanimous entrance into the fair town of Bonnybridge.

Despite our mechanical setback, we had a very good night, and everyone had a good time. The band sounded terrific from the moment we struck up, until the last few bars of music faded away. The applause was long and rapturous.

The next morning, the garage mechanic arrived with our repaired bus. Quite a chunk of our profits disappeared, but we were on our way. We agreed it had been a fantastic adventure and would be keen to do it again next year.

Bill and I fancied a few days off in Dundee staying with our Auntie Nellie. The rest of the band said they would be happy to journey home by themselves and we agreed to bring their luggage with us on our bus.

As Bill and I made our way to Auntie Nellie's prefab, we discussed the band. Although the band sounded great, without constant practice it would fail to keep up with new music. I feared we would now not attain the standard I had in mind.

He disagreed and said, "Don't push them any more Lawrence, they are fed up with practising. Let them go and cruise for a while. We are the top band in the area."

I muttered to myself, "Well, they may be happy to go on cruise-mode, but I certainly am not."

A Cheeky Request

Auntie Nellie came running out to meet us and gave us the usual big hugs and warm welcome. Cousin Alec suggested a variety show at the Palace Theatre, whilst we were in Dundee. We sat in the dress circle. An accordionist came on, and whilst I thought he was very good, the thought occurred to me, that I could do better. His name was Will Hannah and he was well known.

Earlier, at the top of the stairs taking us to the dress circle, I noticed a sign on a door that said, 'The Manager's Office'. This image seemed to stick in my mind throughout the show. During the interval, I came to a decision.

"Where are you going?" Bill said.

"Just through that door over there. I won't be a minute." I replied. I took a deep breath, drew myself up, and then gave two sharp knocks on the manager's door.

"Come in," said a deep male voice. I walked in and saw a surprised-looking slim dark-haired man in a smart black dinner suit, seated behind a desk.

"Oh!" He said, "I was expecting someone else, who are you?"

"My name is Lawrence Adam, I'm an accordionist and wondered if there was any chance of a job here in your lovely theatre please?"

Looking bemused, he put down his pen. "I'm sorry; I don't seem to have heard of you Lawrence. Are you professional?"

"No," I replied. "I've just been on a short tour of the Highlands with my Scottish Country Dance Band. I saw the show and felt the urge to have a word with you." I continued, "Although Will is very good, I think I am better."

He continued to stare at me. "Do you have a day job then?" he asked.

"Oh! Yes, I work as a salesman in the Co-op Drapery in Lochgelly."

"Well, Lawrence," he said, "I have no vacancies at the moment, and I have not as yet heard you play. Are you free this Saturday morning, say, at ten o'clock, to come and audition for me?"

Eagerly, I replied, "Certainly, sir, I'll be here, at 10 o' clock."

"Okay, Lawrence, I'll look forward to hearing you on Saturday. Enjoy the rest of the show." He opened the door for me and I walked away.

"Bye," I said. "See you then." I staggered to my seat feeling quite shaky.

Arriving back with Bill and Alec, they stared at me. Bill said, "Well, what the hell was that all about?"

"The manager offered me an audition on Saturday morning."

"Bloody hell!" said Bill.

"I admire yer cheek young un," said Alec with a grin.

I practised hard during the remainder of the time at Auntie Nellies. On Saturday morning. Bill drove me to the theatre. The manager arrived and shook my hand.

"Good morning Lawrence. Give your music to our pianist, his name's Jack? I'd like him to accompany you. Explain what you are going to play, then go up onto the stage and just...do it!"

It felt amazing to be standing there looking out onto all the seats in the stalls, then up to the dress circle. Any nervousness I felt previously, melted away. I felt as if, 'yes, this is where I belong all right'. I hit a chord and went right into rousing Scottish jigs and reels. The pianist was right on the ball and gave it all a good lift. I announced a rousing famous march, called, 'Blaze Away'. When it came to the bass solo, I swung my left-hand round towards the microphone and played the bass like the trombones of a big brass band, accompanied by the staccato of the trumpets on the right hand of the keyboard. I was grinning from ear to ear.

When I finished, the manager stood up from his seat in the stalls

"Bravo, Lawrence!" he said. "Yes, you are good all right and I will definitely be sending for you some time soon, I promise you. I am going to tell you your wee secret. It is the smile, it's a winner. Never stop that smile. If you look like you are enjoying yourself, then so will the audience. That is the current Scottish accordionists' problem. They all look so bloody miserable! You are the first one I have ever seen smiling as you play. Great, thank you for coming in to play for me."

Bill and I drove straight back home to Lochgelly. As we embarked from the ferry at Newport, I glanced up at a huge poster on the wall. It was advertising the Dundee Palace Theatre. I saw Will Hannah's name written in bold red print and the thought passed my mind, "It might be my turn soon." I felt very hopeful and very encouraged by the whole experience. "Ah well," I thought, as we took the two-hour drive home, "back to the Co-op on Monday. Business as usual."

1958 September Dundee Palace

The following week, a letter from the manager of the Dundee Palace invited me to perform for a week at his theatre. I was jubilant. I managed to get the time off work.

On 29 September 1958, I presented myself on the stage of the Dundee Palace for a rehearsal with the pit orchestra. There was a distinct aroma like no other in a theatre. It could have been the perfumed spray used after a performance, or from the general atmosphere of the place. The musical director was the same pianist who accompanied me at my audition.

He grinned and said, "Hi there son, I thought it wouldn't be long before you were back here again. Good luck to you."

After my rehearsal, the manager took me to a dressing room. When he opened the door, seated in front of a long large mirror was the singer John McIvor. John stood up as the manager entered the room. He was a tall, good-looking man about 35 years of age his black hair swept back and wearing heavy make-up.

"John," he said, "this is Lawrence Adam, he's new to show business. Look after him this week. Show him how to apply stage make-up and give him some production tips about going on and coming off techniques."

John smiled, shook my hand and said, "Certainly, welcome to the business Lawrence. Sit down and I'll explain about the make-up first of all." He looked up at the manager and said, "Goodness me, this take me back to when I started. Leave him to me." The manager gave an appreciative nod, took his leave and closed the door.

John showed me the make-up I needed to buy,

"Only use this brand," he said. "It's called 'Leichner'." He told me where to buy it and what it cost. He explained why it was necessary to wear make-up because the powerful stage lighting and the spotlights bleach out the features.

"You can use my make-up tonight Lawrence, but I'll expect you to have your own by tomorrow night's performance."

He handed me a stick of tan coloured grease paint, about three-quarters of an inch thick. "This is what is called number 9. Place about five dots on your face." I did as he said, thinking this is ridiculous: I look like a Wild West Indian.

"Next" he said, "This is a number 5, do the same thing with this one." This was the same size stick, creamy coloured and again a greasy texture, but with an attractive smell to it. "Rub the number 9 and the number 5 all over you face and right down to your shirt collar line." I did this and took on a very attractive tanned appearance. John then took a brown coloured crayon eye pencil and demonstrated how to use it on my eyebrows, along the bottom edge of my eyes and the edges of my sideburns. I looked at my reflection in the mirror and was surprised at the difference.

"Next is this thin stick of blue grease-paint, dab this on your eyelids and smear it on them to enhance your eyes."

He nodded in satisfaction. "Good, nearly there Lawrence. For this little addition we use the end of a burnt-out match-stick." He held a thin stick of red grease paint and took a very small amount of it onto the end of the matchstick. "Dab this very carefully onto the corner of your eyes. This gives them a sparkle and makes them look lively."

"Take a little of the red onto the tip of your middle finger and gently rub it onto your lips, this makes your teeth look pearly white."

A voice emanating from a small speaker in the corner of the dressing room burst into life with a male voice saying, "Good evening ladies and gentlemen, this is your half hour call, your half hour call. Thank you."

John said, "That means we have half an hour before curtain up Lawrence." I felt a few butterflies take off in my stomach. He produced a red tin with a powder-puff inside marked 'Leichner Blending Powder No.116' on the lid.

"This is the last touch to your make-up. Gently dab this over your face to seal our artwork. You will need to buy yourself a tin of this," as he placed a round silver coloured tin with a blue lid on the make-up table. "It's called 'Crow's Cremine' grease-paint remover. You will also need either a soft toilet roll, which is what I use because it is cheaper, or a box of tissues. I warn you it's a very messy business!"

I said, holding the tin up to my nose. "It's a very attractive smell."

John laughed and said, "Well, that's it, you're hooked. You have now inhaled the intoxicating 'Smell of the Grease-Paint' the next sensation is the 'Roar of the Crowd'. Then you're definitely hooked."

I started to get into my full Highland Dress. Lucky, I thought, I might need this outfit at some point soon. As I accumulated enough money, I bought the outfit bit by bit. Eventually, I possessed a blue silk velvet double-breasted jacket with silver diamond-shaped buttons, with a thistle emblem engraved on them. In contrast to the blue velvet, a white lace jabot (short scarf) was worn at the neck. Pinned to this was a small silver thistle-designed brooch with a cairngorm stone set in it. A gift from my mother. Worn round the waist was a broad black leather belt with a large silver ornate buckle. I decided not to buy a kilt in my own tartan, which was mainly green, but instead chose a bright blue and red tartan of the Macbeth Clan. No one in Scottish show business dared to utter the word 'Macbeth' in a theatre. Artistes thought it brought very bad luck to anyone within hearing distance. I was also to learn that show business folk could be very superstitious. My sporran consisted of silver mountings, which supported a stiff leather-backed bag, made from grey baby-seal skin. This was all finished off with tartan hose, scarlet flashings (fixed to black elastic garters) black highland lace-up brogue patterned shoes with silver engraved buckles.

John McIvor, said, "Well Lawrence, you certainly look the part. That lot's going to look super under the lights, all you have to do now is play as well as you look!"

The tannoy speaker burst into life again with the announcement, "Overture and beginners please, overture and beginners on stage now, please." This time the speaker remained on. I heard the orchestra tuning up, and then go into the overture. I heard a round of applause followed by some rousing music followed by thumping sounds.

"What's that noise John?" I asked.

"Oh! The thumping? That's the dancers doing their high kicks. The speakers stay on throughout the show Lawrence, so that you know when it is near time for your act. It's a good idea by the way, to be standing in the wings during the act before your turn."

I looked at him, puzzling over the word 'wings'?

He laughed and said, "Sorry, you'll learn a different theatrical vocabulary in this job. 'Wings' means the side of the stage. 'Tabs' means curtains. The 'Boards' means the actual stage itself. Then there is the 'Flies'. That's above the stage where they raise and drop in tabs or scenery. 'F.O.H.' means front of house. And there's something else, you'll need to think, about a 'Lighting Plot'."

"A lighting plot?" I asked.

"Yes," said John. "You'll need to know what lighting you require, for the different moods of music you will be playing. Watch my act, when you settle down later in the week you will get some ideas for yourself. You can request different coloured spotlights, foot lights, and F.O.H. lights. It is all part of learning your craft. However, tonight, just concentrate on getting out there and entertaining the crowd, to the very best of your ability. A useful tip to keep in mind Lawrence, always give your very best. You never know who might be watching you out there." I never ever forgot that one.

John stood up, afforded himself a final check-up in the mirror and said, "Right here we go then." With that, he swept out the dressing room door.

I sat for a few minutes, just staring at myself, in the mirror. "How the hell did I get here?" I looked at the programme drawing-pinned to the wall and noted that there was a 'Speciality Act' on before me. I think they were jugglers. I read again, my name in blue print on the programme, 'Lawrence Adam and his Accordion'. I heard John finish his act and thought he received excellent applause.

He walked in, removed his jacket and said, "You'll be okay tonight Lawrence, they are a lovely warm audience."

I stood up, lifted my accordion from its case, put it on and said, "Well, here we go then John, see you later."

"Good luck," he shouted after me as I climbed the stairs leading to the stage and my awaiting fate.

As I climbed the stone stairs, the music and applause became increasingly louder as I neared the top. There I was standing in the wings awaiting my entrance music.

A figure appeared beside me. "Hi! You must be Lawrence. I'm Tommy the stage manager. Your first time on the professional stage I hear?"

I gave a nod and said, "Hi! Tommy."

"Don't worry Lawrence, they love accordionists here and we have a full house tonight."

There was a solid round of applause and the orchestra went right into my entrance music,

'Scotland the Brave' which I must confess, brave I did not feel at that precise moment.

I felt a slight tap on my back from the stage manager accompanied by the words, "Right, yer on kid."

I marched smartly towards the centre of the stage under the very bright warm spotlight to stand in front of the microphone where I gave a chord and straight into a rousing Scottish melody of jigs, strathspeys and reels. The audience soon started to clap encouragingly in time to the music tempo, plus loud "Hoochs!" (whoops!). When I finished the first set, they applauded generously indeed. 'The Bluebell Polka' went even better. The musical director winked and a grinned. I announced the 'Blaze Away' march and was amazed, that when I turned the basses towards the microphone for the bass solo, I was startled to receive a cheer and a burst of appreciative applause. As the orchestra played me off, I heard shouts of 'more...more!' I was astounded and arrived at the side of the stage to be pushed back on again by John McIvor who had been standing at the side.

"On again Lawrence, go on, take another bow, and take your time, count to five." Eventually, I staggered off to the sounds of the next artiste starting his act and realised, rather sadly, that my allotted time-slot had ended.

When I reached the dressing room John said, "Well, how do you feel now?"

I felt in a bit of a daze. I replied, "It was fantastic John, I've never been so happy in my life! It was over all too soon. It felt like I was only on there for just a few short minutes."

"You're going to love this business Lawrence, and I think this business will have a lot to offer you. I warn you though it is not all going to be roses. It is a very hard game in fact. Sadly, theatres like this are in decline and work is getting harder to find all the time."

John was correct regarding the removal of the greasepaint. What a messy business. As I emerged from the stage door with my face still stinging from the effects of the Cremine make-up removal-cream I had another surprise waiting for me.

Three young girls ran towards me with small books and pens in their hands saying, "Can we have your autograph please Lawrence and have you any photographs?" I did not know what to say, this was a completely new experience for me, and one I certainly did not expect, that anyone should want a picture of me, or an autograph!

John was behind me and as we walked away, he said, "Ha ha, that surprised you eh? You will have to get some of what we call 'throw away pictures' done Lawrence for the fans. I'll give you an address: they are not too expensive, and well worthwhile to get your name about.

I was staying at my Aunty Nellie and Uncle Eck's prefab. Mum and Dad travelled over on Saturday with Bill in the band bus. I do not know how Auntie Nellie found the space for us all to stay, but relatives all managed to perform these amazing feats in those days. No one seemed to mind at all where he or she slept. I cannot remember ever hearing any complaints such as 'types of food not being acceptable' or 'beds being too small' or 'too hard' etc. Everyone just mucked in.

Front row seats were booked for Auntie Nellie, her family, Bill, Dad and Mum. I had arranged for a big box of chocolates to be given to my mother after she was seated. I remembered her tale to me relating to this very theatre, when as a child with her siblings, enviously watching little rich children eating delicious chocolates. My mother, and her raggedly dressed urchin brothers and sister, could only afford the very cheapest seats upstairs, but this time they were right in the front in the dearest seats in the stalls.

I was pleased that my act went very well. The manager came backstage to congratulate me and said that he was sure he would hear of me again. I said goodbye to John McIvor and thanked him for his invaluable advice. Sadly, I never worked with John every again. This was something I became used to in the future.

We stayed the night in Dundee, bade farewell the following morning and made our way back home. As we embarked from the ferry, I glanced up at the huge poster advertising last week's show at the Dundee Palace. There was my name! What a moment.

Sixteen
The Carl Levis Show

"Why don't you audition for the famous 'Carol Levis Discovery Show'?" said the customer I was serving. "They are auditioning in Edinburgh this week." I thought about it and decided, why not?

Bill offered to drive me to the auditions. At that time, the 'Carol Levis Discovery Show' was the equivalent of the 21st century 'TV show called 'Britain's got Talent'. The auditions were held in the Empire Theatre Edinburgh. The stalls were packed with folk who amazingly fell into two categories. Accordionists playing Scottish jigs and reels and Highland dancers festooned in medals bouncing up and down upon their chests doing Highland flings or the sword dance. I studied the four judges seated at a long table on the stage. They looked weary and fed up with what was on offer. I also noted, when they called out names from their lists, they were English.

I said to myself, "Well now, to English ears one jig or reel must seem pretty much like the next. If I am to grab their attention I will need to play something different."

Bill nudged me and said, "What are you going to play?"

"My Florence," I replied.

"But you don't know it yet, I've listened to you practising. You only know about half of the piece, you'll look an idiot!" He exclaimed.

My name was called out. I stood up and muttered to Bill, "Here goes an idiot." I walked up onto the stage, put on my accordion and saw a look of utter dismay cross all the judges faces. I knew what they were thinking, "Oh! No! Not another Scottish accordionist!"

"Hullo Lawrence, and what are you going to play for us?" one of the men called out. "I'd like to play an Italian classical piece called 'My Florence'," I replied.

"Did you say a classical piece?" They said in amazement.

"Yes, that's correct."

"Please do carry on," another gentleman said.

I thought, 'Well, here goes, perhaps they might stop me before I reach the end of the bit I know. If not, I might pretend to faint, or something." I glanced at my brother, seated hunch up in the stalls, with his hand up to his mouth and his eyes open wide. He looked more nervous than I felt.

The start of this piece of music was magnificent, big block chords, fast finger rippling-cadenzas, followed by a gentle waltz tempo, and then a sudden change into a brilliant staccato passage. The trouble was I only knew it up to the end of the staccato passage, after that...well!

Just at the precise moment of pending disaster, one of the judges shouted, "Lovely Lawrence, come over to the table for a moment, please." I stopped playing (with great relief) walked over to their table.

"Thank you, Lawrence, for an excellent audition. We've decided to offer you a place in the show. It will take place here in this theatre next week at 8.45 pm on Friday 20 February. Please send some photographs of yourself to this address, along with this signed agreement." He pushed a sheet of paper towards me, which I placed in my pocket. The year 1959 was certainly looking exciting.

As I walked back to join Bill, he shook his head at me and said, "How could you do it? Let's face it: you're just a wee cheat. That was blatantly dishonest, you should be ashamed!"

I just shrugged and said, "I didn't tell any lies, I did what I said I was going to do. Why should I be ashamed?"

When we got home, the first thing Bill did, was to tell my mother what happened.

She roared with laughter, and said, "Well Bill, yer brither's certainly got guts and takes risks, that alone will take him a long way."

Bill transported me once again to the Edinburgh Empire theatre. It was much bigger than the Dundee Palace. I handed over what music I had to the orchestra's Musical Director.

He remarked, "I'm afraid we have a much bigger orchestra than this son, but don't worry, we'll manage to follow you. Keep your eye on me."

I decided to play the exact same act as I did in Dundee. It went well there, and I knew it well. I was quite far down the variety bill and followed a skiffle group, which was all the rage at that time. The theatre was packed with about two thousand people: the biggest crowd I had ever faced.

"Well, I hope you're not going to attempt 'My Florence' tonight?" Bill said.

"No not at all. I'm going to be playing Scottish jigs and reels!" I replied.

"What!" he exclaimed! "They will be expecting a classical piece."

"Well, that's show business," I said, as I walked on to my introduction music. I was convinced I was not going to win, so I decided to enjoy myself. The crowd seemed to appreciate my offerings. I will never ever forget that roar of approval from such a large audience.

At the end of the show, we lined up across the stage. At one side stood a huge clock face with numbers round the edge and a red pointer. Carol Levis explained that the needle moved according to the volume of audience applause. The celebrity Jackie Collins, (authoress and sister of film- star Joan Collins) would stand behind each artiste, raise her hand and that was the cue for the audience to applaud for the act they thought deserved to win. The winning act would appear in the Carol Levis Discovery, BBC Radio Show from the Playhouse Theatre in London. They would also appear in the Carol Levis Discovery, TV Show live from Birmingham.

I listened to all of this and thought 'Lucky devil that wins that lot.' I had resigned myself to the fact that it could not possibly be me. Most likely, it would be the skiffle group, or the girl singer who was pretty good too.

Jackie Collins began her walk from right to left. The audience responded with huge bursts of applause. Carol Levis, in his Canadian drawl, shouted through his microphone, "Oh yes! That was a good one. The highest so far, but we are not done yet. Another burst of applause.

I thought, "Wow, yes that sounds like 'the' one, I think that's the girl singer. I thought she would win."

"Do we have a winner?" shouted Carol Levis. Jackie Collins moved again, getting nearer, to me. Suddenly there was an eruption of loud applause and shouting of 'Encore'. "That was a very good one," shouted Carol Levis again. There followed more bursts of applause. Carol Levis said, "Well ladies and gentlemen, you all saw that needle jump up the clock, but let's just double check that once more." I sensed Jackie Collins move again in my direction back along the line, but I could not see where she ended up from my vantage point. We had been instructed to keep our eyes front and not look behind us. There it was again, thunderous applause, accompanied by Carol Levis shouting down his microphone, "Yes! Oh, yes! We do have a winner. The crowd were cheering loudly, and I felt a push against the small of my back, pitching me forwards towards the footlights.

I thought, "What on earth? Who did that?"

Camera flashbulbs started popping and Carol Levis joined me, took me by the arm and said, "Well done Lawrence Adam, you are our winner." I was flabbergasted!

When we got home, Bill burst into the lounge shouting, "Mum, Dad! He's only gone and bloody won it."

"No need to swear son," Dad, said.

"Well done ma lad," Mum said wiping away a wee tear.

I had a couple of very complimentary press notices in the newspapers. Much more was to come however.

The notification arrived to take part in the Carol Levis Radio Show in London all expenses paid. Sure enough, a letter arrived detailing when the show was to due be broadcast on the BBC from the Playhouse Theatre London on Saturday the 4th April, 1959.

"More time off work Mr. Adam?" grumbled Mr. Lister. "This will have to be deducted from your wages this time I'm afraid."

The train arrived in London at 10.30 am and a taxi took me to the Playhouse Theatre by the River Thames. As I entered the doors into the stalls there was that smell of theatre again. The orchestra were tuning up. A woman materialised in front of me holding a clipboard,

"And you are?" she said in a clipped London accent.

"Lawrence Adam," I replied.

"Ah! Our Scottish accordionist." She said giving me a welcoming smile. "I'm the Production Assistant and my names is Angela. Follow me Lawrence and I'll find you a dressing room."

Angela showed me into a smart brightly lit dressing room and left me there saying, "Just   relax Lawrence. I'll come to fetch you in about 20 minutes or so. When you are finished, you should get a taxi to the booked hotel. Do you have the instructions with you?"

I produced the piece of paper and glanced at it saying, "Yes, all explained thank you." Angela gave a smile then took her leave. I sat down, looked at my reflection in the mirror, thinking back to the Edinburgh Empire Theatre. Did I really win? How on earth did I win? I kept asking myself many questions and replaying the events in my mind.

There was a tap on the door, Angela opened it and said, "Okay, Lawrence, your turn. Don't forget to bring your music along with you for the musicians." She led me onto the stage, which was not very big really. In fact, when I stood and took everything in, the theatre was quite small but had a cosy atmosphere.

The Musical Director took my music and distributed it to the orchestra.

"Now then Lawrence, the show will be recorded tomorrow afternoon. Once we start, we continue to the finish, the recording does not stop, so I hope you are note-perfect. There is a good audience in so please wear what you normally wear for your performance and think of it as a theatre show. Right, let's get started shall we." He raised his baton and we were off.

They were excellent musicians and only required one run-through of each piece. "That's fine Lawrence, enjoy the rest of your day and I'll look forward to seeing you tomorrow. Please be here, at the very least, half an hour before the show and be ready to go when you are called."

After booking into the small hotel, I went for a walk. I crossed the River Thames and stopped to look in the window of a small jewellery shop. A watch caught my eye. I had never seen anything like it. It was gold, and the watch rectangular-shaped face, did not have numbers but instead was marked off with stones. A ruby at 12, 3, 6, and 9. Then diamonds where the remaining numbers would be. It was attached to a thick gold ornate bracelet. I was mesmerised. I looked at the price and thought, 'Why I can definitely afford that. Sadly, the shop was closed. I took out a notebook and pencil and carefully wrote down the owner's name and the address. I intended to write and ask if he would send it to me, when I got home.

I arrived in good time to be greeted by Angela still holding her clipboard. She gave me a big smile. "I'm pleased to tell you that you'll be playing to a full house Lawrence. I'll come for you in good time and accompany you to the stage. Mr. Levis will be introducing you and leading you off when you have finished."

I readied myself with one ear tuned to the small speaker in the corner of my room. First was a comedian who was very funny and seemed to be going well with the audience. Followed by a vocalist. Soon the customary tap on my door heralded Angela's reappearance saying, "Okay, Lawrence, follow me please."

I went into top gear mode as Carol Levis announced me, as

"Here's a young Scot from a small coal-mining town called Lochgelly in Fifeshire. He going to play his accordion for us, so give a big London welcome to Lawrence Adam."

I thought there must be some Scottish folk in here today as they started clapping in time to the music. It was like Dundee Palace all over again. Once more, it was all over too soon, but I was pleased to leave the stage to the sounds of cheering and applause.

Carol Levis announced, "You will be seeing this young man again soon, as we are inviting him to take part in the big show from Birmingham on network television."

Angela escorted me back to my room again and said, "Lawrence that was brilliant. Good luck for the TV show. We will be in touch with you shortly. Do something extra special for that show. It will be seen by millions."

The show was broadcast on Wednesday 15 April and we managed to tape it. My mum sat and cried as she listened to it saying, "Oh dear! Just fancy! Oor Lawrence on oor wireless."

Someone remarked that they saw my name in the Radio Times. There was a small piece in the Lochgelly Times newspaper. However, Sottish people are not prone to making complimentary remarks to one's face. The rest of the weeks went past as usual, magic shows, dance band engagements, appearing at various places in a Top Town Variety Show and working in the Gent's department at the Co-op.

At last, a letter arrived inviting me to appear on the TV show on 21 April, to be televised from Birmingham.

I had been working very hard and felt I had mastered a piece of music called 'The High Level', which was reputed to be the fastest and most difficult of Scottish accordion solos. I had an idea to make it even more special. I did not tell anyone what I had planned. I made a purple velvet fitted-cover for the accordion keyboard and a matching purple velvet eye mask.

I arrived at the TV Studios in Birmingham in good time. The show was scheduled for 7pm. The routine was like the radio show. A Production Assistant introduced me to the band under the directorship of Jerry Allen, a well-known broadcasting musician.

The difference on this occasion was that I was dealing with a floor manager wearing headphones. Instructions were relayed from an unseen producer. He was in a room called a 'Gallery'. There were five large cameras on tripods, with rubber wheels attached, moving silently and swiftly. Men followed the cameras guiding the trailing cables.

In addition to this distraction, a technician pushed around a man who stood on a small metal platform also on rubber wheels. He held a long pole with a large boom microphone. There were so many people buzzing around! Just to add to this new confusion, the production manager told me that when I noticed a camera with a red light lit on top of it, that was the one I must look at. This was quite a bit trickier than a stage show or a radio broadcast.

The floor manager told me the producer wanted to know what I would be wearing, and details of the music I would be playing. I explained as best as I could.

"Okay, Lawrence, just go through your rehearsal now, but I may have to stop you occasionally." The band were absolute top-drawer quality. I came to the High-Level music and I explained about the keyboard cover and the blindfold.

The floor manager said, "Hold it there just a minute please Lawrence." There was a pause: he was obviously listening intently to the producer's instructions. He said, "The producer wants to see you do this now please, for camera angles and lighting."

I obliged and when I had finished the floor manager smiled and signed thumbs up. I felt exhausted and that was only the rehearsal!

I was asked not to leave the building. An evening meal was supplied at the canteen of which I ate very little due to the thoughts of the live televised show approaching.

I dressed in my Highland outfit and resisted the temptation to have a quick practice. I had learned through experience, that if I did not know it by now, I should not be here about to do it. It would be all too easy to make a mistake and then panic, entering the 'What-If' syndrome. The familiar tap on the dressing room door and the production assistant telling me it was show-time.

I stood at the side of the extremely brightly lit stage. The atmosphere was electric. Carol Levis introduced me.

"Next is a young man I discovered in Scotland who comes from a small mining town called Lochgelly, in Fifeshire. He is a virtuoso of the piano accordion, and here he is to play for you. Please give him a big welcome."

I walked into welcoming applause, grinning and playing, the Scottish jigs, strathspeys and reels I had learned so well in the past.

Arriving at the 'risk factor', I said, "I'm going to play for you the fastest and most difficult piece of Scottish music ever written for the piano accordion. (The silence was deafening!) To make things even more difficult, (soft drum roll) I am going to fix this thick velvet cover over the keyboard, so that I cannot feel the shapes of the keys. Just to add more risk, I am going to place this velvet blindfold over my eyes so that I cannot even see the keyboard. Ladies and Gentlemen...the 'High Level'."

The piece starts slow, and then gathers momentum, until it is only just physically possible to play at all. Many years later, someone told me I was relying on a thing called muscle-memory. When I finished, even before I removed the blindfold, I heard the loudest cheering and applause I had ever heard up to that point in my life. To me it was intoxicating stuff. As far as the audience were concerned not to mention the poor producer, it would be great relief. It could have gone horribly wrong. TV was live in those days. What you saw was what you got.

When I arrived home, there were big hugs and my mum said, "Lawrence, what were yi' thinking aboot son wi that blindfold and things? Whit a thing to pull, I thought I was goin' tae hae a hert attack."

Bill chimed in, "Aye, she put her hands up to her mooth and wailed, 'Oh! Ma Goad!'." He carried on laughing as he said, "An dad just froze, stopped puffin' on his pipe wi his eyes oot like organ stops! It really was a great stunt though."

There followed a very good press notice in the 'People's Journal' saying "He could well rival established Scottish stars." A small paragraph appeared in the Lochgelly Times.

Not one member of the Co-op staff mentioned anything about the TV show. However, many customers who came in were full of praise saying that I had put Lochgelly on the map.

The Telephone Call

The big event however, was when Mr. Lister came bounding into the Gent's department, walked up to me, stared at me for a few minutes, then barked,

"Mr. Adam, I am sick and fed up of you getting telephone calls at work. I have told you this before and this is the very last time I am telling you. There is a gentleman on the phone in MY office and he is most insistent that he speaks with you. Please be brief."

With that, he marched off in the direction of his office. I followed him in. I did think he might have given me the courtesy of some privacy, but no, he thumped himself down on his chair and started fiddling about with some papers.

"Hello, Lawrence Adam here."

"Ah! Hullo Lawrence. I am Andy Stewart's manager." Everyone in Scotland knew of Andy Stewart. He had a record in the UK Top music charts called 'A Scottish Soldier'. DJ Terry Wogan played it on his radio show.

"Andy Stewart?" I said. Mr. Lister looked up, then down again.

"Yes, my name is Mr. John Worth. Andy is appearing at the Inverness Empire Theatre this week. Well, he popped out at the interval to the bar next-door. There is a TV set above the bar and he said he saw you on it. He was most impressed and asked me to phone you to ask if you would consider turning professional and joining his show which is about to go on tour."

"Turn professional?" I noticed a podgy little pink hand open a desk drawer, picking up my Employment Cards, and just hover there.

"How much would I be paid?" I asked.

"Well as you are new to show business, we would be prepared to pay you £15 per week."

"What would my hours be, please?" I said.

"Your hours?" he said laughing, "Well, you would be on the stage twice. Once in the first half for about five minutes, then again in the second half for about seven minutes, twelve minutes in all."

"You're going to pay me £15 per week for 12 minutes work a day?" I asked.

"Yes, that's quite correct." I noted the little podgy hand now withdrawing the cards and placing them on the desk. Mr. Worth continued,

"The tour will be at a different venue each night for four weeks, with the possibility of extras."

"Mr. Worth, you are on, when and where do I start?"

"Excellent," he exclaimed, "Andy will be pleased. You will start at the Empire Theatre Inverness and then we move off the following day. You are required to start on Monday of next week!"

"Monday next week? I don't know if that would be all right with my boss." I glanced down and Mr. Lister gave a large definite nod of approval.

"Yes, Mr. Worth that will be fine I'll see you in Inverness on Monday."

He said, "No, no, please arrive on Sunday, come to the theatre and I'll have accommodation fixed up for you and you can meet the rest of the artistes in the show."

Mr. Lister said, "Well, Mr. Adam, looks like you will be leaving us very shortly then?" I nodded. He said, "£15 a week for twelve minutes a day. That is immoral. Why that's more than I get!"

"Yes, and it's certainly a huge pay-rise for me, from £5 per week for about nine hours a day, six and a half days a week," I replied.

I told my folks my news when I arrived home from work. Bill was disappointed and said, "What about the band Lawrence, what are we supposed to do now eh, have you thought of that?"

"I wanted perfection Bill, the band didn't. They were content to drift. I am not. You will get another accordionist easily enough," I retorted.

My Dad said, "Well you know, whilst I am very proud of your achievements, I did think you might have been better with a reliable, steady career."

Mum said, "You go son, that's where your heart is right enough, so follow yer dream and follow yer heart."

Farewells

When I told the band members that this engagement was my last time with them, they were shocked. They told Bill they would be willing to carry on, if he felt he could still get the work in. He said he felt confident he could. We said our farewells and apart from my brother, I never ever saw any of them again.

After the Co-op store closed on Saturday, all the staff gathered at the foot of the wide main carpeted staircase that led to the upper sales floor. Mr. Lister was standing on the stairs. He gave a small speech of farewell and handed me a maroon coloured canvas and leather grip, as a farewell present contributed to by all the staff. He and the staff would be sad to see me go (which, as far as he was concerned, I did not believe for a minute) but he wished me well. This ended with a polite round of applause. There were a few tears especially from Miss Allan. I cannot in all honesty say I was very sad to be leaving. I felt that it was time for a change and I was pleased that my dream looked like coming true. I said my goodbyes and walked out of the door where I had first entered, six years ago as a naive teenager who had ticked the box on his exam paper. During those years, I experienced many changes and would always be grateful for the knowledge and the educational certificates I earned and never forgot the lovely people that I had met: especially Mr. Given, my first mentor.

1958 My first stage appearance at the Palace Theatre Dundee

My first TV appearance as a winner on the famous Carol Levis Show

The Lochgelly Co-op Store, my work-place

The Drapery Salesman

A Youth Club outing to Arbroath

Packing up the Band-Bus after a gig at Wick

THURSO

WICK

GRAND DANCE
in
B.B. Hall, Wick
on
Thursday, 24th July
1958
From 8 p.m. — 12 midnight
Music by Lawrence Adam and
His Thistle Band

ULLAPOOL

1958 Dance Band Tour of Scotland

My first professional Highland Tour of Scotland

My first (and last...great fun but hard work) Scottish Summer Season

The big break that did not work out as expected

I loved the Inverness Empire Theatre

Seventeen
Pastures New and Working with Stars

"A package here for yi son, it came yesterday an' I forgot aw aboot it," shouted my mother, as she prepared the breakfast. I was busy packing a grip-bag in the bedroom.

"I'll be there in a minute, Mum. I'm just finishing my packing. That grip-bag that I got as a present from work has sure come in handy." I walked into the kitchen where I was soon tucking into a big fry-up. Bacon and egg, two slices of black pudding, two slices of haggis and a slice of fried bread. All washed down with a large mug of hot tea. There was an atmosphere of forced joviality underlying some sadness.

"Where's that package Mum?" I asked. She handed to me a well-wrapped box, which revealed the gleaming gold diamond and red ruby encrusted watch I had bought in London. I proudly put it on and I thought it looked good.

Dad said, "Hey, when yi get fed up wi that son, yi kin pass it on to me eh?" We all had a good laugh, and then it went a bit quiet.

Bill broke the silence and said, "Well, we'd better get going if you are to catch yer train." I nodded, stood up put on my coat and grabbed hold of my grip.

"I'll get this fer ye," Bill said, taking up my accordion-case.

There followed long hugs. I noticed a small tear in my mother's eye, as she said, "Take care of yerself son, remember we love yi and we'll be thinking o' yi."

Dad apparently could not find the words to express himself, so he gave a nod. We walked down the stairs and as we reached the bottom, I turned and gave a final wave to two anxious looking parents and then we headed for the railway station.

Bill and I did not say much on the long walk from our house to the station. The train arrived. I clambered on board and had a whole carriage to myself. I lowered the sash window in the carriage door. The guard blew his whistle.

"Hope all goes well Lawrence, I'll try my best to keep our band goin'. See yi in four weeks." Bill said, giving me wave and slowly disappeared into the distance.

1959 Inverness

26 April 1959 found me once more entering the realms of risk, travelling to a new endeavour in show-business.

Standing in the foyer of the Inverness Empire theatre and not quite sure what to do next, the sounds of screaming teenagers came through the doors of the auditorium. I recognised the familiar voice of England's latest pop star singing his hit song, 'A White Sports Coat and a Pink Carnation'. His name was Terry Dene from London.

A tall buxom lass joined me. She was in her late thirties ginger hair up, smelling of sickly sweet perfume, wearing a modest amount of make-up, and dressed in a tight-fitting, green woollen dress. She displayed an air of authority as she introduced herself as Jean, John Worth's Personal Assistant. Her attractive Highland accent struck me as she explained a change of plan. I now had the evening off.

Another woman walking briskly appeared from the auditorium laughing and saying, "My Gawd, it's absolutely packed in there." Jean introduced her as Muriel, the tour Production Manager.

As she shook me by the hand, she said sympathetically, "You must be tired Lawrence. I'll get the car and take you round to your hotel. I'll meet you at the front of the theatre in a couple of minutes." With that, she dashed out. Muriel was a short five feet six inches, slim woman in her twenties I guessed. She had shoulder-length black hair, wore a modern cream coat with a large check design on it and black patent high-heeled shoes. She had this same soft Scottish lilting Highland accent.

As I made my way out, Jean shouted, "By the way, Lawrence, you'll be collected at around 9 am and we will be heading for the town of Mallaig. We do two shows there."

The hotel was small. The room was clean and tidy. I unpacked what I needed and freshened up just as the gong signalled dinnertime. I made my way to the dining room and met a young woman who introduced herself as Margaret MacDonald the vocalist with the show. Margaret was in her twenties, had long auburn hair, a pleasant face, good figure but a condescending manner. She gestured to a seat opposite hers at the table.

Two European looking, people sheepishly entered the dining room and shook hands with everyone introducing themselves as The Skating Marinos a speciality act from Germany.

I asked Margaret where Andy Stewart was, and she replied, "Oh my goodness. He will not be staying here. He'll be in one of the larger hotels. We won't see him until just before the show. Do you know Andy?"

"No," I replied, "I haven't had the pleasure."

"I don't think it will be a pleasure Lawrence," she laughed.

After breakfast, two cars arrived at the front of the hotel. A man in his late forties walked up to me and introduced himself,

"Hullo Lawrence, I'm John Worth, we spoke on the phone." He took my suitcase. "You will be in my car with Margaret." He placed my case in the open boot of his car and went back for Margaret's case who by this time had climbed in and was settling down in the back seat with a magazine. Jean got in the front with John. The others in the cast had their own transport and followed us. John Worth could best be described as an intense bundle of energy. Height about 5 feet 10 inches, slim build, lank black hair cut in the style of the day but could have done with a trim and kept falling over one eye. He had flashing dark eyes that looked very sharp and observant. His dress reminded me of a schoolteacher rather than an entrepreneur. He wore a creased dark coloured jacket, with dark grey trousers, a pair of black unpolished scruffy shoes, a conservative checked shirt and a dark maroon coloured tie. His jacket pockets seemed to be stuffed and carrying a bulky load. I noticed he had a strained expression and darkish bags below his eyes. Patter was easy for him and it flowed continuously without effort.

Malaig

We arrived at Malaig, a small town with an attractive port in Lochaber, on the west coast of the Highlands of Scotland. It had been a long, hot, gruelling journey. I was going to have to adapt to travelling long distances and was concerned that I would have enough energy to perform to a high standard afterwards. A higher wage reflected the longer than 9 am to 5 am of many occupations. The audience were seated when we arrived at The Railway Hall.

As I was first on and given a five minutes spot with John Worth accompanying me on piano. In preparation, I spoke to the Stage Manager. He was a tall, stocky man in a seaman's blue sweater, wafting a stench of body odour, stale tobacco and seaweed.

I said, "I have a lighting plot here for the lighting man."

He laughed and pointed up to the ceiling, and said, "Di ye see that light bulb up yonder laddie?"

"Yes, I do, why?"

"Well...that's yer lights!" He replied.

"Fine, what about tabs?" I asked.

He laughed again and pointed to a rope loop attached to the house curtains.

"You jist nod yer heed an' I'll pull on this rope an' yer on, son."

Minutes later, there I was standing behind the house tabs, in my highland dress, strapped to my accordion. John Worth announced me as that 'Ace accordionist from the Carroll Levis TV show' I gave a nod, a loud chord on my accordion, the tabs swept back, and I was facing the audience. The hall was packed, there was a rousing cheer and the long journey had been worthwhile.

The show was proceeding well when Andy Stewart arrived, fully dressed in his kilt. He received a huge ovation, especially when he sang 'A Scottish Soldier' his international claim to fame. We had an interval of 30 minutes, before doing the same again. I was astonished when the tabs swept back this time, to see the very same audience, sitting in the exact same seats as before! I asked the stage manager how this was.

He said, "The folk here Lawrence are entertainment starved. They dinna have television. Yer compere should have said 'as heard on the wireless'."

After the show we all went back to the hotel, had a bite of supper, then went right off to bed and I slept like a log.

Oban

The following morning, we were off early again, this time to Oban – a four-hour drive through magnificent scenery. We drove past Glencoe, towards Fort William, but it was not such a long journey and I was grateful to have two successive evenings in the same place, although the audiences were not as enthusiastic as the previous shows.

Andy Stewart was a very serious and critical type of person. I noticed that the cast did not readily seek out his company but tended to shy away from him. During lunch in the hotel, I found myself seated with Andy, Margaret MacDonald and Muriel. During the meal Andy leaned over took hold of my wrist and looked at my London watch.

"My Gawd!" he said, "Wull ye jist look at that! That must be the cheapest bloody thing I've ever seen in ma life." He laughed loudly joined by Margaret.

Muriel looked very sympathetic and said, "Well I think it's a braw wee watch Lawrence and I bet it means a lot to you."

"Yes, it certainly does," I replied.

Andy laughed, shook his head and retorted, "Well, aw I kin say is, yer taste is in yer bloody backside!"

I then realised, why no one hovered around him much, or sought out his company.

He came over generally as abrasive sometimes arrogant and rude, but I suspected there was a deeper level to Andy and that underneath the macho image; he was concealing a sense of insecurity.

As the tour continued, I began to understand what it must be like to be like to be the star of a show and I felt sympathy for him in a way. The management or agent books a star quite simply to make a profit. If the takings on a night are down, they let the star know of their displeasure. If they are up, it's arms round the shoulders and drinks a plenty. Therefore, the star feels insecure and exists from performance to performance. Bearing in mind the public are fickle, success is often fleeting and not usually everlasting. I got the impression that Andy recognised my understanding of the situation and we had many little chats.

Andy was known by many as a vocalist, who had a hit record with his rendering of

'A Scottish Soldier' followed up by others such as 'Campbelltown Loch I wish you were Whisky' and 'Donald Where's yer Troosers'. However, he was a very talented comedian and impressionist. I saw him many evenings enjoy a standing ovation from a packed theatre or hall. His Elvis Presley impression was spot on and very funny.

It was a gruelling tour covering many miles and towns within the Scottish Highlands and even over the sea to Skye. Mainly we were well received.

I marvelled at the 'Skating Morinos'. They did their act night after night roller-skating at high speeds, on a circular wooden platform, just wide enough to accommodate them. His very attractive petite, blonde haired wife clung to his neck with her boots, as he wheeled her round at great speed, looking like her head might be smashed in at any moment, as it appeared to be only inches from the floor.

I developed a great admiration for the speciality acts. They were usually quiet polite people, dedicated and deep-thinking perfectionists, who liked to keep to themselves. Most speciality acts are more circus than theatre and live by different highly commendable codes. Theatre folk are all by their very nature, fiercely ambitious and highly competitive. They can seem pushy and abrasive.

Theatre based show business, does not tolerate cruisers or coasters. It is very much a day-to-day, week-by-week existence, never being sure where you will be next or what exciting things might happen or alternately what disappointments await you. Either you love it or you leave. In some ways, it is a 'Calling'. It demands sacrifice, determination, a strong focus and there is nothing else you want to do. Many are called but few are chosen.

The Elgin Experience

The strain on Andy became apparent when we did a late-night show in a cinema in Elgin. We had already completed a show in a village called Cullen, a former royal burgh in Moray on the North Sea coast 20 miles east of Elgin. We were all tired. It was the third week into the tour. There were no dressing rooms, the lighting was poor, and the working area of the stage was narrow. The only backcloth (the curtain at the back of the stage) was the actual cinema screen. This was made of a cellular type of material full of tiny holes. We were warned to be very quiet and careful of what we said as the microphones could pick up any noise.

The show started and as usual, I was first on. The cinema was packed. However, as it was a late show there appeared to be a great many men in the audience the worse for drink and getting louder as the show progressed.

I was okay, Margaret just about scraped by; the acts that followed were booed off plus the added ignominy of a slow handclap. The Skating Morinos abandoned their contribution, when empty beer bottles started bouncing and landing upon their small platform. Andy arrived, and it was obvious he had drunk more than a few whiskeys. He was heard to say behind the perforated cinema screen, "I am not going to even try and entertain these ignorant, drunken, shower o' bastards!"

Every single word could be heard by all loud and clear. There followed a few seconds of absolute hush, then rumblings and beginnings of a full-scale riot. John Worth gave me a shout to grab my accordion, get on there and try to calm them down. Back on I went again, feeling like a gladiator fed to the lions, smiling broadly and merrily playing Scottish jigs and reels for all I was worth. All to no avail and obviously a pitiful futile gesture, as they were now baying for our blood!

The shout went up from Muriel and Jean, "Quick all of you, grab yer stuff and git oot o' the door, the cars are ootside in the alleyway wi' the engines runnin'. Shift yersels. Oot, oot! Quick as ye kin."

We did not need telling twice I dropped into Muriel's car and it sped off to the sounds of screeching burning rubber. Suddenly, the crowd burst through the cinema side-door and immediately started hurling bottles, bricks and anything else they could lay their hands on, which bounced off the cars as they sped away as fast as they could, disappearing into the safety of the night.

Forfar

The tour eventually progressed towards the grand finale tour in a place called Forfar, the county town of Angus. I was feeling the strain as it had proved extremely hard work. However, I had gained much knowledge and realised that I felt like a professional performer now.

I was elated to see on the front row Bill, and Mum and Dad beaming up at me. There was no last night party or bouquets of flowers sent up. The cast just said their goodbyes and departed. John Worth said to 'keep in touch' as he would have more shows for me at the Empire and that I should contact an agent called Ross Bowie in Glasgow for a summer season, as soon as I got home.

The end of my first venture into professional show business. I loved it! It was not be the last I heard from Andy Stewart either but that would be some years in the future.

I came home with my family in Bill's vehicle. He was doing his best with the band, but he was finding it difficult to secure bookings. I was out of work, referred to as 'Resting' with nothing in sight. I did not do any work in fact, until my first summer season show at the Webster Memorial Hall in the seaside resort of Arbroath. Entitled 'The Arbroath Follies of 1959'. It had a large cast and proved to be a big learning curve. The opening date was Friday 26 June. Rehearsals commenced at 10 am on Monday the 22 June.

My very first summer season

The Producer was a roughly spoken Glaswegian called George Clarkson: he 'shot from the hip and took no prisoners!' There were two performances per evening, 6.30 pm and 8.45 pm. The programme changed completely every Wednesday and Thursday. He warned us that no repeats would be tolerated, but that he might relent during the last week of the season. I never saw the light of day. I was in early every morning with the cleaners to learn and practise new pieces of music ready to present to the Musical Director twice a week and practised right up until rehearsal. I was in every musical scene and took part in comedy sketches having to learn words to songs, learn complicated dance moves with the chorus and report for costume fittings.

A comedy duo called Billy Denison and Diane Carol topped the bill. There was young dancing brother and sister act billed as Lindsay Wood and Jeanette who had been in Scottish showbiz for years. There was a female singer called Kay Gordon and another double act called Williams and Moore, vocalists who kept to themselves. Sadly, they were past their sell-by date. The British Actor's Equity rep, Ronald Wayne, did not suffer fools gladly but passed on many helpful tips. Ronnie was English, about six feet tall, well built, blonde-haired and possessed a fine tenor voice.

Finally, there was Jimmy Reid, an elderly man billed as 'The Canadian Scot'. Jimmy was quite portly, grey thinning hair and wore the kilt on stage and off. He had a fine tenor voice and was well known for the song 'Maggie'. I spent lots of time with Jimmy ... me perched on a skip (large hamper) in his small dressing room, listening spellbound to all his stories. One of the artistes said that his wife Maggie came to the theatre regularly every Saturday night and sat in a box. She loved it when he walked over to the box, looked up and sang Maggie to her. Then sadly, his wife died. That evening, he insisted on still going on.

All the cast gathered in the wings, just in case he faltered. He didn't. In fact, when he came to the song Maggie, the audience applauded as usual, and then he slowly walked over to the empty box and sang his song, with tears trickling down his cheeks. He was not the only one crying, so were the cast and the orchestra. Jimmy came from a generation of performers, who firmly believed that whatever happens, 'the show must go on.' I was very fond of Jimmy and he, like Ronnie, offered volumes of advice: How to

- come on stage and go off
- milk applause
- verbally to introduce various pieces of music
- who to contact for orchestral musical arrangements
- how much it should cost me, and
- deal with producers and agents.

This proved particularly useful in my later years of showbiz when I became an agent and a producer myself.

Ronnie said more than once,

"As soon as you finish here, head for England you will never regret it. I've had enough of this bloody country. Due to a shortage of venues, the agents can hammer your money down and get everyone to work very cheap. You will make double the cash in England, Loll, (his nickname for me) so get down there at the first opportunity mate. Do not waste away up here. English summer seasons do not change the programme twice a week, are usually only one performance per night plus the money is far better and you get respect." Ron married a lovely dancer called Esther from Glasgow.

One morning, just as I was setting off from my digs, the landlady, a lovely friendly red-haired

Arbroath lass said, "Can I give you some advice Lawrence?"

"I always listen to any advice," I replied.

"Well, it's about your dress really. You look more like a salesman in a shop than a theatrical artiste."

"Really? Go on."

"Well," she began, "lose the collar and tie for a start, lose the suit and the lace-up shoes. Go for a more casual look. Wear your hair longer, lose the short back and side image. One more thing, your name is not showbiz enough, shorten it to Lawrie."

She only charged me £3.50 a week for full board and even did all my washing. I never had digs that like that again anywhere. I decided to take all her advice went casual, and even shortened my name for future engagements. She was bang on with her observations.

The show closed on Saturday, 22 August. After the Arbroath Follies show, we lined up across the stage as the audience showed their enthusiastic appreciation. Large bouquets of flowers were brought onto the stage and were passed to the women in the company. The applause still came. Presents were handed up to the Producer by the Musical Director and were in turn passed to my mate Ronnie, who then allocated them to various members of the cast. I was delighted to receive some myself.

For the first time, I experienced the sad feeling of a last night finale. In a way, it had been a relief to be able to do repeats for the last week and have some time off for a change.

I appreciated all the dance band experience I had, which I drew upon heavily to arrange the music into two spots of 6 minutes each. I had also learned many new pieces and had accumulated a large repertoire of music, which stood me in good stead for years to come.

The company was offered an extension of two weeks at a resort further up the coast, at the Beach Pavilion Theatre in the town of Montrose. It was a smaller theatre but had a cosy atmosphere.

Next, we had a marathon trip right across the country before catching a ferry to our destination at Dunoon. The scenery was breath taking. The theatre was large and more professional than Arbroath.

I join the famous White Heather Group

On the Friday Robert Wilson's manager contacted me. I was invited to take the place of Scotland top accordionist, Will Star. If agreeable would I join the White Heather Show at Her Majesty's Theatre in Carlisle on the 16 November. The show would run for three weeks before continuing. Will was an accordion hero of mine. What Will was able to play, at the speeds he played at was truly astounding. I was very flattered to be asked.

Robert was a Scottish household name famous for his theme song, 'Down in the Glen'. He was an established EMI recording star, had his own BBC Radio show for years and now toured the world with his 'White Heather Show'.

My pal Ron Wayne exclaimed,

"Loll, you're made! You can work with these guys for the rest of your life. What a golden opportunity for you." I answered and agreed to take the job.

I spent some time in Glasgow with Ron & Esther and stayed in their flat. Ron took me round what scraps of agencies were in Glasgow, but it produced nothing. One of his contacts in England and hired me for a week's cabaret at the Continental Palace Theatre, Hull in Yorkshire.

On 27 September, I arrived in Hull for the music rehearsal or 'Band Call'. I placed my music down in front of the footlights on the stage. First on was the singer, Rosa Macarie. She was very good. Rosa told me that in the 1920's and early 30's, her father was famous and had his own broadcasting accordion band. She asked me if I was interested in earning some extra money.

"Definitely," I said.

She explained that it was a working men's club and we were not supposed to do them according to our contract, so we should keep it quiet. If the management found out, we would never be re-booked. This was a new type of venue to me, which paid very well.

The Continental Palace Theatre was also a new experience for me. It was a traditional theatre but had every other row of seats removed and replaced by small tables. At the rear of the auditorium was a large long bar. Waiters nipped back and forth from the bar to the tables, carrying trays of drinks, plus chicken or scampi and chips in a basket. The trick was getting used to the distraction of movement all the time. In addition, the auditorium was not in darkness like a traditional theatre, so the audience was visible all the time. It was a learning curve and the wage was more than I had earned in Scotland.

I returned home to Lochgelly. Bill was thinking about giving up the band to emigrate to New Zealand. He was fed up and felt like seeking pastures new. I felt sad about that, but I remembered the band did take quite a bit of driving, coaxing and encouraging, and quite appreciated his feelings.

When I told my folks that I was heading for Carlisle to appear in the White Heather show Mum exclaimed,

"Jings son, that's Robert Wilson's show isn't it?"

"Yes, it is Mum and I'm to replace Will Star."

"Oh! I am thrilled son, ye ken, ave admired Robert Wilson fer years. You could be famous noo yersel. It seems like ye have made quick progress."

On Sunday 15 November, I met the cast at a rehearsal at the Majesty's Theatre Carlisle. Robert Wilson was a Scottish gentleman. Terry Duffy the pianist, who had been with Robert for years, went patiently through my music with me.

A young woman called Eileen materialised at my side and said in a firm voice,

"Here, he canny play that ye ken Terry!"

I looked at her, "Why not?" I asked.

"Cause I'm the main accordionist here and I will be playing it, that's why!"

"I didn't know there was another accordionist in the show. I am sorry. I'll find something else."

She gave a curt nod and still stood there glaring at me as I shuffled through some other pieces.

"Okay, I'll do this instead." Passing some other sheets of manuscript to Terry.

Eileen aggressively reached in front of Terry and took hold of the music.

"Or this sonny. I will be playing this during week two."

This went on for some time. In the end Terry said,

"Look Eileen, I think some compromise might be helpful."

We finally agreed on a Scottish selection that satisfied her. However, when I handed over the Carnival of Venice she said, "No, yer no playin' that! This is a Scottish show, naen o' yer classical stuff." I was by this time tiring of this and stuck to my guns.

I rounded on her and said in a firm voice, "I was told by Robert, that I am replacing Will Star. I know for a fact that Will played many show-pieces and continental music, and so do I and I am going to be doing that, and that's final."

She stomped off saying.

"Really! Well we'll just hiv tae see aboot that."

Terry looked up smiling,

"Well you seem to have made a right pal there eh? Welcome to the famous 'White Heather Group'."

We completed the band call and Terry said, "Have you got any digs fixed yet Lawrie?"

I realised I had not and said, "Heck, no, have you any suggestions?"

"Aye, there's room where I'm staying. Nothing fancy but it's cheap. I'll tak ye roond in a minute."

I made my way back to my dressing room. After a few minutes, there was a tap on my door and Eileen entered. She said, "Look Lawrie, we should try to git on."

"Well I'm willing if you are."

She handed me some lists containing titles of tunes and keys written by the side of each one, on a slip of paper

"I don't know if Robert telt yi or no', but you are automatically pert of the 'Kornkisters' group as advertised on the posters."

"What! It's the first I've heard of it."

"Och aye. We stand at the back an' provide the backin' when Robert's on stage dayin his act."

"Well I'm not happy about it, so where is the music?"

She smiled, "There's nae music, we jist play chords an Terry does a' the fillin' in…that's when he's sober that is."

I nodded, walked out and headed for Robert Wilson's dressing room. He shouted, "Come in." I asked him about accompanying him.

"Didn't I mention that? I am sorry Lawrie, but it's always been expected. Will Star did it."

I agreed to do my best but thought I should mention there was no music.

"You'll manage fine I'm sure Lawrie," he replied.

"Can I ask you Robert, why did Will leave? He's been established with your show for years?"

A silence followed, and he looked a bit embarrassed.

"Well now, it's no secret that Will has a drink problem and I put up with a lot for a long time. However, things came to a head and he just had to go. I was very fond of Will and sad to let him go, but there was no other option. I hope you'll be very happy with us Lawrie and feel that you can settle with us."

The digs were grubby, the landlady matched the surroundings and the food was often inedible. The weather for the next three weeks was cold, wet and miserable. None of the cast spoke to each other. It was a most unfriendly show.

Billy Crocket was about the most pleasant but kept to himself with his partner Jeannie. She made an appearance during his act playing a small concertina. She looked very sweet with her long blonde hair, an hourglass figure in a sparkling well-fitting leotard showing off her long slender legs. She seemed very shy and as soon as she came off, she scuttled back into their dressing room. I met Billy years later in a tough nightclub in Wales, who gave me some very useful hints and pointers. Billy was an excellent visual comedian and never failed to register with the Carlisle audiences.

Another long-time serving artiste with the show was a singer and guitarist Sydney Devine. I never managed to have a conversation at all with Sydney. He appeared, nodded, went on stage and I must say went very well indeed with every audience, came off, nodded, then disappeared back into his room.

Eileen was one of these folks whom I found impossible to get along with. She stood in the wings glaring at me with arms folded, every single time I went on stage. When I came off, immediately she turned on her heel and went off to her dressing room. I did not admire her playing very much. She hit all the right notes, playing run-of-the mill Scottish jigs and reels music, but the music was mechanical and soulless.

I did not enjoy playing for Robert either. I felt quite sad listening to his act. He had peaked and was on cruise mode. The high notes were noticeably strained. I held my breath every time he went to hit the high notes. The end was near,

Terry only seemed to be around during the show and then he probably went to the pub. He seemed to have a drink problem and liked the port wine. Sad that many a talented Scottish theatrical became addicted to the bottle.

During the final week of the show, he was late, and I thought for a horrible moment that Eileen and I were going to have to accompany Robert's act ourselves. However, at the last minute, and just in the nick of time, Terry scrambled onto the piano stool. I could smell the boozy port wine aroma wafting over me. We grouped together quite closely as a trio. Robert went into his final song, 'Down in the Glen'. The audience applauded as soon as they recognised the introduction. I felt sorry for the whole cast but realised that the best was in the past and the end was approaching faster than they probably realised. They had all been together for some years and had long since become bored with each other's company. After some serious thought, I concluded that I did not really care to be part of the White Heather Show any more and told Robert I would not be moving on with the show. He said he was sorry to hear that but wished me well. He never asked me why. I suspect he already knew.

Back in Lochgelly, I decided to move to London to try my luck there. Perhaps Ron and Esther were right. They said they were intending to do just that as soon as they could. I managed to get a copy of 'The Stage' newspaper and examined digs addresses in London. I wrote to a woman in Upper Clapton, East London, informing her when I would arrive.

My mother pressed something into my hand. She said, "I ken fine you dinna have much son. I have kept this for you when you started to earn a wage at the Store (the local name for the Co-op) and gave me a contribution to the hoose-keepin'."

It was not a fortune but was very thoughtful of her and certainly all contributions were welcomed. Another new adventure awaited me there so once more, I embarked into the realms of 'risk'. London, here I come!

Eighteen
A Scottish Immigrant in London
The streets were not paved with gold after all!

It was early evening when the train pulled into Kings Cross station London. I grabbed my accordion and suitcase and made my way to the taxi ranks. I asked the taxi driver to take me to Upper Clapton please.

He said, "Where to mate?" I repeated my request. He said, "Sorry son, never heard of it." A great start I thought moving on to the next taxi. I repeated the request to the driver.

"Wouldn't he take you?"

"He said he didn't know where it was," I said. He gave a nod and said, "Okay, get in, I know where that is." And we were off.

It was December and the city lights were shining brightly with Christmas decorations displayed here and there, adding an extra twinkle to the otherwise grey cold night. Eventually we arrived outside a sombre looking row of terraced houses. The dimly lit street was cobbled and looked like a scene straight out of an old wartime black and white movie.

"This is it mate," said the taxi driver in a singing cockney accent. I paid the fare, noting how quickly my funds were diminishing.

Facing me, were about six wide concrete steps, leading up to a stout dark green door. I pushed the well-worn doorbell and waited. A dim hall light went on and the door opened revealing a slim woman with fair hair in her early forties. She had a plain face but not unattractive. Her dress was quite smart, a dark red colour and looked as if it was made of cashmere.

"Good evening," I said, "My name is Lawrie Adam. I'm a theatrical artiste and wrote to you recently."

She looked amazed. "I don't recall receiving a letter, I'm sorry," she replied in a London accent. "In any case, I stopped taking theatricals some time ago. They were not financially reliable. We take reps and lorry drivers now. Sorry." She started to close the door.

"But I've come all the way from Scotland and straight from Kings Cross station. I've nowhere else to go and it's dark and getting late," I pleaded, holding my breath.

"I am so sorry. From Scotland? But we're full up, I have no rooms left I'm afraid." She looked genuinely concerned.

"How old are you?" she asked. I realised I looked younger than my years.

"Only just turned 21."

"Look, I would not want my son wandering the streets around here in the dark. If you do not mind sharing with my teenage son, there is a spare bed in his room. You can have that until a room comes free if you like?"

"That will be fine and very kind of you. Thank you so much."

The small ground floor room was at the end of the entrance hall, facing the front door. Her son's single bed was on one side of the room and on the opposite wall another single bed. There was a small wardrobe, a chair and some teenage clutter and a faded dark coloured carpet covered the floor. Above her son's bed was a large window with cotton drapes that did not close.

"I'll leave you to get settled in then. When you hear the gong in about half an hour, come into the dining room and have a meal."

I was starving, so when the gong went I was first in to the dining room! Half a dozen men came in. Two in suits and four in sweaters with open neck shirts. The landlady came in with her teenage daughter Louise. They served sausages, mash, peas and gravy followed by delicious homemade apple pie and custard. When the guests settled down on the various armchairs or the settee to watch the remainder of the news, mugs of tea were served.

I met the son Peter, who did not say much and was already in bed reading a book when I walked in. I climbed into bed and was soon in dreamland.

In the early hours, I was jolted wide-awake. I saw bright flashing lights running along the wall above my head and a throbbing vibration reverberating throughout the room accompanied by a loud noise like a train passing through the house, which is exactly what it was. Outside the window was a railway track with a train thundering past. This happened at regular intervals throughout the night, but in time, I got used to it.

The following morning, the landlady invited me downstairs for my breakfast in the family dining room. She asked me about my aspirations and myself. She said I could call her Jane. When she mentioned money for lodgings, I decided to be honest with her and asked if I could pay her at the end of next week. She agreed thank goodness, muttering "Huh! Typical theatricals."

I signed on at the nearest dole office. They said bearing in mind, I had experience as a salesman and the fact that I had qualifications, it should not be too difficult to find me work. At two warehouses, I gave poor interviews to avoid being hired. This decided me, that I might fare better studying to the Evening Standard newspaper and applying to advertisements more to my liking.

The first one was in a big posh store on Regent Street. I put on my very best clothes, all topped off with my Co-op-bought raglan-sleeved qualification green overcoat, an RAF regimental coloured cashmere scarf and a green felt Robin-Hood style hat, which were all the rage in Scotland. I presented myself to the store staff-manager who sat behind a huge desk, immaculately dressed in a well-cut expensive looking suit. He bid me to take a seat opposite him, placed his fingertips together, and with a bemused expression playing on his face, asked me a variety of questions. I offered my certificates for his perusal.

He said, "First of all Mr. Adam, I would like to ask you about types of merchandise you have dealt with."

"Certainly," I replied.

He continued, "Let's start at the top shall we? What make of hats have you sold?"

"Attaboy," I said. His eyebrows shot up.

"Never heard of that, what about shirts?"

"Yes, 'Amicus'," I said.

"Never heard of that one either. What about neckties then?"

"Yes, we sold 'Tootal' ties."

He smiled and said, "Ah! Now I have heard of them. Where was it you worked last again Mr. Adam?"

"In the Co-operative Society in Scotland."

He stood up and said "Oh! I do not think so Mr. Adam. Our salesmen deal with film stars, celebrities and even Royalty and I can tell right way, by the merchandise you mentioned, that you are not right at all for us. Thank for calling. Bye." I found myself outside on the busy street!

I had one more interview for a shop called 'Aertex' in Piccadilly Circus. I looked in my wallet. I only had a £5 note left! I just had to get this job! I decided to look in the store window of where I had just been and memorised all the names of the merchandise. I was not going to be caught out again.

Aertex

In the waiting room at Aertex, a group of hopeful salesmen waited but there was no spare chair. The air was thick with cigarette smoke. A door opened, and a balding kindly faced middle-aged man said, "Okay, next one please." As I was already on my feet, I made a hasty decision and dashed inside the door.

As it closed, I heard the muffled angry wails of the waiting men.

"Did you see that? I've been here for bloody hours!" said one.

"What a bloody cheek!" shouted another.

I took no pleasure in my action, but I was desperate and wasted no time in presenting my certificates to the manager who seemed suitably impressed. He asked me about merchandise and I was able to rattle off all the brand names I had memorised a few minutes earlier.

He looked up at me, his glasses resting on the tip of his nose, "When can you start Mr. Adam?"

"Immediately, sir,"

"Really, what about 8 o'clock tomorrow morning?"

I grinned and said, "Thank you very much I'll be here at eight sharp."

I stayed at Aertex until the end of March. During my lunch-hour, I was able to nip out and do auditions for summer seasons. That meant trailing up and down almost every theatrical agency steps in the west end of London.

One agent said, "I remember you now. I saw you in a summer season in a godforsaken seaside town called Arbroath. I thought you were quite good but could have done with a bit more practice."

"Sir," I said, "I had to learn two different acts a week from early summer until September. That's one reason I am in England." His comment did stick in my mind however, and I was determined to practise hard and aim for perfection.

Most of the many agents said they had nothing at present but would keep my details on file. A stock answer I realised. One agent called Don Ross Agency assured me that he would get in touch later, probably in the autumn as he could use my act in some of his northern venues. His handshake was particularly warm and held on to my hand far longer than was necessary!

I struck it lucky. I had an appointment at the Max Rivers rehearsal-rooms in Denmark Street playing for Hedley Claxton. He ran many summer seasons playing in many English resorts. He liked accordionists and if I went well, I could look forward to at least five years summer work with him.

"Okay, Lawrie, I'll book you. I will pay you £18 per week (that was £4 up on Arbroath). The show changes programme five times during the season. You will need five good polished 12-minute acts (that was music to my ears, considering I did about 25 at Arbroath!). You will start in Southsea at the Parade Pier Theatre for three weeks, and then travel to the Summer Hoe Pavilion Theatre in Plymouth for the remainder of the season. I will require you to rehearse in London for two weeks."

Mr. Pratt, said to me one day, Mr. Adam, I hope you don't mind me asking, but that is either a very large typewriter you keep bringing in here or a musical instrument?"

"It's a piano accordion, sir."

"Well, when we are closed tonight, why don't you give us all a tune on it?"

I did, and he said he enjoyed it very much. When the staff had all gone and I was putting my accordion away, he said, "You really are very professional on that you know. I play piano myself. I think you could do that for a living Mr. Adam."

"Funny you should say that Mr. Pratt, but I was about to hand my notice in to you. I agreed a contract for a summer season today."

"Where would that be?" he asked.

"Well, after two weeks rehearsal here in London, I go to Southsea for three weeks, then on to Plymouth for the remainder of the season."

He provided me with a glowing reference should I ever need one in the future. He was an excellent employer. I had experienced how the very rich shopped as opposed to the coal miners' wives in Lochgelly. They bought one shirt. At Aertex, they usually bought goods in half dozens and at triple the price of the Lochgelly prices. No Tootal ties here, only pure 100 per cent silk. Best quality Egyptian cotton shirts and Jaeger jackets that would have cost my Dad

2 months' wages. The quality was first class and taught me the lesson that, you get what you pay for.

In London, as soon as you open the front door in the morning the meter starts running. I never made much of a profit. By the time I had paid my digs and bus into and out of the West End, the balance left was small. I loved the city though, the smells the noises, the shops, the pub lunches (my luncheon voucher helped) and going to Leicester Square to watch the musicians, strongmen acts and jugglers all vying for attention from the crowds on a Saturday. My favourites were two men and a woman. The men had small moustaches, leotards and bowler hats. They were called 'The Happy Wanderers' and were hilarious. I sometimes treated myself to a bag of hot chestnuts sold from carts by the roadside. I managed to see two theatre shows in London, the 'Amorous Prawn', starring fellow Scot, Stanley Baxter and at the Victoria Palace, 'Bud Flanagan and the Crazy Gang'.

I never did change bedrooms at my digs. Peter said he liked having me in his room and requested me to stay there. I ate my meals with the family who could not have been kinder to me.

Nineteen
My First English Summer Season

The London rehearsals had gone well, and I had purchased a cabin-trunk to send on by train in advance to the theatre in Southsea. I felt at home here in England and Southsea was a pleasant town. The theatre company quickly became a tightly knit supportive group completely different to my previous summer season.

Southsea

The show was much classier than Arbroath. The top of the bill was a well know comedian called George Lacey. George kept to himself very much and had a bit of a short fuse.

Three weeks soon passed. The Company Manager herded us onto a train taking us south towards sunny Devon. Accommodation being scarce, I shared a room with the stage manager, Brian Seddon.

Plymouth

In the same digs were two women in their late forties. They performed as a double act and played in top class theatres all their lives. They were billed as 'The Munks Twins' and were well known for their 'mirror act'. One of them danced in front of a large gold frame, supposed to be a mirror, the other acted out her reflected image and only gave the game away at the last moment. To us they were Nancy and Mollie and were genteel for theatricals. They drove around in a very old-fashioned car, which reminded me of my Dad's Hillman Minx. They spoke impeccable English and sounded very posh. I later found out that they lived in a huge mansion house, complete with a maid, in Bayswater London.

Dave Allen

Comedian Dave Allen completed the set. Dave went on to become a household name and have his own television show. Brian and I made for the theatre on Plymouth Hoe and we could not possibly miss it. We just stood there taking in the sight before us. It was a huge white marquee. At first, I thought it must be a circus. However, when we got up to the large showcase outside the entrance, there was my name and my photograph. I managed to obtain the poster and still have it to this very day.

Inside, the band were rehearsing the overture. The stage was equipped with footlights and sets of tabs. However, protruding from the front of the stage, right in the middle, was a main support tent pole. We ventured backstage to find dressing rooms with our names stuck on the doors. The star had his own room. The Munks Twins and the girl vocalist Margaret McKechnie shared another. The soubrette, (a vocalist and lead dancer), a glamorous young friendly northern lass called Dorothy Holgate, and the dancers were in another. Finally, the second comic Dave Allen (who did his own stand-up act and was comedy-feed to the star) plus Tony Castle (lead dancer), Barry Daniels the baritone singer and myself.

That first Devon summer season the weather was brilliant, the audiences were warm and receptive, and the company became like family. John Soutar arrived with news from Lochgelly. John watched the show many times during his stay.

Dave had a real impish sense of humour and often played pranks on the Company. He painted bull's eyes inside Dorothy's bra with thick greasepaint. We thought someone was being murdered on hearing her screams, as she removed her bra during a quick change.

One morning the Munks twins came down for breakfast (last gasp as usual) with white hair and deathly white faces. Dave had covered their pillow in talcum powder.

Then it was my turn. He exclaimed that there was an almost complete circle of a dark brown ring on my arm.

"I don't want to worry you Lawrie," he said, "but that looks like Ring-Worm and should that circle close, it could be fatal!"

Tony said, "Oh! My God Dave, I've heard of that."

Dave said, "Do not touch it or allow anyone else to either. Get straight round to the doctors in the morning."

I hardly slept all night but as I stood outside the surgery door in the morning, the Munks twins came running up to me, "Lawrie, Dave's up to his jokes again. It's not ringworm it was make up he dabbed on your arm."

His biggest and most public joke was the night when our dressing room mate Tony, a young lad in his early twenties described as 'camp' was late in returning from his visits during the show to the Cobwebs pub. Brian was always furious with him. Although he never actually missed his cue, he came near it many times and only managed to get his costume on in the nick of time. This night, he was late again.

Brian looked in and said angrily,

"Bloody hell! Do not tell me he is not back yet?" Dave walked over to Tony's corner and took his white tights that he was due to wear in the looming ballet scene.

He ran the crutch under the cold tap, folded them up again and placing them behind a biscuit tin that served as our waste-bin, saying,

"This should be interesting. Say nothing just keep staring at your reflection in the mirror like I will." Barry and I did as requested with straight faces. Tony dashed in.

Brian opened the door saying in a very terse voice,

"I am responsible for the smooth running of this show, and you are a pain in the arse. Get ready this minute, or you will miss your cue. Hedley is sitting out there third row from the front (Hedley would turn up unexpectedly to see how his shows were going)

and you *are* going to be on that stage, even if I have to throw you on!"

Tony looked very panicky, "Okay, keep your hair on Brian, where's my tights? Where are they?"

Brian grabbed them from behind the tin saying,

"Here they are you nit, now quick get them on, they are coming up to your entrance music."

Tony threw his blue satin top over his head, grabbed his tights, pulled them up and went, "Eeee!"

Brian grabbed his ballet pumps and shouted,

"Get these on and get out there." We followed them quietly and stood at the side of the stage. The dancers stood in a circle. Dorothy took up her position in the middle ready to jump into Tony's arms. He lifted her into the air and held her there in a pose. The music gathered momentum then stopped suddenly. That was Tony's cue to take a flying leap onto the stage, pick up Dorothy and raise her high above his head. Everything went quiet for a few seconds. The musicians tried to stifle their smirks and giggles, as they looked up and spotted a large dark wet patch on Tony's crutch. The audience also started to giggle then laugh loudly. The dancers also noticed, and their legs started to buckle slightly.

Brian looked then uttered,

"Oh! Shit! Look at that, Hedley's going to be round here any minute raising merry hell."

I suspect he had a good laugh himself on the quiet. The show was a resounding success and we were offered a further two weeks at the Festival Theatre in Paignton.

Dave was not happy with his act. His style was all wrong for him. He spoke with an American accent and sounded like Jerry Lewis. He went to Australia, returned as simply himself, the lovable Irishman with a mischievous twinkle in his eye, and became a big TV star.

Before we left Plymouth, we had a last night party. We all chipped in for a complete set of clothes for Dave, as we noticed he had worn the same clothes all season. He was overjoyed with his gift. He stripped off, put on his new outfit and threw the old ones in the bin. Dave's present to me was a brass statue of the three wise monkeys, which I still have.

Paignton

Paignton was next door to Torquay the Naples of England. The theatre was much larger than Plymouth with a huge semi-circular stage. The audience were under canvas but this time it was at least dark blue and from an artiste's point of view was like playing a proper theatre.

Before the show finished, Hedley suggested I could work for him again for the following summer season 1963 here in Paignton with a pay-rise.

"The contract will be in the post," he said. "Meanwhile, as you have agreed to do the summer season, I can now offer you a short Easter season at the Palace Theatre Morecambe. Would you like that?" I agreed.

"Good," he said. "If they like you up there then it will be easier for me to book you in perhaps the year after for a summer season. That's my longest one and runs for 25 weeks, Only the Central Pier in Blackpool, beats us by one week to the title of the longest running summer season in the British Isles. I will put that contract in the post as well. Have a good winter Lawrie and I am sure we will enjoy a long partnership." We shook hands.

I set about going 'ooop north' (as the southerners jokingly say) to look for more work to see me through the winter months. I chose Manchester as many of the pro's (short for professionals) said there was a big boom of work coming in by way of clubs.

Twenty
1960 The Manchester Experience

The train from London pulled into Manchester station: I had never been in this city before. I placed all my cases in the left luggage department then ventured out on to the busy city streets. My first port of call was to the Town Hall, where I hoped to obtain some lists of available accommodation. Theatrical pals had advised me to try for a bed-sit or a flat instead of Bed and Breakfast as it was cheaper with fewer restrictions. Having obtained a quantity of lists I popped inside a phone box on Albert Square and made some calls. First place was a bus-ride to an area called Didsbury: a lovely flat but too posh for me and the price was formidable!

Next stop on my list was an area called Rusholme. The address sounded good. Park Crescent, 144 Denison Road. It was a small bed-sit and very basic consisting of a bed, a small table, a chair, and for heating, a gas fire. The cooker was on the landing outside my door, shared with a South African man who occupied the room in the opposite bed-sit. The price was excellent so I moved in.

Lewis's store

Cash flow was sorely needed once more. From a newspaper, I booked an interview with a large store on Piccadilly in the heart of the city called 'Lewis's'. The wage was far from a showbiz wage but turned out to be better value than in London. My certificates together with the reference from Aertex London eased my passage in to work in the Radio and Television department and paid a wage plus commission on sales.

Lewis's was very similar to many other stores in London. Two salesmen worked on the Radio and Television floor alongside myself and they let it be known that they had first pick of the customers. Commission on sales was involved.

One day, I decided to play a little trick. They regarded me as a rookie compared to themselves. When they were at lunch, I went around three popular selling TV sets. On two, I twiddled a few knobs. On the third and incidentally the one carrying the best commission rate, I fiddle the knobs again making sure that the picture looked far superior to the other two. No sooner done, and then in walked a couple requesting a TV set. Just in time, as 'Bill and Ben' as I nicknamed them, returned from their pub lunch and watched me selling. I got the couple interested in the two not so good tellies, and then I said, "Of course you really must make up your own minds, I don't want to force anything upon you." Upon seeing the picture on the third set, that was their immediate choice. Bill and Ben had been trying to sell this set for weeks but failed. I felt very pleased with myself and gained their immediate respect from then onwards.

We were inundated with young men, killing time during their lunch hour asking us all sorts of daft questions about various products. Many times, they lost us sales by plying us with questions but never intended to buy anything.

We had just received a stock of the latest new transistor radios.

I was asked, "Look here, what's the difference between 3 transistors and 4 transistors?"

I quipped up very quickly, "One transistor?" He went straight to the manager and complained. I received a ticking off although I got the feeling the manager was trying hard not to laugh.

Another time, a very attractive young woman came up to me and said, "Excuse me young man, where can I get felt?"

Again, the words just automatically came out "Back here in half an hour madam!" I found myself back with the manager and another ticking off!

I met up with some fellow theatricals in the canteen one day who gave me a few city agent contacts. One remarked, "You haven't got a car Lawrie? You would do far better if you had a car. There's a lot of money to be made doing two or three different clubs a night but a car is essential."

The singers asked if I knew anyone who could transpose their music for them to a key that suited them. I told them I could do that for them. They told me the rate they normally paid. I said I would do it cheaper and they could have it back the same day. They were ecstatic.

From then onwards, every morning when the man in a grey overall, slowly pushed a large metal cart on wheels round the various departments collecting the rubbish and upon reaching the Radio and TV department, looked furtively about, then slipped a bundle of music plus requests to me, together with a small brown envelope, containing pound notes. He returned once more just before closing whereupon I placed the finished music in his truck. Another income!

My first motor car

There was a garage on the Oxford road near where I lived. They had a blue Issetta three-wheeler car for sale (known as a Bubble Car) at nearly £300. Dad had said to me, "Lawrie, one day you will decide to buy a car. Don't buy a second-hand one, go for a new one, keep it three years then part-exchange it for another new one." Poor dad, he could never do that, but perhaps I could.

I went inside and spoke to the salesman. He told me the terms. If I bought it on hire purchase, I could pay for it monthly. I decided to proceed. As he handed me the keys. I said, "I can't drive, could you drive it over the road for me?"

He laughed and replied, "Yes certainly, but what then?"

"Oh! I'll learn," I said cheerfully.

Next day I bought a book entitled, 'Teach yourself how to drive and pass the test in three weeks!' I focused on the book and the car and did that very thing! Of course, I had to drive myself around the streets surrounding my digs every available moment breaking the law, as I had no 'L' plates no insurance and no driver's license. I am a focused risk-taker.

For practice, I drove up to Scotland to pay a visit to my Mum, Dad and Bill for a long weekend. That was a bit daunting. There were no big motorways then however just A-roads. Mum was very proud to be driven by her son in his new car even if it was a bit on the small side.

I plucked up the courage to drive through the busy city traffic into work. I even managed to get a parking place right next to all the management cars by doing a deal with the car park manager, who was a singer. I agreed to transpose his music at reduced prices.

"How the hell does he pull that off?" remarked Bill to Ben. "I've been asking years for that privilege and always turned down."

Sadly, at Easter I had to hand in my notice as I had 11 days' work in Morecambe at the Palace Theatre. The manager said he was very sorry to lose me, but he would treat it as a holiday and I could return if I wished. I certainly did.

Morecambe

I kept the bedsit on and made my way to Morecambe in my new car. I had applied for the Road Test and received a date, which would be when I returned to Manchester. I arrived at the theatre and during a conversation, Hedley was astounded to learn that I had not passed my test but was driving a car. He forbade me to drive whilst I worked for him.

Another artiste called Reg Daponte, who did a ventriloquist act, looked on sympathetically and said, "Look here Hedley, we can get some L plates and I'll drive with him." Hedley agreed.

Reg said, "Okay, Lawrie, come with me in my car we'll buy some L plates and then return."

He had a white open-top sports car. Reg, in his thirties, and a Londoner, reminded me a bit of a Rex Harrison type figure as he appeared in the film 'My Fair Lady'. He spoke very well, wore a modern checked soft hat, black-rimmed glasses, collar and tie, the smart latest shorty light fawn coloured coat, with a college scarf, which had one end thrown over his shoulder. We jumped into his car and took off. When we stopped at traffic lights, I noticed he received some admiring glances from passing girls. He gave them a big grin, doffed his hat and said, "Hullo there girls." Turning to me, he said, "It's the car Lawrie, it works wonders you know."

I remarked, "Thank you for this Reg, it's really very good of you. How long have you been driving?"

"Oh! Years, Lawrie."

"How long since you passed the driving test?"

He laughed and replied, "I haven't passed my test, but that will be our secret." I liked Reg immediately.

He gave a big grin and said, "Did you know that many folk call us theatricals sophisticated gypsies? I suppose we are in a way." One day in the future, I would employ Reg in one of my shows.

Hedley's show was a resounding success and received a tip off that I would be certain to be offered a summer season there soon. I liked the town of Morecambe, the theatre and the people. After the show, I returned to Manchester.

Back to Manchester

Clubland was a growing lucrative industry. Now with wheels, I was able to race between venues all over the city, doing about three different clubs a night. They were packed out and featured approximately 18 acts per night. I worked regularly with people such as Colin Crompton, Frank Carson, Duggie Brown and many others who went on to become household names in a TV show called, 'The Comedians.' The working conditions could be tough and so could the audiences, but I was making more money than I ever expected to earn. I was not playing the sort of music I preferred, but that which pleased the crowds. I suppose, thinking about it, I had become a musical prostitute!

I spent a long day serving customers in the store, then made my way round the various venues such as, The College Club, The Princess and Domino Club, The Yew-tree Hotel and many more. The audiences sat at red Formica-topped tables with waiters to serve up the drinks and food; chicken and chips in a basket, or scampi and chips in a basket. These dishes came on a red paper serviette in a basket. These venues were known as 'Theatre Clubs'.

Then there were the Working Men's Clubs. A similar layout, but food was mainly pies. It was quite normal to be half-way through your act when a man appeared selling pies from a large basket strung round his neck. There was always a game of Bingo. The distractions were many, so the artiste had to be able to command attention and be on the attack. The complete opposite from a theatre technique.

The Northern Sports Club was quite well known. The man who owned this club had one eye and a huge mean-looking Alsatian accompanied him always. One night, I had a disagreement with him over the fee. He totally lost it and threw me down quite a long staircase. He threatened to put his Alsatian dog on me unless I left. He had mental issues and was known as 'One eyed McCall.' The golden rule was, I was later informed, never speak to him and avoid contact at all costs. It was as if the Klondike gold-rush days had come to Manchester.

I was pleased with the occasional week, Monday to Saturday, at the Continental Palace Theatre Huddersfield, which was more of a theatre type venue and a relief from the harder Manchester clubs. I was able to play music better appreciated by theatre audiences. I had to set off immediately from work, drive 'over the top' as they called it and do a show. Then back to Manchester to be ready for work the following morning.

During one of these weeks, I was working with a singer/actress from London called Jessie Robbins. Jessie was a very large Jewish lady with a big personality. She strolled down into the audience singing 'Let me entertain you' whilst sitting on various men's knees, stroke their (usually bald) heads and cause much mirth.

One evening however, Jessie had decided to pay a quick visit to the toilet and nearly missed her cue. I banged on the toilet door and shouted to her that she was on. She came dashing out just as her intro music started to play. She grabbed the microphone and walked on singing her song, heading for the nearest man seated near the stage. Unfortunately, unbeknown to her, and in her haste, the back of her long black evening dress was tucked into the back of her knickers! The audience went into immediate hysterics. As she sat down on the elderly man's knee, the audience were in fits of laughter. I thought the poor man was going to have a heart attack! Jessie went through her whole 15-minute act, came off and said to me in passing, "You've got a great audience tonight Lawrie, did you hear that? I went a bomb!"

Beryl

Later in the week she introduced me to a relative of hers from Halifax called Beryl.

I thought she was quite pretty and had a drink at her family's table after my act finished. We kept in touch and I promised to pay her a visit when next I came her way. She was a quiet shy type of girl and worked as a typist for a law firm. Her father had his own grocery business she said. She also had two brothers.

I did pay them a visit later. They lived in a quaint little area called Southowram, which sat just above the town of Halifax. It was a trip into the past. The old-fashioned brick houses formed a square. They had a 'communal toilet' consisting of a brick building, containing a long wooden plank with three holes. I presume three people could sit together and enjoy each other's company! There was a communal washhouse containing washtubs etc., and a huge iron mangle. Beryl's house did not have electricity but still used gas mantles. I never did find out how many bedrooms they had but it was a very small house.

Her mother was pleasant and kept everything clean and homely. Her Dad's grocery business turned out to be a large stall in Halifax Market. I saw her as and when I could. She visited me and stayed in a hotel on the crescent of Victoria Park. She said she did not really care for showbiz people and hoped I might get a 'proper job' one day. I cannot remember becoming engaged, but I must have done. I took her to Scotland to meet my folks and remember my mother saying, "Bonnie lassie, bit she's no the wan fer you son."

An Accident

One winter's night, it was very frosty and had been snowing. Whilst travelling to play the Huddersfield Continental and going 'over the top' my little bubble car went into a sideways skid, then it started to roll like an Easter egg. The noise of scraping and banging was extremely loud. I just kept calm, wrapped myself round the steering wheel and hung on. Sparks flew above my head. The canvas sunroof ripped off. The wheel-jack, normally kept under the seat, rattled and banged around the cabin a few times, then disappeared through the open roof. The car then rolled on its side heading for the side of the road, where I knew there was a long steep drop, down to a ravine below.

"This is it then, I thought, any minute now!" Suddenly, everything stopped dead, followed by a complete eerie silence. I waited a few seconds, and then slowly reached up for the door handle. Very carefully, I turned it and gently pushed outwards. The steering wheel in an Issetta bubble car is attached to the door. The front of the car consisted of 'the door'. I opened it, gingerly stepped out and noted that a ridge of snow at the side of the road had stopped me going over the side to certain death.

I was aware of two cars skidding to a halt and people running over to me asking if I was okay. "Get a blanket," shouted one.

"He'll be in shock!" shouted another.

In fact, I was unhurt. My only concern was getting my accordion out of the back and getting to the theatre. This was kindly done. I was able to phone a garage, phone Beryl and they put me up for a couple of nights. I phoned Lewis's and told them I was ill. I collected my repaired car a few days later. However, I was shocked to find that the tartan seat covers, the carpet and anything else that was removable had been stripped out. This was quite normal for a car left on the Yorkshire hills overnight, I was told. As I drove back to Manchester. I thought, "Well, that's one of my nine lives used up!"

Driving Test

The day arrived for my driving test. The examiner was a large man who had some difficulty cramming himself into my small bubble car and let me know that he was not happy at all. I had a plastic 'L' plate stuck on the front of the car which fell off.

The examiner said impatiently, "Just get it and give it here."

He threw it on the back shelf. Then the car started to buck backwards and forwards. He said, "What the hell is going on?"

I replied, "I'm so sorry, I need to switch over to the reserve tank." I moved a small lever at the back of his seat and thank goodness, all was well. He shook his head and gave a sort of snorting noise.

As we went through the various parts of the test, I thought to myself, "Of all the places to take a test, I pick the city of Manchester!"

He broke into my thoughts saying,

"Now Mr. Adam, when I slap my clipboard onto my knee, you will perform an emergency stop."

I nodded nervously. Suddenly he did just that, and immediately I hit the brake. He pitched forward banging his bald head with a mighty thump on the front window - no seat belts. I thought he was knocked out, but he revived. Shaking his head and muttering, he marked something else on his clipboard.

"Pull over here Mr. Adam," indicating a parking space outside Victoria Station. He presented me with a small sheet of paper.

I looked at him and said, "So, I've failed then?"

"No Mr. Adam, you have passed."

I went to shake his hand, but he said, "No, no! You must not do that, we never shake hands with clients. I will just catch a bus back to the depot Mr. Adam. You have a good day and drive safe. He heaved his huge lumbering frame out of the car, waved and left me there.

I got out and thought I would treat myself to a cup of tea and a bun in the station. As I walked around, I noticed I was receiving some funny looks and smirks. A group of girls in the café went into fits of giggles and shrieks of laughter. I checked my trouser-flies were not undone, then said, "Okay, what's funny?"

One of then reached behind my back and handed me the 'L' plate that had fallen off during the test. "Well, well that examiner must have stuck that on my back," I thought, "Driving test examiners do have a sense of humour after all."

I was booked to appear at the Victoria Railway Club opposite the station entrance. I came out of my bedsit to face by something entirely new to me, dense fog! I climbed into the car and realised I could not see more than a yard in front of me. However, once a theatrical pro accepts a booking, the golden rule is 'you turn up whatever'. I made it to the park gates and carefully onto the main Oxford Road. I decided to follow the rear lights of a bus in front of me. I guessed the way to the station and thought I was doing fine until someone banged on my side window. I lowered the window to discover a railway porter holding a lamp.

He said, "And where the hell do you think you're going young man?"

"I'm looking for the Railway Club, please?" I replied.

He laughed heartily, "Well son, you have managed to drive onto platform 3. On your right, is the guards van, which can take you and your car to Kings Cross Station, London."

I did manage to find the club.

Morecambe

Offers of good theatre dates started coming in, so I handed in my notice at Lewis's and headed for Morecambe to appear once more in the 'Easter Revels Show' at the Palace Theatre.

Scotland

When that ended, I headed up north to Scotland again for John Worth to appear at the Empire Inverness with a star act called 'The Joe Gordon Folk Four'. I stayed another week to perform with recording singer Calum Kennedy.

Over to Ayr on the west coast then for a week at the Gaiety Theatre, with a rising star called Chic Murray. It was a lovely intimate theatre to work.

I managed a spell at home with my folks who eagerly pumped me for all my news. Bill said he was due to leave for New Zealand towards the autumn and perhaps we could meet up in London before he sailed.

Everyone seemed in good spirits as I took my leave to head back down south to Leeds City Varieties theatre in a show entitled, 'Halt, Who Goes Bare?' I realised this might signal the demise of variety. The top of the bill was a stripper. I noticed as I was leaving that the name of the show for the week following was 'Journey into Spice!' I was correct, family audiences did depart. I was pleased to be heading once more down to Devon for a summer season at the Summer Pavilion in Paignton.

Twenty-One
A Summer Season in Glorious Devon

In glorious sunshine, I drove along the promenade toward the Summer Pavilion Theatre. Brightly coloured show bills were displayed everywhere. It seemed The 'Gaytime Show' was going up in the world. Topping the bill was famous recording star David Hughes. The rest of the cast were unknown to me, as I would be to them.

Back at the theatre, Hedley addressed the assembled cast who appeared very friendly, and introduced David Hughes, a polite quiet man. He had his own pianist, Derek New, who was also the Musical Director for the show. He was also a composer who became well known for his hit composition 'Cross-Hands Boogie', which he had written for Winifred Atwell. Winifred was popular in Britain and had a series of ragtime hits.

I shared a dressing room with the choreographer, the comedy-feed, and the lead dancer. The comedian, Bryan Burden, was the son of Albert Burdon, who starred in many early black and white feature films. Albert was also well known for his 'Comedy Magic Illusion Act'. The singer, Jean Barrington had just finished a stint with the 'D'Oyly Carte Opera Company'. Later we appeared in other shows together.

For a publicity photograph, David Hughes had us all drape ourselves on and in his huge white American convertible limo. Bryan drove a red convertible

Triumph Sports. My car looked very humble and small by comparison to those two but at least I was fortunate to have one, as the rest of the cast did not.

The rehearsals and opening night went extremely well. Many of the scenes from Plymouth and the Easter programmes in Morecambe were repeats, so I was very comfortable and able to concentrate on my own act.

I managed to stop the show on the first night! Stopping the show is a term used when the applause keeps going far longer than normal, and the audience demands more. Not that everyone was impressed. As I came off, the star said with a note of sarcasm, "Well...follow that!" turned on his heel and went into his dressing room slamming the door.

Mum and Dad came down for a week's holiday, which coincided with my friend John Soutar's visit. Mum and Dad said they loved the show. They sat on the bench outside the theatre on a warm summer's evening, watching the boats on the sea and listening for their son's act. I was able to spend quite a lot of time with them and show them the sights. It was very sad to see them and John leave for home.

I appeared in Sunday concerts with stars such as Rosemary Squires, and the Springfields, before Dusty struck out on her own. Beryl Reid was a great laugh who used to perch on my dressing room table and we cracked jokes together. Bryan Johnson, winner of the Euro-Vision Song Contest with his song 'Singing High High High' and was related to Teddy Johnson of

'Teddy Johnston and Pearl Carr' fame was a very pleasant man.

Terry Hall and Lennie the Lion went down well, but Peter Brough and Archie Andrews fell a bit flat. I used to listen to his radio show regularly as a kid. He was very nervous before a show and admitted he smoked a large Havana cigar to hide his mouth. He was not really a ventriloquist and had reason to be nervous.

I practised six hours a day to maintain the standard that I had achieved. One late afternoon I was just finishing when this tallish debonair man, burst through the auditorium doors and came striding down the centre isle taking off his jacket and throwing it over a seat. He looked up and said, "Hullo, are you finished rehearsing?"

"Yes," I replied, removing my accordion.

"I'm Alberto Semprini."

I told him who I was. He sat down at the grand piano on stage and did a few chords and a couple of impressive arpeggios remarking,

"Good piano. I don't know about you but if I don't practise every day, I know I'm not as good as I should be. If I miss a day, the audience notice I'm not as good as I should be. If I miss another day, the theatre bookers notice that I'm not as good as I should be."

I replied, "Thank you Mr. Semprini, that's something I will never forget.

He grinned, "Are you new to show business Lawrie?"

"Yes, this is only my third summer season," I said.

"Well, here's another tip for you which has served me well, if you fail to prepare, then prepare to fail!" I have never forgotten his advice. That evening, he gave a brilliant performance.

David Hughes was quite insistent that he did not just do his act but wanted to be in as many comedy sketches and musical scenes as possible. One evening David had a heart attack and was immediately spirited away to hospital. We were all shocked and saddened to hear that he died. However, the show must go on and Lester Ferguson a well-known Canadian singing star replaced him immediately. Lester registered very well, endorsing the saying that no one is indispensable.

End of the season

It had been a glorious and successful season and so I was very pleased when Hedley said I had been requested to return for next summer season together with Jean, Bryan and Lester. He could manage a small pay-rise. I accepted at once.

After the final curtain, I had a few dates in my diary. A week in Dublin at the Olympia theatre with Tommy Fields (Gracie's brother) and a week in Germany playing to the American troops in and around Wiesbaden.

I flew to Germany where I struggled with the language, but the German audiences were most appreciative. The American troops were not so easily entertained.

London

I returned to London where I found a bedsit with an upmarket address for a very reasonable price. It was, Flat 1, One Priory Park Mansions, Priory Park Road, Maida Vale. It was just down the road from the Kilburn Cinema and in the Irish quarter of the city. There were fights every Saturday night without fail. The room was small. I do not know when it had last been decorated. The dark brown wallpaper was all faded and in one corner not only had it come away from the wall, but also, so had about a yard of the plaster. The slats were clearly visible. I consoled myself with the fact that I was just passing through, would be out all day and if I could manage it, most evenings as well!

Selfridges

Once again, I needed cash and managed to obtain a job as a salesman in Selfridges, the famous store on Oxford Street, in the tie department. The store was very busy,
and I recognised quite a few well-known film and TV stars doing their shopping.

Showbiz work was very scarce and all I managed to get were some scrappy low-paid concerts around the city. I did manage to get two bookings for the Dome at Brighton on Sundays, which I enjoyed.

Bill to New Zealand

Bill had written to say he was coming down to get the ship to New Zealand. Could he stay with me in my flat in London for a couple of days? When he walked through the door of my humble bed-sit, he gave a gasp and said, "Oh Ma Goad! Look at the state o' this place. Lawrence, it's a slum! Wait 'till I tell mum and dad where yer living."

I asked him not to. It was only temporary. We spent a lovely time together then I saw him off. The streamers fell, the brass band music played through the loud speakers, then it went quiet and he was gone. It was 43 years before I was to see him again. He died soon after.

It was December and it snowed quite heavily. I usually caught the tube into Oxford Street Station. It was crammed full and I always had to stand. I will never forget the haunting sounds of the train screaming into the station, the rush of folk to jam themselves in, then the shout, "Mind the doors!" As I climbed the stairs jostling with all the commuters and finally arrived at the exit door on Oxford Street, a precious sight met my eyes causing me to stop to drink it in. The snow was softly falling. Walking along the kerbside in single file, were six bedraggled looking musicians playing the Christmas Carol, 'In the Bleak Mid-Winter'. I smiled, "Well Lawrie, you wouldn't get a sight like this one in Lochgelly!"

As soon as I arrived at my store counter, a young lad who worked as 'the runner' to bring change for me, when I rang a bell and put my hand up, whispered "Mr. Adam, there is an urgent phone call for you." I thanked him and quietly stole away. A London agent had tracked me down. Was I be interested and available to appear in Blackpool at the 'Movenpick Restaurant' over Christmas? The money offered was far more than I would have made in Selfridges and so I accepted. I was surprised to hear from the department manager that if I wanted to he could keep my job open for me upon my return in January. I agreed.

Blackpool

In Blackpool, I met Norman Teal the local agent who had arranged accommodation for me in a hotel. After my opening show, which went very well, Norman asked if I would be interested in earning quite a bit of extra money. He booked many other venues in the town and I found myself running all over the town doing extra work for which he paid me in cash. I made a small fortune. After the Christmas run he said, "Shame you're not local Lawrie. Your act would be in great demand in and around Blackpool. Let me know when you are here again."

January Sales

I returned to London and Selfridges and picked up where I left off. I was just in time for the famous January Sales. The floor manager announced that the honour for this year, to open the doors was to go to a Mr. Lawrie Adam from the Tie Department.

Come the fateful morning, there was a 'countdown'. Then a bell sounded my cue to unlock the main Oxford Street doors to the eager waiting public. Some had been camping out all night on the pavement. The countdown started. The bell rang. I opened the doors...and was promptly knocked flat on my back as the wild herd of shoppers violently pushed me this way and that screaming as they went! What an experience.

Manchester

Deciding to return to Manchester to find work, I managed to strike lucky and got my bed-sit back. However, there were no vacancies at Lewis's but got a job for a company called 'Rylands' just off Piccadilly Square. They were a wholesale company and I was employed as a warehouseman, preparing the orders for the reps to collect. I did not like working there one bit.

Once more, I was busy with club work and taking home a good wage. I bought myself a radio and heard an accordionist in a variety programme. I wrote to the producer and said, "I was better!" He kindly answered and invited me to audition at the BBC. I did, and was offered a broadcast for newcomers to radio. He said if I did well I would be on the BBC's books and invited to do more broadcasting.

I enrolled on a correspondence course to learn how to orchestrate music. Originally, I did it to save myself money on arrangements, but was delighted when other artistes hired me to write and orchestrate their music. Another income!

Eventually, summer season-time arrived once more, and I headed down to Paignton.

Decisions made during this season were pivotal and would affect the remainder of my life.

My very first English
Summer Season.
The Hoe Summer Theatre
Plymouth, Devon.

We travelled many miles performing in Sunday Concerts.

My first English Summer Season. The Hoe Summer Theatre Plymouth

It turned out to be a huge marque, but the audiences were great

A Publicity
Carnival Float
in a street
procession

Comedian Dave Alan

Members of the company

Twenty-Two
The Love of My Life

St. Andrews Church Hall, yes that was the correct address right enough and this old red brick building seemed to be it. I suppose the theatre was staging a pre-season show and that was the reason we had been farmed out to this hall for our summer season rehearsals. As I got out of my bubble car, I heard the distinct noise of a piano and someone singing. It sounded like the soprano Jean Barrington. What a lovely voice she had.

I made my way up the few concrete steps, opened the large old wooden door and spotted my pal from last year's show, comedian Bryan Burdon. He was sitting on a bench at the side of the hall and I joined him. We exchanged pleasantries and catching up, when suddenly, a group of dancers in black leotards burst into the hall followed by the choreographer telling them to line up, please.

As he started to put them through their paces, my eyes were drawn towards a very attractive tall willowy blonde girl. I could not take my eyes of her. I was thinking how beautiful she looked and how gracefully she moved when Bryan gave me a sharp dig in the ribs.

He murmured out of the side of his mouth, "Bloody hell Lawrie, these girls are all gorgeous. I don't half fancy that blonde one."

I glared at him and said, "Hands off mate, she's mine!"

He laughed and said, "Oh! Yeah, well we'll just have to see about that."

There was a short coffee break, so I made my move. This was her first summer season. She was ballet trained at a posh boarding school called Bush Davies in Sussex. Her name was Wendy Shipley from Scunthorpe. Unfortunately, I was called away allowing Bryan to move in. The pianist explained I could chose my own music in a forthcoming Gypsy scene and a Scottish scene.

Back to resume my conversation with Wendy. I found she seemed to have lost interest. It was not until some weeks later, that she enlightened me about the conversation with Bryan. It was, "See you've met our Lawrie. Of course, he's gay you know, bless him."

No wonder it took me some considerable time to get her to take me seriously. The old saying proved to be true in my case, 'faint heart doesn't win fair lady.' However, I had a saying of my own, 'Never take no for an answer!'

Accommodation proved to be a problem. There was only one guesthouse available and no room of my own until later in the season. I had to agree to move around, meantime and had to leave my belongings there still in the suitcase. The first couple of weeks were only just bearable.

I explained my plight to Bryan who said, "Come back with me to my digs. My landlady is great. She is Swedish and lots of fun. She lives with her daughter." I met Jane who lived in a lovely part of Paignton overlooking the sea in a modern dormer bungalow.

Jane did not quite have a complete grip on the command of English. This was apparent when she went into a music shop and asked for a recording of 'Kenny Jazzmen and His Balls'.

As the season progressed, I regularly asked Wendy for a date only to be fobbed off by some excuse or other. Meanwhile Bryan looked serious about a very pretty, black-haired dancer called Andrea, known as Andy by her friends. Andy was also friends with Wendy and said she would do what she could to bring us together. We went on a few excursions to the lovely beaches around Devon. Whenever I tried to get friendly, Wendy retorted, "Oh! Leave me alone Lawrie." I was getting nowhere.

I hatched a plan with some of the cast who were sworn to secrecy. We would all go to the Marine Drive in Torquay. I would take Wendy in my car and tell her that I had 'L' plates and would be happy to teach her how to drive. She agreed. The plan was we would all stand facing the sea and have a pebble skipping competition. Quietly they would slowly steal away and fade into the darkness until we realised we were on our own. Poor innocent Wendy fell for it hook line and sinker!

"Here! Where has everyone gone?" she exclaimed looking a bit concerned.

I replied, "Don't worry. My car is parked just up the hill there. Come on. I will start you off on your first driving lesson then I will run you back." I stuck on the 'L' plates and we got into my car. I told her how to start the engine, which she did. I explained how to get into first gear. She managed to drive slowly forward. I reached my arm round the back of her and switched the lever from the reserve tank to the empty one. The result was that as we set off, all went normal for about 30 seconds before the car started to jerk and jolt then the engine cut out and we slowly drifted to a halt.

"Oh dear!" I said, "You're not going to believe this, but I've run out of petrol."

She looked a bit panicky and said in a quiet voice,

"But how are we going to get home now?"

I said, "Well, it is a problem, as all the garages will be closed. I am very sorry. It looks like we'll have to spend the night in the car."

"Oh dear!" she replied. "I'm not very happy about this."

I put my arm round her shoulders to comfort her and said, "Don't worry, we'll be safe enough here until morning." She was not convinced.

Unexpectedly, the whole front of the car opened (the front was the door) and a bright flashlight shone in my face and a voice said, "Well, well, and what have we got here then?"

I spotted the patrol car with the word 'Police' emblazoned on the side.

Wendy said, "Oh! Officer, thank goodness you are here. We've run out of petrol and have got to get to Paignton."

"Don't worry moi lover," he said in a thick Devon accent. "Ned and oi always keep a spare can especially for emergencies like this."

In no time at all, we were on our merry way. "Grrr, foiled again," I thought.

Bryan and Andy invited us both to Andy's flat for a meal. We played a game of cards. Bryan whispered to me,

"Don't worry mate, I'm going to suggest a game of strip poker, but I won't call it that. Girls are useless at it. Believe me this is your lucky night."

After a few drinks, I noted that Wendy was stone cold sober! We started the game, but I was shocked to realise that Bryan and I were not winning, and they were both grinning from ear to ear.

Andy finally said. "Okay, boys, you must think we are a couple of chumps. I've played this before and I make sure I never lose!"

As I got up to go, I thanked Andy for her hospitality and gave her a little kiss on the cheek. Wendy said she would help Andy with the washing up. I went to give her a kiss on the cheek as well, but instead planted a huge meaningful kiss on her lips, bent her backwards, and made it last a long time. She was gasping for breath when I finished. I took my leave and said, "Good night all."

I did not realise it at the time, but that act of desperation was the one thing that worked. From that moment on, we clicked and were an item, like two peas in a pod as Wendy did agree to go on a date at last. I took her to the cinema to see Blue Hawaii starring Elvis Presley. My heart gave a flip-over every time I saw her and thought she got more beautiful every day. I realised I was in love.

Our show had record attendances every night and I was enjoying the show very much. The star Lester Ferguson was great fun. There were smashing after show parties where we made friends with some of the actors at the repertory theatre, Jimmy Perry who was a regular visitor to see his wife Gelda, an actress in the show. Jimmy went on to be famous with his TV scripts of 'Dad's Army', 'It Ain't Half Hot Mum', 'Hi de Hi' and many other popular shows.

An Unexpected Wedding Invitation

Everything was going well until Jean Barrington came into my dressing room one evening before the show, waving a piece of card. "Look at this Lawrie. It seems I have an invitation to your wedding reception! Apparently, you are marrying a lass called Beryl."

I laughed, "Oh yeah? And where is that then?"

She replied, "In the Southgate Cafe in Halifax!"

"Are you serious?" I asked.

Jean passed the small card to me and everyone crowded round to have a look. Sure enough, she was quite correct. "But I haven't even proposed, never mind agree to a wedding date!" I exclaimed. "Surely I should have been consulted."

Bryan said, "Well, they want their daughter off their hands soon as possible mate and have you in their sights."

I had decided to write to her and try to let her down gently. Lester Ferguson walked in and asked what the problem was. I explained it to him. He said,

"Come into my dressing room Lawrie and I'll solve this for you. I have personal experience to draw on."

He explained his plan, which I agreed to go along with. A few days later I received a letter on smart headed notepaper from the world-famous Harlem Globetrotters in New York USA. It was an invitation to join them for a 12-month world tour as soon as I finished my summer season. They used musical acts before their game to warm up their audience.

I wrote to Beryl telling her of the offer, enclosed the letter and pointed out to her that I had not agreed to any wedding date or indeed reception. She replied saying I had to decide: it was either her or the Harlem Globetrotters! I did not hesitate in my reply confirming the latter.

I thanked Lester for his advice and help and said, "Thank the boys for their offer, but I will decline if they don't mind."

"What offer?" laughed Lester, "They would deny it anyway."

The season continued with various Sunday concerts with stars such as Ann Shelton who was a lovely woman and Carol Carr who was not. On Sundays, if I wasn't working, Wendy and I would visit the theatre and listen to some of the country's top military Brass Bands. There was a charity cricket match, which was great entertainment. I took pleasure in showing Wendy my favourite secluded peaceful spot when I wanted to be alone, to enjoy the fantastic view. We enjoyed some picnics with Bryan and Andy and then there was a boat trip on the sea with the cast.

The sky always seemed to be blue and the sunshine warm as I wandered hand in hand with my girl.

Meeting Wendy's Parents

Wendy's mother, father and her little brother John arrived one day. I met John first. We had been on the beach and all I was wearing were a pair of shorts and sandals. We pulled up in front of where they were staying. The canvas roof was open to the warm blue sky, which suddenly went dark.

A voice from above said, "Hello, this is a cute little car." It was Wendy's brother John. She may have referred to him as her little brother, but he was taller than I was!

"You go up," I said to Wendy. "I'll slip into a pair of trousers then join you in a minute."

I am told when she entered the flat, her mother said, "Well where is this Lawrie you are always telling us about?"

"He won't be a minute. He hasn't got his trousers on." That got some reactionary stares and gasps. She hurriedly explained. The family were warm and friendly, and we got on famously during the remainder of their holiday.

I had been warned it would take five years to become established, but as the season ended, I realised more agents and bookers acknowledged me. I had achieved success in three.

Starting in October, I had a contract to tour southern Ireland in a big variety show for eight weeks followed by a pantomime in December, taking me through to January at the Richmond Theatre in Surrey. I had return bookings for Leeds City Varieties theatre and Huddersfield and Hull Continental Palace theatres. I had no need for a job this time but could do what I loved doing best and be paid very well for doing it.

To put the cream on everything, Hedley asked if I would like to appear in his longest running summer show at the Palace theatre Morecambe: a total of 25 weeks agreed on condition that he booked Wendy as a dancer. He replied, "No problem with that, she can work for me any time: she's a first-class dancer."

Bubble swapped for a Van

The bubble car was showing signs of fatigue. It was only a small engine intended as a town or city runabout and I had thrashed it up and down the country. I swapped the car for a brand new mini-van.

I offered to drive Wendy back home to Scunthorpe and was delighted when she agreed. I stayed a few days and met her friends. Her best friend June ran a dancing school where Wendy assisted in teaching the children. We visited a very posh house in its own grounds, which was where June's parents lived. Then I met June's husband Peter. By the time I left for my Irish tour, I felt like the prize bull after many farmers had wandered round me considering my future, or if I had one.

Dublin

I took the plane to Dublin and on by taxi to the first engagement to meet the cast. The star and producer was a well-known Irish comedian called Jack Cruise. It was a very large prestigious variety show, which included two speciality acts from Europe both performing death defying stunts: two male vocalists who were famous in their country for radio and recording work; the folk singer Willy Brady; a soprano known to TV audiences called Patricia Cahill, and others.

Willy insisted I stay with his family in Dublin when we were appearing in that area. His wife and two children made me very welcome. The tour covered a larger area than the one with Andy Stewart. The venues were much bigger and were all in proper theatres. Willy knew where to stay, and I was content to follow. The audiences were entertainment starved and loved the accordion.

The folk all seemed to have a sort of 'pinched' look about them. Most of the men appeared to wear fawn raglan-sleeved gabardine raincoats and a black beret on their heads. (That could be where Frank Spencer got his fashion idea from for his TV series!) Many rode about on upright bicycles. It explained why they walked about the town with cycle-clips round their ankles. Most of the cars were battered looking VW Beetles. No road test was required. The car salesman advised you how to drive it, and then you were off! One tip was, when you park never leave your hand brake on as folk preferred to bump out of a parking space.

One of my press notices said that, 'I was the best on the accordion since the visit of world famous Toralf Tollefsen'. That was praise indeed.

Every night was a different town, a different party or ceilidh, and a different bar, but always with a pint of creamy Guinness in my hand. My accordion had to go as well, together with Willy's guitar. At the interval, newspaper packages were handed round. "Ah! Fish and Chips," I thought eagerly. No, not so. When I opened my package, four cooked pig's trotters met my gaze.

Willy laughed and said, "Git it down ye, you'll love them." I did, and he was correct!

By the time we arrived in the city of Cork, we were all shattered. Willy had a driver and his car was a solid black saloon called a Mayflower. It had leather upholstery, which needed a good clean and the driver, Gerry, could have done with a bit of a spruce up as well. He looked smartish in a dark suit (slightly crumpled) with collar and tie and was a very obliging chap. I was invited to do a TV show from Dublin if I could fit it in. Gerry made sure I arrived in time. It certainly gave a boost to my act as most of Ireland watched the show.

Many times, I spoke to Willy about Wendy. He said to me one night after the show, "Now three things are going to happen tonight here in Cork. One, Mrs. Quirk, the hotel owner will want to sing Danny Boy. When she hits the high note, and her eyes roll back in their sockets do not dare to laugh or smirk. Two, I have secretly recorded your act and sent off the tape to my record company in New York. I didn't tell you that I am their representative here in Ireland. Well, they have sent back a contract for you to sign and want you to make an LP Album in Dublin after the tour."

I exclaimed, "Goodness me that's fantastic Willy." A short silence followed, and then I said, "What's the third thing?"

He put down his Guinness, looked at me in the eye and said in an even voice, "You are going to go into that phone box outside the hotel, dial Wendy's number and for God's sake propose to her. If she is as beautiful and wonderful as you keep harping on about every day and night, you had better not lose her. I nearly lost my lovely wife. Don't you do the same!"

I dialled the number…Wendy answered.

I said, "Will you marry me?" There was a brief silence. My heart turned over.

"Yes," she said. I was on cloud nine for the remainder of the tour. I promised to get her an engagement ring as soon as I got back.

Engaged

I arrived in Scunthorpe and knew she would be in the Co-operative Tea Rooms having a break from the dancing class. My heart gave a lurch when I spotted her sitting in the window wearing a Black Watch tartan dress drinking her coffee. Her blonde hair was shining in the sun and yes, she was indeed beautiful.

We visited a jeweller to buy the ring and received a large free box of chocolates as a gift.

We were very excited as we started to plan for our wedding. We paid a visit to my home in Scotland. I had written my mother telling her my news and the reply was favourable. It was snowing and a very cold December. Mum and Dad took to Wendy right away. I could tell they had become very fond of her and she was like the daughter they had longed for. Mum whispered in my ear,

"Aye son, she's the wan richt enough. Nae nonsense wi' her an' as straight as a die."

As we both had pantomime commitments we reluctantly had to leave. I was bound for Richmond and Wendy was to appear in Sunderland. I knew she would be well looked after because she was working with two of our pals from Paignton, Bryan and his girlfriend Andy. They would be the next ones planning a wedding we thought. Sadly, we went our separate ways and I promised to try to visit Sunderland to see her if it was at all possible. I did manage it, but it was after the two weeks rehearsals and after the Christmas shows that I decided to risk the journey in my little mini-van.

Twenty-Three
1963 A Lifelong Partnership is in the Making

Conceived implausible situations never ceased to amaze me. These were justified as theatrical license when described to me by the producer of Dick Whittington, my first pantomime. The script said, 'Appear dressed as a very portly rotund Arab'. The reason being as I discovered, was because I whip back my burnoose to reveal an accordion dangling from my neck! Thus, an excuse to go into my act. In the middle of the Sahara Desert?

My part included comedy moments. It was a big thrill to hear the children all laugh, shout and scream at me. It was good to work with Jean Barrington who was playing the principal part of Dick.

Many regarded Richmond Surrey as posh rich area of London where celebrities such as film producer and actor Richard Attenborough lived. The lovely old-style theatre itself was a prestigious venue overlooking the green. Over the Christmas period, the two performances on weekdays, plus the three on Saturdays were booked to capacity. The cast, mainly consisting of straight actors who tended to look down on variety folk. Sadie Corry, who played the cat, was by all accounts the best 'Whittington cat' in the business. I ended up standing next to her when she muttered some very caustic asides, spaced out with the odd four-lettered word, but only audible to me, sending me into fits of stifled giggles, which I dare not show to the upturned studious little faces of the audience.

Bob Rolls, a man about my age was the theatre manager. He lived locally and invited me to his home to meet his family who were equally charming.

My accommodation was a comfortable bedroom with breakfast included. During the Christmas period, I sat in my room listening to all the festivities going on below me. I thought, "Now, if this was Scotland, I would have been invited downstairs." I could not wait to drive up north to see Wendy. We phoned each other every night.

Journey to Sunderland

One Saturday I made up my mind I was going to hit the road to Sunderland as soon as the last performance had finished. I told Jean my plans and she tried her hardest to persuade me not to attempt it. "In the first place," she said, "your contract states that you must not go any further than 25 miles from the theatre. In the second place, after doing three performances, you are going to be too tired to drive all that way: it must be over 250 miles!"

I said, "Yes, and in the third place?"

"It's bloody snowing out there and the roads will be very dangerous, especially in that small mini-van of yours!"

I replied, "Good points Jean, but I am still going and that's that, so do not breathe a word to anyone."

She shook her head and said. "Why have you got to go?"

I smiled, "Love?"

It was a long haul of a journey. The roads were very bad and the further north I went the colder it became. The long-distance haulage trucks seemed huge as they roared past overtaking my small mini throwing up blinding slush over my windscreen. I pulled in for some refreshments at one of the many transport cafes and I made for the lorry drivers section. The food was cheaper, the portions more generous and there was always a big steaming mug of hot tea to finish. It was a luxury to get in out of the freezing cold dank air and into bright yellow florescent lighting, the smell of toast and cooked food. I grabbed a brown plastic tray and asked for the cooked breakfast. The young woman loaded up my large white plate with bacon, fried egg, beans, chips and two thick slices of buttered toast plus the traditional large mug of steaming hot tea of course.

Finally, I arrived at the Roker Guest House, situated on the blustery wild seafront in Sunderland. Wendy, who waited up for me, ushered me inside. There was a coal fire in the lounge, but it was still freezing cold. It was good to see Bryan and Andy again who assured me they were looking after her.

Their pantomime was at the Empire Theatre with a star I had never heard of from Northern Ireland, called Donna Douglas. Their show had a longer run than mine did by a few weeks. It meant I could return and stay with them until their show finished. I could then run Wendy home.

At the end of my show, I drove up the long lonely A1 in weather like my last trip and was so pleased to stagger into the Roker Guest house. Wendy's show had not finished so I just settled down in front of the fire. The landlady opened the door and shuffled in wearing large baggy slippers. She was a grey haired old lady in a pinny with a worn faded pale blue jumper underneath. As she walked, she carried before her a small shovel. I presumed it was coal for the fire. All her concentration was on her little shovel.

She murmured in a strong Geordie accent, "They'll be 'ome soon, I'll jist build oop the fire for yi' lad."

She dumped her shovelful on the glowing fire and I thought she had put it out. It was dross, coal dust. Eventually they all came waltzing in and made me very welcome.

During that couple of weeks in Sunderland, I enjoyed their company and their show, which was better than ours was. Bryan was an excellent Buttons. However, the biggest thrill for me was watching my fiancée dance. She stood out ahead of everyone else, always finding that extra inch. It was obvious why I never had any trouble getting her accepted in any show.

Mum and Dad to New Zealand

About this time, Mum and Dad wrote to tell me they intended joining Bill in New Zealand and they had everything arranged. Their date for sailing was in March. Wendy and I decided to pop up to see them. It was good to go home, but there was an undertone of sadness too. We spent a few days with them and promised to see them off from London Docks.

We visited Ron and Mary in their home where Wendy met their children, Wee Ronnie and Carol. John Soutar came to visit and said how sad he was that the Adam family would not be there anymore.

We walked down the outside staircase for the last time with Mum and Dad. It felt very sad to realise I would not be back in the house of my birth ever again. So many memories: all the Christmases and Happy New Years; the laughter still ringing through the years; all the musical evenings with the Johnstone couple banging on their ceilings because of the noise. Happy times and sad times now at an end.

On the 22 March 1963, Wendy and I journeyed to meet Mum and Dad who gave us our visitors' boarding passes. The ship was called the 'Ruahine' I took many pictures of us all. Poor Mum could not help showing regret at leaving us for the unknown. She said, "You do right by that lassie Lawrie, she's smashing, and we are leaving you in good hands."

Dad hugged me and said in my ear, "When you feel the time is right son, let us know and we'll try and help you with the fare, so you can join us."

All too soon, there was a long loud horn blast and a hollow sounding disembodied voice saying, "Will all visitors leave the ship now please." There were long hugs from my mother and father as we reluctantly said our goodbyes and slowly made our way down the wobbly gangplank. In fact, I wasn't too sure if it was the gangplank wobbling, or if it was my legs. Wendy had a firm encouraging grip of my arm. I sensed that she knew exactly how sad my feelings were.

The ropes and chains unhitched and gave the Ruahine her freedom. She gave a few hoots from her horn. Through the speakers, a brass band struck up played the stirring but emotional music of 'Auld Lang Syne'. The ship's mighty propellers started churning the water into a frothy cauldron, as the ship slowly left the dock and started out on her long journey for New Zealand. Streamers were thrown from the ship to the shore. Many folks were in tears as they waved their loved one's farewell, not knowing if they would ever see them again. I could just make out my Dad with his arm placed firmly around my Mum's sagging shoulders as she gave a wave that seemed full of sadness. Then they were gone.

I have always associated a scene such as this one like bereavement. Someone nearby says, "That's it, they are gone." However, in a space of time, other voices will take up the call of, "Here they come!"

Scunthorpe

The winter passed. I stayed in Scunthorpe working various clubs in the Lincolnshire and Yorkshire area. The audiences were tougher than the west coast and the shows not as professionally presented.

A show in Grimsby had a small stage. Beside me, was a small card-table and on it was a long white enamel dish containing a raw side of pig, covered in blood. This was the raffle prize. I remarked to the audience,

"I'd better be good tonight if that's what happened to last night's act!" It broke the ice and got a good laugh.

We didn't have much money and were trying to save up as much as we could to get married. It was very good of Wendy's parents to house and feed me. In the evenings, we would all watch television, or play card or board games. Wendy's brother John was full of fun and felt like another brother to me. He was very skilled at painting model soldiers to the exact replica of the real thing. Ultimately, he acquired his own model shop. Both the other married brothers visited occasionally. Bryan and Joan were cheerful, but Colin and Irene were much more serious and quieter.

Summer in Morecambe

It was a lovely sunny day as we drove down the Morecambe promenade. We were eager to start our summer season at the Palace Theatre. The theatre was not new to me as I had already performed a couple of Easter shows there, but it was a new experience for Wendy. The show was very popular with the holiday crowds visiting Morecambe. As soon as the trains arrived at the station, the people made their way to the theatre to book their seats. There always seemed to be a queue at the box office. Every performance sold out.

There were four theatres in the town including ours. The number one show was at the huge Winter Gardens theatre on the front. However, the seating capacity was in four figures and they could never fill it. It was regarded as a white elephant. Some years on, I played this theatre with comedian Al Read and the TV star from Coronation Street called Barbara Knocks, who possessed a very good singing voice. However, it was only a quarter full. Eventually it closed. Further along the front from our show was the Alhambra Theatre where I played some years later. Finally, there was the Pier theatre, which was more of a smallish concert party show.

Our show was the longest running summer show in the British Isles excepting only the Central Pier in Blackpool, which beat the Palace by one week, which infuriated Hedley Claxton.

I was to have quite a long association with Morecambe. I soon had a full diary of Sunday Concerts as I became more known by bookers.

Llandudno

At Llandudno, I appeared alongside such acts as Mikie and Griff. They had a hit record with a song called 'A Little Bittie Tear,' Bob and Alf Pearson who had been big radio stars in their heyday and Irish tenor Joseph Locke, who had lookouts posted on the end on the pier for the police or the Inland Revenue. He owed thousands of pounds in back-taxes. As soon as he finished his show, he was whisked away back to Ireland. Joe had a magical personality with a voice to match and left the stage to a standing ovation.

Bonnie Scotland

A tobacco company called Gallagher, asked me to join their variety show for a theatre tour of Scotland with stars Mike and Bernie Winters. Unfortunately, it started three weeks before I finished at Morecambe. They said they had tried to book me last year. They were prepared to put a stand-in act called Reed and Delroy for the three weeks, and they really were keen for me to join them. The money was excellent, and I agreed.

It was a big lavish show in The Gaiety in Ayr. I had an enjoyable tour, until that is when we played the Glasgow Metropole theatre. It was the last week of the tour and Wendy joined me from her home in Scunthorpe. During the performance, Mike and Bernie who, not wishing to be unkind, had not enjoyed a successful experience with Scottish audiences, dropped in a few sarcastic insults about the Scots during their finale speech. We were all on stage in a line. As soon as they had uttered their words of doom, it went very quiet, and then objects started pinging at much speed towards the artistes, followed by much booing. The objects were pennies. The curtains were lowered, and it was a repeat of the 'Andy Stewart syndrome'. All departed speedily to their cars and vanished as soon as they could be heading for safety and south of the border.

Pantomimes in Richmond Surrey

Wendy and I were soon packing for pantomime season, but this time our separate venues were much closer to each other. I returned to the Richmond theatre in Jack and the Beanstalk once more with my friend Jean Barrington. Wendy was nearby appearing in Puss in Boots at the Theatre Royal in Windsor, under the shadow of Windsor Castle. Little did we realise then that we would be invited to spend many happy short breaks staying as guests in this impressive royal historic castle in later years.

Two memorable events happened at the Richmond theatre. The first was a visit backstage from a TV Producer who was very enthusiastic about my act and wanted me to appear in her current TV series called the Stars & Garters Show starring vocalist Kathy Kirby and compered by a Jewish comedian called Ray Martine. The producer assured me that this would be the making of me, but it would mean having three days off from the pantomime. I was thrilled, as I knew how popular the show was.

I was stunned therefore when Mr. Pritchard, the owner of the theatre refused me permission to have time off. I telephoned the producer who said, "Darling, it's either a yes or a no with me. Why don't you just take the time off anyway? I'm going to pay you more money than you are probably getting for the whole run of his bloody pantomime."

"He said he would sue me if I did and that I would never work around here ever again. In any case, it's not my style to break a contractual agreement," I replied.

"Right" she replied, "So, it's a no then, goodbye Lawrie, shame that." and put the phone down.

The other event involved the impresario Gerald Palmer, who produced the big successful Ice shows every year at the Wembley Stadium. He offered me a number one summer season on the Isle of Man at the Palace Theatre appearing in The Dickie Valentine Show. Moreover, he agreed that if Wendy was good enough to be in a Windsor pantomime, then she was certainly good enough to appear in his show as well. The money was more than I had ever received up to that date, and he intimated that he could probably give me an extra winter show in Dublin at the same money. I signed his contract.

I began to realise a strange thing: the more prestigious the work, and the more money I was paid, the less I was expected to do for it!

Wendy and I had lovely digs with an elderly couple who took a fond liking to Wendy. After our shows finished, they invited us down to their warm cosy kitchen for a light bite of supper and a game of cards. During the card game, we ate sticks of crisp celery and cream cheese along with tea from bone china crockery. Regretfully, they told us that they were unable to have children.

They had a very old sheep dog who lay in a basket in the corner. On many occasions, it produced the most awful stench, and Mrs. Guerny apologised immediately. I must confess, celery and cream cheese have an adverse effect on me and I found myself joining the dog in the aroma department. Mrs. Guerny presumed it was the dog and so I became quite content with the arrangement. However, after some weeks, there was I sitting there and farting away, quite content, when without warning, Mrs. Guerny muttered, as she dealt out a hand of cards, "By the way Mr. Adam, Lilly, our dog died yesterday."

Twenty-Four
Till Death Us Do Part

"I have my best flat coming available in a week Lawrie," said the landlord. "Bring Wendy over and I will do a special deal on it for you."

Wendy visited the Dennison Road flat in Manchester, but she was not keen on it.

"It seems like dead money. Would it not better to buy something and then sell later?" she said. We did not settle on anything, but time was drawing close to the wedding date. Wendy went home, and I stayed on in Manchester for club engagements.

A speciality act called The Keddellos, heard of my plight and they said they had the perfect solution. Wendy and I were invited for lunch with them in their home. We arrived at the address and were surprised to discover they lived in a caravan on a site along the banks of the Mersey called Ford Lane, near a small town called Northenden. It was a warm sunny day. The sky was deep blue and cloudless. Swans glided gracefully up and down the calm water.

"What a lovely peaceful scene." Wendy remarked, looking all around her and smiling "I love it here."

As I locked the door of our minivan, Peter appeared. "Ah! Here you are, come on in, Doreen has lunch all ready."

As soon as we stepped inside their caravan, we felt at home. We had a good chat over a tasty home-cooked lunch. Doreen said, "We've lived here for quite some time. It used to be a fairground. In fact the owner Mary Rylands still lives on the site in her gypsy caravan."

Peter added, "It's not easy to park here. There is always a heavy demand, but there is a space coming available and if you want it Mary said she is prepared to let you have it. However, you can't shillyshally, she needs a quick decision."

I looked at Wendy. Her little face was full of concern. I said to them, "But we haven't even got a caravan to put on a site."

Peter grinned, "I can fix that for you today if you like. I know of a caravan sale minutes away in fact. They have brand new caravans: latest state of the art designs and you could buy it on hire purchase."

"Well we've nothing to lose, no harm in having a look," Wendy said.

We were astounded at the variety of caravans. Peter gave us a guide as the size Mary allowed on the plot. The one that took our fancy was a Summerdale Santa-Fe. It was 21 feet long and 9 feet 6 inches wide: a pale yellow around the bottom half and white on the upper half. It had an attractive large bay window almost the full width of the front, a good-sized lounge with two windows on both sides and a solid fuel fire.

Wendy exclaimed, "I love this, and we won't have to buy any furniture or carpets. Everything is here that we need."

We accompanied the salesman into the office and completed the Hire Purchase agreement.

"We can deliver this caravan on site middle of next week," The salesman said, "That should be fine,

I'll arrange with Mary to supply a power line," Pete said.

It felt entirely right. We had to return to Scunthrope as I was working there in clubs in Lincolnshire and Yorkshire.

Pete and Doreen said, "Leave it all to us and don't worry we will arrange everything for you."

Wendy and her Mum carried on with all of the wedding preparations, thank goodness, and her father paid and did not stint on a thing. I developed a closer relationship with Wendy's brother John, than I had done with my own brothers. When I did manage to be in Scunthorpe, Wendy showed to me the growing accumulation of articles for our bottom drawer.

Dublin recording

Avoca Records USA wrote to advise me that a recording session was being set up for me in the Dublin Recording Studios. Members of the Television Orchestra required orchestrated parts for the session. It was not the Company's policy to pay royalties to recording artistes, but they paid a fee, which was generous. I signed the contract and busied myself practising and writing out the music parts. The album was called 'A Scottish Dance Party' played by Lawrie Adam. There would be a picture of me on the front and another on the back with biographical notes. I was elated at the thought of having my own record album. All that dance band experience I had way back in

Lochgelly and the recording sessions we did in Edinburgh would prove very useful.

Wendy and I arrived in Dublin all geared up for the session. On the day of recording, Wendy sat in the gallery with the recording producer while I ran through the music with the band who were professional session men and they breezed through the numbers. Avoca Records had requested that the contents be all Scottish Country Dances. All went well. It would take a year before the record was finished.

18 April 1964

The day of the wedding arrived. John Soutar arrived to be my best man. Ronnie and Mary travelled down from Scotland with their two children Ron and Carol. Ronnie explained he had been working as a postman in Lochgelly, but they intended to emigrate to New Zealand and join Mum and Dad.

John and I stayed overnight with a neighbour a couple of doors away from the Shipleys so that tradition could be upheld. The big day arrived. It was dry but a bit grey and breezy. Wendy wanted a Highland wedding, so after some breakfast, John and I donned our kilts. Our car arrived and off we went to St. Lawrence's Church in the town to take our places where the vicar endeavoured to put us at our ease.

We had arranged to record the service for my parents in New Zealand. The wait seemed an eternity while we sat in the front pew. The church was full.

The organist started to play some incidental religious music. I was more nervous than I would have been performing in a big show. The choir filed in to take their places.

"It won't be long now Lawrence, just remember what we did at the rehearsal last night and all will be fine," said the vicar, who then mounted the chancel steps to take his place. The organist burst into a fanfare, the choir stood up. That was our cue. I stood up but my stomach stayed where it was. The music started to play 'Here comes the Bride' the choir sang. John and I walked towards the chancel steps, took up our position and stood still.

I heard a few gasps behind me and could not resist quickly turning around. The sight that met my eyes was simply breath taking. Wendy looked like a radiant white angel walking towards me on her father's arm. I looked at her and was astounded to see how beautiful she looked. Her blonde hair was swept up and held by a bandeau of seed pearls supporting a white nylon tulle veil. She wore a full-length Nottingham lace sheath dress, trimmed with Guipure lace, with a train of lace and tulle. Her bouquet was her favourite flowers, freesias. As she arrived at my side, I was aware of her hand gently taking my arm. Our eyes met, and I felt as if I could have melted on the spot. The words were spoken, the promises to each other were made, 'Till death us do part'. My old friend John passed me the ring. The vicar blessed the ring. The ring was placed on her elegant finger. We were pronounced man & wife.

After the ceremony, the wedding party went into the vestry to sign the registers. Wendy's parents were there, her chief bridesmaid, and friend of long-standing, June. My little niece Carol, the flower girl, looked lovely and my nephew wee Ronnie our pageboy looked resplendent in his Gordon Tartan kilt. There were hugs and kisses all round. We signed the registers, received the marriage certificate, then all processed out of the church into the bright sunshine.

We walked out under an archway of pink ballet shoes attached to long poles and held by many of the children that Wendy had taught at June's dancing school over the years. Photographs captured memories of a very special day. Sadly, as I look at the pictures now, many of our dear friends and relatives have gone. A reminder of how quickly time passes. The parents of Bob Roll's (a friend from Richmond pantomime days) made a video of the day.

The next step of the journey was to a venue in Scunthorpe called the Wortley Hotel. We were seated, and the waiters started serving the food, which was delicious.

I heard wee Ronnie say in a piping broad Scots accent say to the waiter, what sounded like,

"Excuse me, ser, bit a hivna' goat a fuckin knife." The waiter froze, then stared at him. Ronnie was small: the table wasn't far below his wee chin.

The headwaiter appeared, "What did he say?"

Just as the waiter was about to repeat what he thought he heard, I explained.

"Ah! He is saying that he does not have a knife and fork. He got it the wrong way around, a fork'n knife, but in a broad Scots accent."

With a sigh of relief, they sorted him out immediately. Giggles all round!

After the meal came the speeches, the cake cutting and finally a dance to a four-piece band. Meanwhile, I collected messages from various folk on the tape recorder to send to my parents in New Zealand. Eventually Wendy and I retired to the bridal suite, paid for by Wendy's Dad. Apart from the proverbial apple-pie bed, we enjoyed our first night of heavenly married bliss.

The following day, after breakfast, we collected the best man John from Mr. & Mrs. Shipley's house and made our way in our mini-van to Scotland for our honeymoon. There were large paper signs stuck on the side of the vehicle saying, 'Just Married'. Someone had tied a string of tin cans to our exhaust pipe for a joke. This was to have a knock-on effect unfortunately, because when we got to Glencoe the exhaust pipe fell off! We dropped John off in Edinburgh where he was living and journeyed on to Dundee. Wendy met my relatives and we were made royally welcome.

Northenden and the Caravan

The week was soon over and we headed for Northenden to take up residence in our new home. Pete and Doreen Keddello were as good as their word and had seen to the delivery of the caravan on the bank of the river. On the other side of the river was a golf course affording a great feeling of space and countryside although we were only minutes from Manchester city centre.

I visited the site owner, Mary Rylands. Mary was a small wiry woman who had the look of experience about her. She lived in a rosewood gypsy caravan. As the van was quite high up on wagon wheels, I had to climb a steep ladder. I knocked on her door, was invited in and was surprised at how compact and cosy her van was. There was a large expensive looking cut-glass mirror and everything else was fitted and built to last in shiny rosewood. She explained how her family owned this land it had been passed on to her as her parents were now dead. With a tear in her eyes, she told me of times gone by when this had been a favourite place for families. There were fairground rides and boats to hire on the river. Now it was much quieter. We settled how much I was going to pay (it was much cheaper than the flat would have been, and eventually we owned our caravan) however, there were some drawbacks. No telephone. She would undertake to accept messages for me but usually these were all muddled up. I dread to think how many engagements I must have lost! Pete and Doreen told me they had the very same problem.

Isle of Man

We had hardly settled in it seemed, when it was time to travel to the Isle of Man for our summer season. We arrived in Douglas at a previously booked a flat overlooking the bay. We made our way to the Palace Theatre also on the front and the largest theatre on the island. Our posters advertising the Dickie Valentine show were everywhere.

I sat in the stalls alongside Gerald Palmer the producer who had booked me. He was a very friendly fatherly type of figure and very easy to chat to. I watched the acts go before me and rehearse with the orchestra who sounded brilliant. The musical director Hall Chambers was also Dickie's pianist. There were two speciality acts. One was a very slick dancing adagio act, called 'The Konyots' and the other was an illusion act, 'Van Buren and Greta'. Their billing said they were Dutch, but later I learned they were from Wigan! They were fantastic. Don Smoothie from London, the comedian introduced me to the game of golf on free days. Wendy was one of a very glamorous team of leggy dancers. A vocalist called Wendy Wayne was next. She sounded average but was pretty to look at.

Gerald tapped me on the arm and remarked, "She will not improve until she knows heartache." She was to prove heartache to Dickie's wife and two children as he left them for her.

Finally was something I had never heard of before, 'Peppy and His Amazing Penguins. His rehearsal was a mess. He stepped forward to the footlights to explain to Gerald that they had not yet settled down after their journey, but they would, and he was not to worry. Gerald seemed to accept that.

The orchestra had no problem at all with my music. I only had one spot to do of about 12 minutes in addition to an appearance in the French scene playing my accordion dressed as a French artist. Wendy worked very hard especially doing the Can-Can at great energetic speed.

The show opened to a reasonable capacity but was not by any means full. Dickie had been a big star in the radio days and had recorded many hit songs but the competition on the island was very strong. Current hit-parade artistes Susan Maughen together with Freddie and the Dreamers and well-known bands were all taking a large share of the market.

The show went well, until that is, Peppy and his Penguins took to the stage. He had various large props for the penguins. The penguins had dirty white coloured nappies on them and Peppy did not seem to have any control over them whatsoever. There were four of them wandering all over the stage. He picked one up and placed it on the rung of the steps leading to a slide of about 8 feet high. He patted its bottom, enclosed in a dirty nappy, which gave of a sort of squelching sound, and it looked like it was full of green coloured liquid.

"Come along now Penny, up you go on the slide for the ladies and gentlemen." It took ages to eventually get to the top, it skidded part of the way down then fell off with a thump to the accompaniment of anguished "Ohs" and "Ah's" from the audience. Meanwhile one of them had wandered over to the footlights and toppled into the orchestra pit entangling itself in the wires of the open grand piano making many strange plinks and plonks. The curtain came down and Peppy was relegated to daytime activities in the theatre foyer billed as, "See Peppy feeding the penguins daily at 2 pm."

Sadly, it looked likely that the show was going to have to close earlier than billed. However, Dickie called a cast meeting and said in his opinion it was a lovely show and he had faith in it. He was willing to take a considerable cut in his salary. If we could all take a reasonable cut, the show could carry on. The cast agreed with this plan. The audiences remained on the thin side until the end of the run.

We heard later that Dickie, whilst doing cabaret dates in Wales, had suffered a fatal accident in his car. It had been a pleasure to know and work with him. He was very talented and a gentleman.

Back to Northenden

We returned home to our caravan in Northenden. Wendy made some lovely red Wallace tartan curtains, and seat covers, which made it very homely. We did have electricity to the van but no running water. The water had to be fetched by me in a large white plastic container from a tap. Another privation was the chemical toilet. This was collected once a week by a council truck that could be smelt from some distance away.

Dublin

We were only home a short time, before making our way to Dublin to appear in a big show which came from the Wembley Stadium in London called 'The Carnival on Ice'. It was very lavishly costumed and produced by Gerald Palmer. The National Stadium was a huge place. It was necessary to wear metal studs on my shoes to grip the ice, however, it was a very vulnerable feeling walking about with a heavy accordion on hard shiny wet glistening ice. If I had fallen frontwards, my accordion would crash into my chest. I had to be very aware all the time but look as if I was enjoying myself. The audiences were superb, and I could not go wrong. They loved the kilt and the Scottish music. The skaters were a very humorous bunch and very clever. I marvelled at the speeds they travelled at and the complicated moves they made on the ice. The electrics were not all they appeared to be. I had taped the show and a group of the artistes (not the skaters) wanted to hear themselves. We gathered in a dressing room, set up the tape recorder only to realise that the plugs on the recorder were a different type to the wall sockets.

I said, "Not to worry, I'll remove the plug and just jam the wires in to the sockets with a matchstick."

Suddenly there was a bang and a flash, and all the lights went out.

Impressionist George Meaton came in to the room illuminated by his cigarette lighter and said, "Lawrie, grab the tape recorder and hide it. Every bloody light in the building has gone off. The skaters are colliding with each other and some have gone over the edge into the audience. There are others on their hands and knees trying to get back to base. The language used, is very unpleasant." I did as requested and no one ever knew any different!

WHAT A PRIVILEDGE TO WORK WITH SUCH STARS

Anne Shelton

Sunday Celebrity Concerts kept me very busy

Weymouth Alexandra Gardens Theatre. 1960

My pal comedian Bryan Burdon   Some of the company

Wendy, the dancer   We had somne great parties in Paignton

A new chapter begins with the love of my life.

1964 Wendy & our first home.
A Summerdale Santa fe' at Northenden

Twenty-Five
1965 The New Arrival

We celebrated New Year in our very own home and looked forward to happy times ahead. Waking up to the sounds of birds chirping outside our caravan home, with little traffic in Ford Lane, it was country living and we loved it. This peaceful setting was so far removed from our working conditions of noise, music, audience laughter and applause.

A loud knock on the door startled us from our breakfast at the kitchen table. Mary, our landowner had brought us some letters. The advert in the Stage Newspaper informing agents of our new address had paid off. There was an offer of a summer season at Skegness. Duggie Chapman, the writer of the letter, topped the bill and I would be second top.

"Please phone if interested."

Another letter arrived a few days later from a radio show producer. I was thrilled to bits to receive a reply to the cheeky letter I had sent to him after listening to an accordionist one day. I thought I was as good if not better and on the off chance, wrote to the producer to tell him so. He offered me a radio spot called 'Air Break' for newcomers to broadcasting at the Playhouse Theatre in Manchester on the 17 February. I accepted both offers. This was an excellent start to 1965, particularly with the extra responsibility for my beautiful wife.

The BBC broadcast went well. The producer complimented me afterwards and said I was now registered on the BBC's list of performers to be contacted for future shows.

An air mail letter from Mum and Dad assured us they were doing fine in New Zealand. They had both gone back to work, which was providing some extra cash. They had agreed a 50 50 split on the mortgage on a bungalow with Bill. Photographs showed them looking happy and well.

Flooding

Not everything remained idyllic. One morning we woke up to very heavy rain battering on the roof of the caravan. This torrent continued all day. We were just finishing our evening meal, when there was a loud banging on our door.

A strong voice shouted, "River's over in an hour!" I rushed to open the door to be confronted by a tall policeman. Water was dripping off his helmet and running down his cape.

"What do you mean, the river's over in an hour?"

"Over where?" I asked.

"Over here. sir. If you don't book the tractor at the foot of the lane to tow you off, soon as, you will be under water here." With that, he turned and made for another caravan.

I threw on a tracksuit and dashed out the door, leaving Wendy hastily packing whatever she could whilst I ran down the lane to request the tractor. It was only a short distance, but by the time I reached the tractor my hair was plastered to my head and I was soaked through. I shouted above the din of the tractor and the driving rain, pointing to our caravan which I could see was already surrounded by a growing pool of water.

"I'm on my way mister. Get everyone out onto higher ground now!"

As I ran back up the flooding lane, my feet were now under three inches of water. Wendy, now at the door was surprised to see the swirling water making inroads around our caravan and panic showed on her face.

"Out now love, the tractors coming to pull us off," I shouted. The tractor hooked up our home and towed it to higher ground. As soon as he moved it away from the site, the water rushed in swirling all around creating a deep pool. A minute later and we would have been flooded out and the interior ruined. We were saved in the nick of time. It only happened that once to us, but flooding did happen there periodically.

"So much for the elegant swans gracefully gliding down the beautiful river," I thought.

Germany

The three-week engagement at the American Officers clubs on the bases around Weisbaden in Germany was an enjoyable experience, although I missed my wife every day. Other English artistes gave me a few helpful pointers. Two Manchester lads, Dick and Paul who did a song and tap dance act took me to a fish and chip shop. I remarked it seemed a bit on the posh side bearing in mind I was not earning a fortune. The walls were lined with glass tanks containing fish leisurely swimming about. We sat down and were soon engrossed in our catch-up chat about the similar clubs we had played in England. A waiter arrived at our table with a pad and pencil poised at the ready, giving us the German glare of expectancy.

Paul said, "Just point to a fish Lawrie, he'll know what you mean." I looked at the fish all swimming about and pointed to one that looked a bit cute and reminded me of an agent I knew. All that was missing was the big cigar in its mouth. We kept on chatting. I became aware that a man with a net was removing some of the fish from our tank. Soon our fish and chips arrived.

"Well, that was delicious," I said to my pals. "They tasted so fresh, like they had just been caught."

Dick laughed, finishing off his last chip and remarked, "Well they were freshly caught. You pointed to your choice fish. He removed it, killed it, cooked it and served it up for you." I felt a bit queasy suddenly!

Pregnant

Upon returning to the comforts of our little Northenden nest, Wendy had some wonderful news. She was pregnant! I was over the moon. Fancy, me a Dad! It seemed unbelievable. We did not care if we had a boy or a girl. Just the thought of a little baby was enough. Preparations started right away. We did a bit of calculation and realised the baby would be born at some point during the summer. I had signed a contract for Skegness to appear in Duggie Chapman's 'Old Time Music Hall Show'. This was a long engagement. It included a week's rehearsal in Manchester followed by a pre-summer tour lasting four weeks. The final week's tour-date was Weymouth following which I had to be back in Germany again ready to open in Frankfurt the following Monday for three weeks. It was going to be very tight, as I was required to be in Skegness for rehearsals the day after I finished in Germany.

Wendy's brother John and my friend John Soutar said they would like to go with me to Germany, as they had never been there. I would be glad of the company. Most folk seem to believe that in show business you are always surrounded by people, having loads of fun and attending lots of wild parties. In fact, during the day if it wasn't possible to go in to a theatre early and put in three or four hours hard accordion practice, I very often had time to kill, the choice was to wander around the towns or city's shops: perhaps see a movie.

Theatrical digs, meal times were usually adjusted to suit theatrical hours. Breakfast extended to 11 am and dinner was at 5pm. The trick was to have a full English breakfast as late as you could get away with it, and then skip lunch. Many theatricals spent the time in pubs and betting shops between the two meals of the day. I never ever felt the need to do this myself.

After the show, it was the practice to relax and wind down by having a few drinks, or if you were financially flush and still hungry, dine out in a restaurant. Perhaps Indian or Chinese, which were increasing in number as opposed to Fish and Chips. Not really a long-term healthy way of life, as I was to find out to my cost many years later.

Changes were in the air however. With the closures of many theatres up and down the country and the emergence of theatre-clubs such as the Batley Variety Club, the Wakefield Theatre Club and Manchester's Golden Garter and many similar venues in the south, together with night-clubs and even large working men's clubs offering a full weeks' employment, the old style theatrical digs were disappearing. There was a change of culture on the way and audience tastes were changing.

Traumatic Journey

It was a very a very hard winter and we experienced a very traumatic time whilst travelling 'over the top'. Wendy and I were in our mini-van heading for Scunthorpe. We intended performing in the Lincolnshire clubs before departing on the first leg of the Olde Tyme Music Hall Show tour before going to Germany. As we entered Yorkshire driving up a very steep climb, heading for Todmorden, the snow was getting heavier and thicker. The road became very slippery and we found ourselves in the middle of a full-scale blizzard. I could barely see in front of me.

A huge black shape, which I realised was the truck I was following slewed to the side, blocking the narrowing road completely and came to a stop. I got out. Looking back as far as possible (which wasn't far) all I could see was a long line of vehicles grinding to a halt. I climbed back in, covered in wet cold snow trying its hardest to get down the back of my neck. The inside of a mini-van is just metal with no insulation or lining.

Wendy remarked. "Look darling, icicles are forming on the roof!"

"I'll keep the engine running for a few minutes," I said.

"Look, now the snow is getting higher round the outside of the doors. We won't be able to get out. In fact, at this rate we could be buried over in no time!" she exclaimed.

I tried to calm her by saying I would open the doors periodically. This I did until it became impossible to get them open.

She looked at me thoughtfully then said, "Do you think we are going to die?"

"No, no! Don't even think that, we'll be rescued soon," I replied. We sat in the van for ages with the freezing cold causing us to shiver. Our teeth chattered uncontrollably. Our breath froze on the windscreen. I had to keep scraping it off to keep watch on what was happening in the eerily quiet white world outside.

At last, someone banging on our window broke the silence. I managed to get the window open.

Crouching down outside was an AA man who said, "Are you two okay in there?"

"Yes, thanks any signs of us getting out of here yet?" I asked.

"Yes son, don't worry. There are two snow ploughs working towards you. One in front and one coming from behind. It was a lorry-driver who decided to execute a turn in front of you, got stuck and blocked the road. Then at the bottom of the hill, another lorry-driver decided he would try the same, unfortunately, with the same results, daft buggers." He said shaking his head. "Just hold tight."

Eventually, they dug us out and we followed a snow plough for the remainder of the journey until we spotted a pub with welcoming lights twinkling in the darkness. We parked very carefully ensuring our exit was clear. At least the snow had stopped falling. We staggered into the welcoming warmth and made for a big blazing log fire. After a few minutes of thawing out, and feeling human again I went to the bar, and ordered us two hot drinks and two meals. Whilst the food was being prepared, Wendy popped into the pub phone-box, phoned her Mum and Dad, assuring them that we were okay, and would be with them soon. What an adventure.

After that experience, we could not wait to swap the van for something bigger and safer. The very next day at a garage in Scunthorpe, we part-exchange ours mini-van for a luxurious big black Rover 90: real-leather seats, the interior all lined in fawn woollen type material and a walnut dashboard. The salesman said it was nicknamed as the 'poor man's Rolls-Royce'. I must say I felt like a millionaire when driving it. We loved that car and kept it for ages.

Wendy accompanied me for part of the tour. They were a friendly little company under the directorship of Duggie Chapman. I found Duggie friendly and straightforward in his dealing with me and I enjoyed working with him.

Duggie played the part of Chairman of the Music Hall and had some good balanced ideas as to the running and programme of a show. My billing was good, and I closed the first half of the show. The programme described me as 'Avoca Records USA, Recording Star Lawrie Adam'. We did good business and the revival of the olde time music hall appealed to many folks.

Wendy returned home after a few weeks, to await my return from Germany. We would both journey on to Skegness in Lincolnshire for the summer season. The last week of the tour, was at the Pavilion Theatre in Weymouth. The two Johns arrived. I had booked them into the show for the final performance. After the show we had a meal, journeyed on towards Dover, caught the ferry over to France then continued the drive to Frankfurt Germany.

The hotel on Bleacher Strasse was a dump! A bit like the London bed-sit I had years ago. Our room was next door to the rather smelly shared toilet on the landing. Nevertheless, we still had a great time and enjoyed ourselves immensely. The weather was glorious. We visited the Rhine and other tourist attractions. Preparations were under way for a visit from our Queen and they were busy decorating the streets.

When playing in an up-market nightclub I found German audiences very appreciative. During my rendering of 'Variations of the Carnival of Venice' they applauded various tricky sequences. At first, it threw me, not being used to this in England. It happened again when playing my own arrangement of Offenbach's Can-Can featuring a tricky bass solo.

Skegness

The trip back to England was a bit of a nightmare. I had to drive from Frankfurt to Calais, aboard the ferry to Dover, journey up to King's Cross Station in London where John Soutar would catch his train. From there, I set off heading for the A1 up to Scunthorpe, drop off Wendy's brother John, collect Wendy and immediately drive up to Skegness.

The Summer Show rehearsals started at 6pm. It would have been impossible to meet the deadline, but for a fellow artiste giving me a bottle of 'pep-pills'. I know not what they contained, but they certainly did the trick and I performed the feat. He warned there could be a big downer the following day. In fact, I never experienced it at all. When I strode into rehearsals, no one would believe that I had just driven all night and day (apart from the ferry) from Germany.

The show was going well indeed but the dressing room situation was very cramped. In fact, there was only one dressing room for the whole company. We all became *very* friendly but not really through choice!

Wendy booked us into a flat within the attic of a large house where we were very comfortable. She was showing a very large lump by this time but still looked beautiful. She had been busy during my absence by making fashionable maternity dresses for herself. We inherited a collection of baby clothes ready for the expected arrival. We were thrilled at the prospect of becoming a family.

My brother Ronnie and his family arrived to spend a couple of weeks with us. He said he hoped to be there when the birth took place but alas, it was not to be.

In the early hours of Friday morning, I was jolted awake.

"Darling, you had better grab the suitcase and get me to the Cottage Hospital as soon as possible please!"

I was more panicked than she was. I ran tripping and stumbling down the back stairs in my pyjamas with Wendy running after me. We jumped into the car and set off at speed racing through the town. A police car overtook me and forced me to an abrupt Halt. He walked slowly back to our car. I wound the window down.

He shone his torch into the car and I noticed a quick expression of reconnection in his eyes as he said, "Like the pyjamas. Been to a wild show-business party, have we?"

"Certainly not officer, my wife is about to give birth and I'm rushing her to hospital."

"Oh yeah?" He replied. "I've heard that one before I'm afraid. Oh! My God!" he said shining his torch into the back and spotting Wendy groaning and clutching her swollen stomach.

"Follow me. I'll get you there the quickest way." With that, he took off with his blue light flashing all the way to the front door of the hospital. He must have phoned in advance, as the doors were already open with two nurses and a wheelchair at the ready. I gave her a quick kiss, telling her that I would see her later in the morning, then she was gone, and the doors firmly shut. I felt deserted and alone.

The following morning my first task was to visit Wendy. She was propped up in bed and looking very comfortable. She said that nothing had happened so far, but they were keeping her in as anything could happen at any time. Eventually, I returned to the flat then onto the show.

A Baby is Born

On Saturday evening 3 July, I was at the side of the stage waiting for my introduction and play-on music when I received a tap on the arm. I looked round and standing behind me was a tallish, well-built man, who spoke with an educated Scottish accent.

"Good evening Mr. Adam, my name is Doctor Jamieson. Eh have come doon here to tell you thet et ten pest seven this evening you became the fetherr of a bonnie wee baby girl."

As I thanked him very much, I heard my name ring out on stage together with my introduction music. I staggered on and my mind was blank! I just stared at the audience and then down at the musicians who were poised and looking at me waiting for me to start. The news I had just heard was still sinking in and I seemed to be in some sort of stunned shock.

Someone whispered in Duggie's ear. He grabbed the microphone and announced, "Please excuse Lawrie, Ladies and Gentlemen. He has only this minute been informed, that he has just become the father of a little baby girl." There was a big round of applause. Duggie continued,

"And when his wife finds out she'll bloody kill 'im!" a big laugh, as he said to me. "Scarper son you're not in any fit state to entertain this lot tonight."

To the shouts from my fellow artistes of "Congratulations Lawrie!" I made for the door and jumped in the car, still in full make-up and still in full highland dress.

At the hospital, I was recognised and shown to my dear wife and baby. Near to tears, I hugged them both and picked up the beautiful little bundle wrapped up in a white shawl and weighing just 6lbs 6 oz. I am sure she recognised her Daddy, because when I touched her tiny fragile hand, gazing in wonder at her little nails she grabbed my finger and seemed reluctant to let go. What an immense thrill that was. It was indescribable. I did not really want to leave them, but I could see my lovely wife was tired out and on the edge of much needed sleep. The nurse took hold of our precious little bundle and told me I should go now but could return tomorrow. In those days, new mothers stayed in hospital considerably longer than today's generation.

I collected Wendy and our daughter 10 days later and brought them back to our flat. Baby Tracey duties filled the days and nights. We were so frightened because she was so tiny. The least cough or grunt sent us scurrying to her cot in case we were getting something wrong. I was glad I had an evening job, as I was fortunate to have the daytime in which to recover!

Record from America

My record Album from America arrived, and I ordered a quantity to sell to audiences. They had a very attractive red sleeve front and back and I could not get enough copies to satisfy the demand. I was making more money selling the records than Duggie was paying me and added together made a considerable salary. I had the idea of having souvenir photographs plugging the record label and they sold even faster than the records. Duggie soon got the idea and followed suit with a souvenir picture of himself and the cast. He was more than happy with the extra income and publicity.

Duggie had a small 10 feet Bluebird caravan and asked if I would be interested in buying it. I thought what a great idea. It would not only mean we could all travel together everywhere, but also save money on accommodation. We agreed to buy it from him for a well-spent £85.

At the end of the season, the whole company went on tour and so did we in our newly acquired caravan. Fortunately, the Rover pulled it easily, although it felt a little strange at first towing. I soon got the hang of it. Reversing was the tricky part. We played a theatre in Kidderminster and that was Tracey's first theatre dressing room. Funny, she never cried in the theatre. She was just 11 weeks old.

The final date of the tour was the Grand Theatre in Swansea, South Wales. The weather had turned to heavy torrential rain. I battled as well as possible with bad conditions and was doing OK until faced with a very steep hill. Tracey was fast asleep on the back seat tucked into her portable pram-cot. As we got about three-quarter way up the hill, it became obvious that the engine was struggling to keep going. I had dropped down to my lowest gear.

Wendy said, "Oooh! What's that horrible burning plastic smell, is that us?" Tracey must have noticed it too and started to object by wailing louder and louder. The car ground to a stop, I hit the brakes, but we started to slide slowly backwards down the hill.

"Quick! Grab a couple of bricks from that wall there and jam them under the wheels, I'll try and hold it with the brakes!" I shouted at Wendy,

By this time, I was also pulling on the hand brake, but we were still moving backwards. Wendy leapt out of the car, grabbed two bricks and jammed them under the wheels. We gained a moment of relief. I looked to my left and spotted an entrance to a park or something. My intention was to drive through the gap, execute a turn, then go back down the hill and look for another more level route. Poor Wendy was soaked through.

Just as she was sagging back into her seat she noticed what I was attempting and said, "What are you doing? This is someone's big palatial home."

"Tough," I said. "We'll be in and out before anyone even notices us." I entered the large gated entrance, noticing at the foot of the drive a very large mansion house. As I did a wide turn, meaning I had to cut across a well-kept lawn in the process, leaving behind me deep scores from the car and the caravan, then finally coming to a stop with smoke pouring from the engine. I switched off.

In the deafening silence I said, "Well, at least we are off that awful steep hill, but I suspect we have a burnt-out clutch."

"That sounds serious, what now?"

"I'm going to have to go down to that house and ask if I can use the phone. I'll ring the theatre, tell them I'm going to be late for rehearsal and ask if they could send a mechanic to come and fix the car." I got out of the car and made my way down to the house. As I reached the huge dark oak metal studded door, I put out my hand to ring the doorbell, the door swung open and there was a tall balding man in his fifties glaring at me in a very hostile manner. I explained who I was, what had happened and asked if I could please use his telephone.

He shouted, "Certainly not! You are the thug who has just scored over my lovely lawn with that bloody car and that bloody caravan. And now you want to use my phone!" Thank goodness, two things happened simultaneously. Wendy appeared by my side cradling a whimpering baby Tracey, and the man's wife appeared from behind him, nudging him to the side displaying a look of compassion saying, "Oh, do come inside out of the rain, and of course you may use the phone." We did not need asking twice.

She looked at her husband and said, "Charles, please go and put the kettle on and make us all some tea." He gave a grunt and left.

People seem interested in theatrical folk and we allowed her to question us until the breakdown truck arrived. They sorted us out and as we left, we thanked them for their kindness. He just gave another grunt.

Swansea

The top of the bill was a fading star called Dorothy Squires. Being the star and acting like one, Dorothy totally ignored the rest of the cast demanding that she had to rehearse with the orchestra and her pianist first. She took ages and did a full rehearsal.

A young lad walked across the stage towards her saying, "Can we go now please, I'm hungry."

Everyone gave a sudden intake of breath and I heard a mutter of, "My God there is no mistaking who that lad's father is."

I turned to one of the acts sitting next to me in the stalls, "Who?" I asked.

"Can't you see it, Roger Moore, the film star? For goodness sake, do not say anything. She has a very quick awful temper. Give her a wide berth. She's violent."

The show was going very well indeed until, from nowhere, a short man in a dark suit, white shirt and tie, topped off with a flat cap, appeared and tapped me on the arm whispering in a thick Welsh accent, "Excuse me young man, would that door be Dorothy Squires' dressing room please?"

I said, in a low voice, "Yes, it is, why?"

"Well, you see," he continued, "I'm the concert secretary for the Tredegar Working Men's Club see, up in the valleys you know. Dorothy used to do a turn for us years ago before she became a big international star see."

"Oh! Really," I said.

"Well we were thinking see, as she's not such a big star anymore and on her way down, so to speak, if I asked her nicely, she might do us a favour and come back and sing for us like." I remembered a similar conversation some years ago outside the Scottish star Andy Stewart's dressing room when his headmaster asked to see him. It was time for a repeat performance.

I said to him, "Knock on her door, she'll shout 'Come!'. Enter and tell her in those very endearing words you have just used to me and see what she says. After all, she can only say no." He gave a smile, turned and tapped on her door.

"Come!" she bellowed. In he went. The door flew open seconds later. He came running out like a scalded cat, followed by various objects flying after him accompanied by an unrepeatable stream of adjectives which were not only heard by the stage crew but by most of the cast. The loud slam of her dressing room door followed. That is show business!

Scunthorpe then Scotland

When the tour concluded we went to Scunthorpe, as Wendy's family were eager to see their newest addition. We stayed there for a week then it was time to hitch up our small caravan again and hit the road up north.

I had a contract to appear in Scotland for a five-week winter season at The Gaiety Theatre in Ayr. We had some time off before I was due for rehearsals and so we visited Ronnie in Lochgelly who were still preparing to leave for New Zealand. We wanted to show off our little daughter who was proving to be a smash hit everywhere we went.

We parked our caravan on a large caravan park just outside Ayr and became firm friends with the owners Jimmy and Myra Mayberry. They loved having theatre folk on their site and made a great fuss of us and especially Tracey. Jimmy walked with a bit of a swagger and earned himself the nickname of 'The Sheriff'. The site was the love of his life. We were to visit them many times in future years.

The Gaiety shows were quite lavish affairs and I enjoyed playing there immensely. Mr. Popplewell, the owner, asked if I was interested in a summer season there but on balance, it would have been a step backwards. All those changes of programme again, twice nightly and the money was far less than I was offered in England. I turned him down and headed back south.

Northenden

There was plenty of cabaret work within the nearby Manchester city and so we spent the remainder of that winter, tucked up snugly in our big caravan in Northenden. When the fire was crackling merrily away together with the delicious smell of Wendy cooking and Tracey happily gurgling away contentedly on my lap, I realised that it is quite true, there really is 'no place like home'.

Twenty-Six
1966 A Real Mixed Bag

"I'm sorry, but I don't care what the water is like in Germany, or the food, so I insist that we take our own water and tins of food too," said Wendy.

"The caravan will weigh a ton," Wendy's brother John said.

"I know John," I replied, "but she will not be moved, so just give me a hand to get all these tins on board then I'll go and get the water."

"And another thing," said my lovely wife, "the chemical toilet cannot just sit here for five weeks, can you just imagine that?"

"Ah! I've thought on that one already," I replied, "and I have dug a deep hole round the back of the van. Just before we go I'll tip the toilet contents into it."

John gave a laugh and said, "I'd love to be a fly on the wall should anyone walk round the back of your caravan."

Finally, we set off on our journey heading for the port of Dover. It was getting dark by the time we reached Coventry. I pulled over on a quiet well-lit road with housing on both sides and room to park.

"Sorry folks but I seriously need to take a massive leak."

"What, where are you going to do that?" Wendy asked.

"In the van." I replied. "I'll just chuck it out, and then we're off. Easy peasy."

I disappeared inside the van and relieved myself in a plastic bucket. Meanwhile, Wendy and John sat quietly gazing out the front window. Running towards the van was a man in shorts. John said, "Uh! Oh! You know what's about to happen, here don't you?"

Wendy put her hands up to her face and exclaimed, "Oh! No, surely not."

Just as the runner drew level with the caravan, the door flew open and the steaming contents of a plastic bucket came flying all over the poor fellow. He gave his head a shake, spluttered a bit, but kept his pace the same, leaving behind him a set of wet footprints. Gasping with horror, I wasted no time in jumping back in the car and took off at some speed!

At Dover, we found ourselves at the head of the queue. A ship's officer appeared at the side of the window and suggested we unhitch the caravan and manhandle it down the steep gradient and make sure it was flush against the wall of the ship.

I said, "Eh! It's quite heavy you know."

He just laughed and said, "I am sure two strapping lads like you can manage that fine. Off you go then, quick as you can, please."

I said to John, "Okay, you go to the other side of the bracket, I'll lift it off the car towing ball, and then we'll take it easy down the ramp. Let's go." I undid the jockey wheel. With considerable difficulty, I managed to lift the van clear of the car towing-ball. Suddenly, it took off! It flew down the ramp at great speed with the two of us trying our best to keep up with it. I could feel the wind in my hair as it gathered momentum! The damn thing had a life of its own and seemed to be enjoying its freedom. With a mighty dong, which sounded like a large cathedral bell, it connected violently with the side of the ship. I glanced over at the officer. Speechless, he stared at us with his mouth gaping wide open.

I returned to the car at the top of the ramp and climbed into the driver's seat. Wendy slowly turned her head and just stared at me, but never said a word. I just drove the car down the ramp and parked up. We got out and made for the lounge area.

"Bloody hell Lawrie, I thought we going to go right through the side of the ship then," John muttered in my ear,

"Yes, from his expression so did the ship's officer," I replied.

Thankfully, getting off the ferry was easier than getting on and so we headed for Germany and our camping site.

Keeping on the right-hand side of the road, was tricky at times, especially when we hit a roundabout. We realised we were lost. I stopped the car and said I would go and knock on the door of the house. A large well-built German woman answered. She had blonde hair in plaits and a face resembling a bag of chisels.

"Ya?" She barked glaring at me. I tried my best to convey we were lost. She waved her arm in a gesture that meant, 'go away' and if she had spoken English, I am sure the last the word she used was, "Off!"

Meanwhile, Wendy continued changing our little daughter's nappy, a task badly needed, as the smell was breath taking.

As I got back in the car, Wendy said, "What a rude woman." She wound down her window, "Here," she added, "you can have this English souvenir with our compliments!" and threw the full brown-tinted soggy nappy up into the air. It landed on the woman's drive with a mighty 'shhhlopp'. I departed quickly.

By this time, we were hungry. I spotted a portable cart selling something to two or three people at the side of the road. I stopped the car and popped over. He was selling Bratwurst (a large cream coloured thick German sausage) placed on a piece of greaseproof paper together with a dollop of mustard. We consumed them within minutes. A taxi stopped for a snack. Getting out of the car, I crossed the road again and asked him if he knew the location of our camping platz.

"Ya, that's not out of my way. Just follow me and I take you there."

It was dark when the helpful taxi driver stopped and pointed to large entrance gates to our site. I flashed my lights in thanks as he drove away. We drove through the gates into inky darkness. We could not see a thing. Some yards away we could just make out some ghostly caravan shapes. I decided to make for them and park alongside. The grass was bumpy and uneven, as we drove across it. We parked up and jacked the caravan legs down. We just wanted to fall into bed. We were all exhausted.

The Bluebird caravan was only 10 feet long but quite compact inside. Wendy and I had a double bed made up of a supporting board (the tabletop) and an arrangement of cushions. It was very comfortable. Tracey slept in her pram-carry-cot and John had a clever arrangement of a canvas hammock, supported by two stout wooden poles down each side. He hung just below the ceiling. We were all unconscious within seconds.

All was quiet and peaceful. I was aware of the sun streaming through the curtains and lighting up the interior. Tracey started to make grunting noises that meant she was ready for a feed. We all got up and sorted ourselves out. As Wendy prepared Tracey's feed and our breakfast, I drew back the curtains and received the shock of my life. Many faces pressed up against all the windows confronted me. They were ignoring us but pointing to various items within our caravan and jabbering away to each other. At first, I was very annoyed then I realised they probably had not seen a British caravan before, especially nothing like our old Bluebird. Eventually, they melted away.

I opened the door to look around and muttered "Oh! Bloody hell, will you look at that!" John and Wendy looked out of the window and gasped in horror. Last night we had ploughed through a massive flowerbed leaving a set of tyre tracks right up to our caravan. "I had better go and apologise to the site owner and book us in."

The tall thin stooped balding man stood behind the counter and glared at me. He was wearing a white shirt and black waistcoat. As I pointed to our caravan and offered my profuse apologies, he muttered something in German shook his head in disgust but accepted my money. We were there for some weeks. It was an excellent site with walkways, a shop, a restaurant, very clean shower and toilet blocks and even a large man-made lake.

The work in United States Army camps was not always pleasant and the travelling was hard. One evening the show arrived at a large camp and we were warned that the men had been out on manoeuvres and might be a bit unresponsive and tired. What an understatement! I was first on and every single soldier (about 100) was sound asleep across the tables. We carried on with the show regardless. The comic, who usually did 20 minutes, only did about 10 due to not one laugh. Not one solitary soldier looked up at us. In the main, the audiences were very tough and not particularly interested. The soldiers, were not there through choice, but ordered to attend. Apart from having Wendy, Tracey and John with me, I cannot say I enjoyed the experience very much.

When I enquired from a German agent why she did not send us to any British Army camps, she gave a laugh and said, "They cannot afford any entertainment, darlink."

I pondered, "And we think we won the war?"

After my final engagement, we hitched up the caravan and sped off for the ferry.

Changes in the theatres

The theatre profession was changing. Summer seasons were getting shorter, pantomimes runs were reducing from three months to a run of three weeks. There were only two ways to obtain engagements in the Working Men's Clubs. One was to go through an agent, the other to hoof it round various clubs in the evenings yourself and talk the Concert Secretary into booking you. They were drunk with power and the set fees were *not* negotiable, so much for a vocalist, a speciality act or a musical act. The comics got the most, but as they relied on audience participation, which was not always forthcoming I noticed. I reckoned they deserved the extra. My type of act was deemed a safe bet.

After an artiste had finished his stint, he or she would often have to chase after the concert secretary for his cash. Sometimes, if he was an absolute idiot, he delighted in paying you out one note at a time in public concluding with a remark such as, "Bloody hell, I have to work bloody hours for a wage like you're getting."

It was often demoralising to arrive at a club to be told that you were expected to do four spots and sometimes the audience like to get up and have a dance. In a theatre, a musical act was expected to do two spots at the most but usually just the one. The musical accompaniment was also unreliable, as very often the organist and drummer could not read music. Sometimes the audience did not even bother to applaud, but just tap their pint mugs on their tabletops. The artiste was expected to perform during all manner of distractions. The sale of raffle tickets or bingo tickets. A loud cry greeted the arrival of the meat-pies. A man would walk around the audience, like a cinema usherette selling ice cream, but with a tray full of pies, just like 'Simple Simon', shouting, "Pies have come!" However, a religious silence was demanded when it was Bingo time'.

Many a time when I arrived at a club and lugged my heavy accordion case up the stairs to the concert room with the smell of stale beer pervading the nostrils. The pulsating gavel-like vocal sounds of "4 and 4, 44. Two little ducks 22," followed by the audience shouting "Quack-quack!" "1 and 7, 17. Legs 11" (and here everyone gave a loud wolf-whistle). If I dared make a noise there be a loud, "shush" from all the concentrating bingo addicts. Even when someone shouted, "House," after the disappointed, "Ah, dammits!" there followed an even louder silence, while the winner's card was checked off by a balding man in a dark suit sporting a large badge on his lapel which said, 'Committee'. That meant power! What a complete depressing contrast to playing a theatre.

However, theatres were thinning out at an alarming rate and to feed my family and pay the bills, I had no alternative but to grit my teeth and take what was on offer.

Manchester

In Manchester, I took a seat alongside about fifteen other artistes in the agent's office who booked theatre clubs in the city. I had been there an hour and it was now my turn to go in, when the entrance door opened and in walked the singing star Matt Munroe. He looked very grand and suave in an expensive-looking black leather coat.

The office door opened, the agent, Gerry Millman, glanced at me then spotted Matt and beamed as he said, "Ah! Matt, lovely to see you, come in come in." Then he looked me briefly up and down and said in a dry tone, "That's it for today kid, try me another time," then closed the door. I met Matt again some years down the line when I played a big theatre club in Cardiff and I reminded him of this event.

Morecambe

It was a relief to hitch up the caravan and head for Morecambe to the Alhambra Theatre for our summer season. I had good billing alongside Scottish comedian star Johnny Victory. Rumour had it that he could be very difficult to work with and had a short-fuse temper. Personally, I found him to be very polite and easy to get along with.

Johnny had his own digs by way of a motor home that he shared with his charming Irish partner Kay. He tended to keep to himself and was a private type of person. He, like many fellow Scottish artistes, struggled with the language barrier, as he was a very broad Glaswegian. I had come to terms with this, years ago. Partly because a Fifeshire accent is softer than a Glasgow one and easier to tone down although it did take a bit of study and working on. I loved to hear the various accents within the British Isles anyway and often mimicked them to good effect...or so my wife told me.

A male vocalist called Robert Earl, who had enjoyed a hit record in his time and managed the Opportunity Knocks winner Julie De-Marco, was also in the show. Although Wendy and I found them both charming people, Julie had obviously developed an extreme dislike for Robert.

Wendy choreographed the show and took on the role of Head Girl. The producer obviously admired her skills and I was very proud of the way she accepted the task and undertook the job of working with the six dancers. All went well during the season until Wendy was elected to bring a complaint to the notice of the management. The promised support of the dancers melted away when faced by a questioning management.

"No surprises there then!" concluded my wife.

We were very fortunate to be able to park up our caravan in the lovely lush grounds of the olde worlde 'Greyhound' pub, nestling by the River Lune in the small village of Halton. We were only 16 miles from the theatre and away from the holiday crowds. After some weeks, whilst having a relaxing drink, Graham, the pub landlord, said Wendy and I would make an excellent team running a pub such as theirs. I must admit it did seem an attractive idea that had not occurred to me. Wendy asked his wife what it would be like for her.

She replied, "Don't even think about it Wendy. Just watch me one evening. You will note that I have a cigarette burning in every ashtray up and down the bar. I never used to smoke! You will see me with a glass of gin beside every ashtray. The punters like to see you drink 'their' drink they have bought you. Not only am I expected listen, but to give my full attention to everyone's problems. To get distracted invites offence and even sometimes abuse!"

Graham, said, "Well, yes I suppose in a way it's a bit like your business Lawrie. It looks glamorous, but behind the scenes, there is hard work. Changing barrels, arranging brewery deliveries, staff problems and management. Even after the punters have gone home we still have to cash-up, then clean up before we stagger into bed well past midnight or into the early hours." We required no more convincing!

We soon settled into the routine of the show. It was a doddle. Once nightly, and no changes of programme. It was a very comfortable type of show with reasonable house attendances and the theatre was a pleasure to work in. It possessed a good atmosphere. It was funny to take a walk past the Palace Theatre, further down the seafront, pushing the pram with little Tracey happily gurgling away and reminisce the happy times we had there in past Easter and summer shows. I had moved out of Hedley's price-range but would always be grateful to him for a good start in English summer shows. He taught me an awful lot.

Once more, I received many attractive offers of Sunday concerts. The trouble was they were all over England! Wendy encouraged me to take them and said that both she and Tracey (now one year old and getting cuter by the day) would come with me.

Weymouth was an over 660 miles round-trip and over 5 hours travelling each way to appear with Alfred Marks.

Blackpool's big new ABC Theatre to appear with The Seekers.

'The Floral Hall', Scarborough, was over 320 miles round-trip and over 3 hours each way, Frankie Howard, was impressed with me and offered me a place in his show scheduled to tour abroad starting in Borneo! However, when he placed his hand on my thigh I decided it was not a good idea!

The famous impresario, Sir Bernard Delfont, booked me for Sundays in Great Yarmouth over 300 miles each way and over 5 hours driving each way with such stars as Dick Emery, Edmund Hockeridge, and Vera Lynn.

I introduced Vera at a concert memorable above all others.

Yarmouth was an awkward trip cutting across country. I was always grateful for my family's company on these long hauls. We had to set off at dawn sometimes. Have a packed lunch then an afternoon band-call with an orchestra. Usually, I performed one spot of about 10-15 minutes and then I could leave. The long mileages were the hardest part. The weather was good, and we had some time between the rehearsal and the show to have a walk around the town. As soon as we finished our part in the show, it was in the car, the nearest fish and chip shop, then off home. We arrived back in the early hours of the morning. I was paid well, and they were all prestigious shows. Tracey was as good as gold in the dressing room. It was as if she knew she was in a theatre and had to behave and be quiet. However, at the Vera Lynn concert I came off to find Wendy very distraught.

"What's up?" I asked.

Wringing her hands and near to tears as she said, "I can't find Tracey. I just popped to the side of the stage to see where you were up to. It could only have been a couple of minutes, when I returned, she was gone!"

The stage manager was walking past at that point, I said to him, "Our little baby daughter is missing."

He laughed, "Don't worry, she's perfectly fine, Vera took her into her dressing room." We found her cooing away and staring up at this female international icon who was cooing back at her as she cradled her in her arms.

Vera looked up and said, "I hope you are not angry with me, I knocked on your door, opened it and spotted this beautiful little bundle and just had to kidnap her. Can I keep her a few minutes longer please?" We were so relieved.

When I went to the side of the stage to introduce Vera to a packed house, I found her pacing up and down wringing her hands in anguish and looking very nervous.

"Vera, whatever is the matter?"

"It's all right. I'm always like this before a performance."

I said, "Well, I doubt if I will even get so far as announcing your name tonight before you receive an outstanding ovation." Sure enough, I walked on, started her introduction, the band struck up her famous song, 'We'll meet again' and all hell broke loose. As she walked on, I felt the wave of sheer love coming over the footlights. She received a standing ovation before she even sang a single note. Here was a genuine star and a lovely sincere person. I wished I could have known her better. She was so nervous it made me feel very humble. I believe she was worried in case she was not good enough for all the people who had travelled the miles to see her.

Not all the stars were of the same quality I realised. The following Sunday we parked a little way down the street from the stage door of the Floral Hall in Scarborough. I had just finished my rehearsal. As we sat and ate a packed lunch, we noticed the Crackerjack TV star Leslie Crowther, making his way past the growing queue of folk buying tickets. At our end, there was a large party of disabled children with their carers. Leslie stopped and spent time with nearly every single one of them. "Well!" I said to Wendy, "that shows you something about Leslie's character."

A few minutes later along came comedian and singer, Des O'Connor with two minders. One in front and one behind. Little hands shot out in front of him offering up their treasured autograph books. Sadly, Des and his minders waved them aside as he made his way quickly to the stage door.

Wendy added, "Yes, and that shows something about Mr. O'Connor's character doesn't it."

It was sad to see, but I added, "Ah well! Perhaps he is running late."

Fish and Chips

One evening after the show during the final week, I said to Wendy, "Do you fancy fish and chips, save you cooking when we get home." I parked outside the stage door and a couple of shops further back was a fish and chip shop.

"Go on then," she said. I walked into the shop and ordered fish and chips twice. The surly tall man behind the counter glared at me and grunted when I ordered fish and chips twice. He seemed to be having a go at the woman standing next to him.

"Domestic squabble," I thought to myself. He duly delivered my fish and chips and took my money just as the door squeaked open and a small middle-aged woman walked in marched up to the counter and placed a huge order.

"Oh! Bloody hell love. You really should have given us warning for such a big order you know!" She looked near to tears.

"Excuse me, where is the salt and vinegar please?" I asked.

"Over there on that bench, are you blind?" He growled. His customer service techniques were not impressive. I shook the vinegar bottle over the golden-coloured appetising fish and chips and they smelled delicious. I replaced the bottle and reached for the salt, which was in an aluminium jar about 5 inches high by about 3 inches diameter. It had a screw-on top punched with holes. I turned it upside down and gave it a shake. The top flew off and the contents dumped all over my prized fish and chips! I slowly walked back to the counter holding out my ruined package in front of the grumpy owner.

He glared down at the mess, and then with a smirk, growled, "You've made a right mess of that…SIR!"

I replied, "Yes, but not my fault. The fault is yours, I'm afraid."

His large podgy hand was poised over the huge mound of steaming fish and chips he was preparing for the woman who was just staring in horror at my fish and chips.

He glared at me and said, "I didn't do it, you did…SIR."

"Yes, but I was using YOUR salt holder, in YOUR shop which is YOUR responsibility to keep in usable order. I suggest either a refund, or a replacement." I replied.

His voice rose in pitch and got louder. **"No bloody way, now just get out!"**

I said calmly, "I am truly sorry you have taken that attitude. I must tell you that my hand is getting very tired holding this package over the large order you have just prepared. Wouldn't it be terrible if it accidentally fell on to this lady's order? Now, I am only asking to be treated fairly here, what do you say?"

"I'll tell you what I say," he shouted. "Fuck off! That's what I bloody say!"

"Oh dear, how sad, what a pity," I replied, "Sadly, I thought that might be your answer." My hand tipped the salt sodden fish and chips right on top of the lady's order.

"Now look what you've made me go and do." I said. The woman turned and headed for the door. The owner went purple in the face, scooped up a handful of the chips and threw them at me. He missed, so he tried again.

By this time, I was opening the door and said, "Well, good night then." However, a tall policeman blocked my exit. He was just in time to receive a huge dollop of fish, chips and batter on his helmet!

He shouted in a voice like thunder, "Enough! What is going on in here?"

Whilst his wife was calming down the owner, I explained the happenings to the policeman.

He was very sympathetic and said, "I think it best if you just go, sir, I'll deal with this. It's not the first time we have had problems here." I did not need to be asked twice.

I jumped in the car and said to Wendy who had been asleep, "Sorry dearest, looks like you are cooking after all!"

Blackpool Night

A letter arrived from the BBC inviting me to take part in their prestigious long-running radio show called Blackpool Night. I accepted. As it was recorded during the day, there was no difficulty in getting time off. I arrived by train, took a taxi and asked the driver to take me to the Jubilee Theatre.

"Yes, that's the old Co-operative Hall. Are you on tonight then?" He replied.

"Yes, I am, but the Co-operative Hall? Not a theatre then?" He shook his head and giggled. Sure enough, I was deposited outside the Co-op Hall. As I walked up the stairs, I could hear a very large orchestra. It was Bernard Herrmann and the Northern Dance Orchestra (the NDO). It took up about a third of the hall. What a change from what I had imagined. We would gather round the radio at home in Lochgelly and imagined a red plush-seated theatre, somewhere in Blackpool.

As I walked into the dressing room, which was just one big, ante-room, the star Jimmy Clitheroe (the Clitheroe Kid) greeted me warmly. He told me he used to play the accordion himself. He asked if this was my first big radio show. I told him it was.

He said, "Don't be nervous Lawrie, they are going to love you. Just enjoy playing with the biggest and best orchestra in Britain."

Then a woman in a fur coat called Winifred Attwell shook me by the hand saying, "I know it's summer, but I am freezing."

Mr. Blackpool, otherwise known as Reginald Dixon, was charming.

What an honour to be working with such famous artistes.

My knees were knocking as I took my place in front of this huge orchestra. Bernard, the conductor, put me at my ease with a beaming smile. I played some jigs and reels, as I would be wearing Highland Dress. Then the Petite Waltz, which was very tricky. I finished with my arrangement of the Can-Can from Orpheus in the Underworld. I was astounded at how wonderful it was to play with such high-quality musicians. As for the show itself I need not have worried, I could not have gone any better than I did.

When I came off, Jimmy shook my hand and said, "I told you didn't I? We'll work together again Lawrie." And we did. In fact, I ended up employing Jimmy and becoming his manager. Life takes many twists and turns.

Enter Jason

One bright warm sunny morning, Graham, the landlord knocked on our caravan door and said, "Our dog has just had pups. I don't suppose you might be interested in one by any chance?" He had a basket with about five little cute black Labrador-cross pups in it all fighting for space.

Wendy came up behind me and said, "Ah! How cute." She reached out and picked one up, gave it a cuddle then looked at me pleadingly.

"Okay then." We named him Jason (for no reason). He was fine around Tracey who was one year old and taking an interest in everything.

On Father's Day, I received a lovely gift; Tracey walked her first few steps. Wendy and I were thrilled to bits. Everything she grabbed in her hands went straight into her mouth! Then she started to talk, Mummy and Daddy were her first words followed by "Oh dear!" I realised Wendy said this a lot and so she was copied. I noticed that Jason would sneakily creep into her cot at some point during the night and was fast asleep beside her in the morning. Both looking like butter would not melt in their mouths!

One night, Tracey made it on to the stage and paused there like a deer caught in headlights just staring transfixed at the audience. She received a big laugh and a huge round of applause. She gave them a big grin and toddled off.

I thought, "She's a natural!" During the last night finale of the show, she received more presents sent up over the footlights than we did!

Twenty-Seven
A Change of Address

I managed to keep the wolf from the door by immersing myself in the Manchester Theatre Club circuit. On the plus side: They paid far better money than working men's clubs and were run more professionally.

The theatre clubs had more seating capacity however: Although only one spot was required, a longer time on the stage was expected and the stages were larger. When the audience did not like what you offered, you knew right away. I felt like a Christian going into the arena to face the lions. Fortunately, my considerable experience helped me to know instinctively what would be acceptable, and thus kept me in work. Sadly, some acts were shown the door.

I never knew who would be on the bill until I arrived. Some, such as Frank Carson, Colin Crompton, George Roper and many more became TV celebrities in the ITV show called The Comedians. Equally, I could be following on an already famous star such as Brenda Lee or Craig Douglas. Then the audience would chant throughout my performance "We want XXX," but the show had to carry on. On one occasion, the club hosted a Stag Night featuring strippers, drag acts, or foul-mouthed comedians. A drag act such as Terry Durham was far more glamorous than the prettiest looking stripper and often funnier than the comics.

It was a relief when an agent called Nelson Firth booked me into a venue called 'The Planet Room' within the Winter Gardens in Blackpool. Nelson was a man who was always immaculately dressed and presented excellent quality floorshows for big business events and dinners and he paid well. The show was a cabaret, timed to entertain people who had booked seats for the Opera House Theatre. Unfortunately, the audience would start to drift off eventually, to take up their seats in the theatre upstairs.

The exciting summer season offer - to appear in a Number One summer show at the 'Floral Hall Theatre' in Scarborough with Jimmy Clitheroe as the star - was a big leap up for me. Wendy was hired as one of the dancers. The money offered was the most I had ever earned for a season. We really looked forward to that one.

Whilst working at a club in the Manchester area, I made friends with a fellow Scot called Matt McKenzie, who like myself dressed in Highland regalia. He sang Scottish songs and did some comedy. We realised that Wendy had worked with his wife Kim some years back. They too had a young child about Tracey's age and lived in an impressively large caravan at Church Minshull, Cheshire near Crewe. There was no risk of flooding at their site. It had more safe space for Tracey to play in and seemed friendly. Matt said he could enable us to move and we decided to do so.

Once we had moved, we discovered one snag. Jason our dog had grown to his full size and did not like the little yappy poodle next door. When he went outside the poodle started barking at him. He never barked back but just stood quite dignified, staring at it.

One day, Jason was outside with a whole pack of other dogs. Out flew the little poodle and yapped louder than ever. Jason made a dive and in seconds, he was standing straddled over it. It was lying on its back, just staring up at him. He did not bite or attack it. What he did do, with all his pals gathered round watching him, was peed on it. Slowly, he strolled away, leaving a soaked, shaking, petrified poodle with clouds of steam rising from it. It never bothered him again.

New towing caravan

We bought and towed a new, slightly bigger touring caravan to Scarborough to a pitch on a site just outside the town about 15 minutes away by car. Wendy told me she had many memories of this resort as when she was a little girl her family went there quite a lot and they all loved it. I was able to do Sundays at many holiday camps in the area. For us it was a luxury, as we did not have to travel miles to get to any of them. I did a Warner's camp and came face to face with an old chum from my very first summer season in Arbroath, Ronnie Wayne. He was Entertainments Manager. He said he was pleased I was doing so well and that the advice he gave me to leave Scotland was correct. It certainly was.

When we turned up for rehearsals, Jimmy Clitheroe came up to me and with a grin said, "Well Lawrie, I told you we would work together again."

He made a fuss of Tracey and warmed to Wendy right away. The boss's partner informed me that they only required me to do about 8 minutes towards the end of the first half. The dancers, dressed in Scottish costumes, introduced me and danced to a Scottish pop song. Under my direction, The Arthur Blake Singers whistled at the side of the stage to a new pop number called 'I Was Kaiser-Bills Batman'. Bill Pethers was conductor of the full theatre orchestra.

The show comedian, Derek Dene provided curry parties for the cast at his rented house, which were a lot of fun, although mostly Derek's curries were hot Vindaloos and inedible!

Fishing

A fishing trip was organised for the men in the cast on a genuine fishing boat. We left very early in the morning and set out to sea. We just kept hauling large cod on board until we decided we had more than enough. We were all exhausted when we arrived back in the harbour. One day in the future, I would once again set out in a fishing boat from Scarborough, as a director with a film crew producing a documentary. I would also have a title in front of my name. If I had been told this, I would not have believed it.

Golfing

I was encouraged to try my hand at golf by Jimmy Clitheroe's comedy feed, Billy Windsor. We played three mornings a week on a small golf course of nine holes. Jimmy came with us one morning and said I should try a real game of golf on an 18-hole course. That turned out to be an absolute disaster!

Jimmy and I met up one lovely warm morning at the Scarborough Golf Course. We were in the clubroom when in walked three stars called the Bachelors closely followed by Derek Dene who was the Vaudeville Golfing Society top player. They decided to join us. I hired a set of clubs, but I made the point that I had not played much.

They just laughed and said, "Yes, a Scotsman said that to us once before and he wiped the course with us."

The first tee-off was by a bus stop near the main road. There were about 10 people waiting for a bus. One of the woman exclaimed,

"Ooooh! Look! It's the Bachelors!" They started to wave.

Another said, "Yes, and there's Jimmy Clitheroe!"

I heard another remark "Who are the other two? Don't know who they are."

The Bachelors hit their balls beautifully. Derek Dene smacked his right down the fairway.

Jimmy muttered, "Now, don't be nervous Lawrie, you'll be fine, just keep calm." Jimmy hit the ball with his specially made driver. It went like a rocket.

I noted that the bus had arrived thank goodness. The door opened and as I hit my ball, it slewed off right into the open door of the bus, which drove off with my ball inside it. Jimmy was in hysterics and doubled up laughing.

"It could have been worse Lawrie, you could have killed someone!"

Fortunately, the Bachelors and Derek were already some way down the fairway concentrating on where their shots had landed. As we walked after them, Jimmy said, "Thank goodness we're not playing for money. You would be bankrupt by the 8th hole!"

BBC Seaside Special

The BBC asked me to appear in their Seaside Special radio series called 'On Stage Scarborough'. The stars were Jimmy Clitheroe and The Bachelors.

I still did my quota of Sunday concerts. I did a couple in Blackpool at the Opera House with Ken Dodd, Harry Secombe and Max Bygraves. Closer to home was a Holiday Camp called 'Collies Camp'. I should not really have done this as it was within my 25-mile limit barring clause in my contract. However, the agent (and owner of Flamingo Park) David Cook assured me he would keep it very quiet, and he paid me very well indeed.

Wendy and I fell in love with Scarborough, as did Tracey. We returned there many times on holidays. During boat rides in the lovely Peasholme Park, Tracey thrilled watching the battle-ships warfare, explosions and battles between ships and even airplanes zooming overhead dropping bombs on submarines. A trip on a pirate ship' to an island looking for treasure. Happy times on the beach and the fairground. Wendy's Mum and Dad visited us and we all went to Flamingo Park Zoo. We visited a great Steam Engine Rally and Fair in Pickering. Tracey had her first candyfloss and was not sure how to eat it. There seemed so much to do. I acquired a cine camera and filmed anything that moved.

I enjoyed getting up early on our caravan site and going for a walk with Jason. It was so quiet and peaceful and gave me quality 'thinking-time'. However, one morning, Jason slipped his lead. He had a mischievous streak in him and did not always come back when called. He was in the middle of the still quiet road, when a car came roaring round the bend and hit him sending him up in the air like a little toy. The driver did not even falter but kept on racing out of sight. I knelt by his side and cradled his head. He was still alive, but only just. I managed to carry him back to the site and met the owner. He had been a Squadron Leader in the war and did not speak much to any of his tenants.

However, this time he showed compassion.

"I'm very sorry, Mr. Adam," he said in a low voice, "but your dog is dead." I felt tears trickling down my cheeks. He put his hand on my shoulder and said, "You go and tell your family what's happened and give your dog to me. I'll bury him for you."

We all cried when I broke the news. We cried again when we looked at his little food bowl and realised I still had his lead in my hand. At the end of that week, the cast surprised us with a gift of a small, attractive, longhaired, black, cute dog. It was a Brier, which we named 'Dee-Dee'.

We briefly returned to Church Minshull and then on to Blackpool to work the Christmas season in the hotels. We stayed in Blackpool with friends of the Shipleys, Phyllis and her husband Arthur, both retired, and Phyllis' father lived in a roomy terraced house. We rented an upstairs lounge/kitchen and a double bedroom with a bed for Tracey.

Working in hotels was very hard and strange in many ways. The strangest were the small guesthouses. The landlady would introduce me and in I would walk in full stage dress and usually stood in front of the fireplace, playing my accordion. The audience sat on armchairs, dining chairs, sofas or on the floor. My performance only lasted 15 minutes before I dashed on to the next hotel. The onlookers were appreciative, lively audiences.

The agent, Norman Teal provided me with a list to work through. Most of them were on the front, North Shore then onto the South shore. I played at 12 hotels per night. The fee covering the whole arrangement was satisfactory. Working over the three or four days at Christmastime paid more than pantomime.

We spent a very happy Christmas at Phyllis and Arthur's house. Wendy's Mum and Dad came over from Scunthorpe to be with us. Tracey was mesmerised by all her presents from many people... and of course, Santa.

Meantime, Andy Stewart's manager, Jimmy Warren contacted me to offer me a tour in Canada and USA for 8 weeks with the White Heather Show starring the Alexander Brothers in the spring of 1968. Once again, the money was more than I had ever earned so far in show business. This reminded me that, one never knew who was in the audience and to always to do the absolute best every night.

The proud Dad shows off his daughter to Duggie Chapman & Myrna Rose. Mummy looks on.

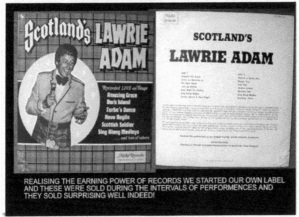

REALISING THE EARNING POWER OF RECORDS WE STARTED OUR OWN LABEL AND THESE WERE SOLD DURING THE INTERVALS OF PERFORMANCES AND THEY SOLD SURPRISING WELL INDEED!

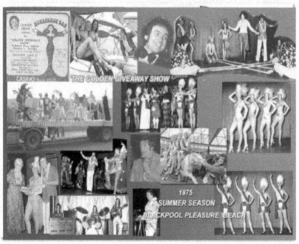

Twenty-Eight
Pastures New. The Carnegie Hall
New York USA

"Good morning Lawrie, my name is Eric Wright of Fosters Agency London. I wondered if you would be interested in being represented by our agency."

"Thank you for ringing Eric, I believe you also represent a very good friend of mine called Bryan Burdon," I replied.

"Why yes we do!" he said. "Bryan has been with us for some years and I think he would agree that we have done very well for him."

"From what I know of Bryan you certainly have," I said.

He continued, "Why don't you pop down and meet me and we can have a chat."

I phoned Bryan and he invited us to stay with him and Andy in their bungalow in south-west London. Andy was very taken with Tracey and made a big fuss of her.

Bryan noticed Dee-Dee our dog and said, "Bring your dog in too Lawrie." Andy did not seem too keen but Bryan insisted so in she came. Andy proudly showed us round their new home bequeathed to them by Bryan's mother. She finished telling us how much they had paid out for their expensive carpets, when Dee-Dee, who must have been a bit nervous of her new surroundings, went into a squat position and peed on the lovely carpet. All went quiet for a few seconds, then Andy and Wendy burst into overdrive cleaning it up whilst I scolded the poor wee dog who slunk away into the hall head down and tail between her legs.

The phone rang, and Bryan shouted,

"Lawrie get that for me, will you?" There was no furniture at all in the square shaped hall and the phone was on the floor. I squatted down and it was Eric for me requesting a time to meet. I hung up. In horror, I noticed that by my right elbow was in a liquid pool of dog-poo about 5 inches in diameter. There was a stiff brown A5 envelope on the floor. Tearing off the flap, I managed to scoop the poo into the envelope.

Eric telephoned back to speak to Bryan. I handed him the phone as I attempted to get back on my feet. Bryan said excitedly,

"That's Great Eric, hang on I'll write that down." He glanced around and said, "Lawrie pass me that envelope, will you?"

"I'll get you some paper."

"Lawrie, stop messing about and give me that bloody envelope, will you?"

Reluctantly I passed it into his hands. Placing it on the floor, he started to write and as he pressed, the smelly brown substance started to ooze out.

"Oh! My God!" he exclaimed. "Eric I'm afraid I'm going to have to call you back, something has happened here...I'm in the middle of a disaster!"

Mortified, I could only apologies to my friend most profusely. He looked at the scene then burst out laughing, put his arm round my shoulder then said in a low tone between convulsed stifled giggles,

"Go and keep Andy busy while I clean this lot up mate." What a forgiving pal Bryan was.

Later that evening we had been watching some home-movies of our escapades in Paignton. Bryan had his cigarettes and lighter between our armchairs. He reached down to get them, curled his fingers under the packet then looked up at me and motioned with his head for me to look down. As his fingers pressed into the carpet, they created bubbles of liquid. Dee-Dee had struck again!

I met up with Eric Wright in quite a classy restaurant for lunch. When he visited Bryan at Paignton, he said he was very impressed with my act. Because placing artistes was becoming increasingly difficult, he offered a trial year. He had spoken of me to a Light Entertainment Producer at the BBC who seemed interested and accepted some photographs of me. Eric had arranged for me to play for him tomorrow at 11 am.

Inside the BBC, I was shown into a modest sized rehearsal room with a grand piano. A few minutes later a charming elderly, distinguished looking man walked in, who instantly reminded me of my old drapery boss Mr. Given, same dark navy suite, grey hair. He shook hands and thanked me for coming in to see him. A few minutes later, a tall thin man nodded and smiled as he joined us and took his seat at the piano. I gave him some music. I played the 'Carnival of Venice' then a Jazzy number called Nola, followed by the Petite Waltz. The producer picked up the telephone.

"Right, Lawrie," he said, "I've fixed for you to appear in the Rolf Harris show. He will want to play something with you. He also plays accordion but of course, not in your league." He walked towards the door saying, "Follow me. Let me introduce you to our producer, Ernest Maxim who is at this moment in the studio doing 'International Cabaret'." Goodness me, I had seen this show. It was very professional and compered by the Carry-On film star Kenneth Williams.

We entered a very large studio and watched a hive of activity. Ernest Maxim was perched high up on a crane, beside the camera operator. They had finished filming the Beverley Sisters.

My contact shouted to Ernest, "Please come and meet one of your guests Ernest, he will be excellent in one of the shows."

"Oh dear! Frank, I am right in the thick of this at present. If you think he is ok, then that's good enough for me."

Unbelievable, I was going to be on two big BBC star TV shows. This could make me. Wait until I tell Wendy this. I shook hands with the producer as he said with a broad smile, "I'll be in touch with your agent Lawrie, and we will get all this in a contract to you."

I hurried back to Bryan and Andy's house to tell them the good news.

Two days past and I heard nothing from Eric. Bryan suggested I ring him up, which I did only to hear,

"Oh dear! Lawrie, have you not heard? Frank died, it was very sudden."

"I'm very sorry to hear that Eric. Does that mean the work he mentioned no longer exists?"

"I'm afraid so chum. Whoever succeeds Frank will have their own ideas and their own artistes as well. Line dead I am afraid. However, I do have a month's work for you up north. It is in working men's clubs in the Sheffield area. Do you want it?"

I still had two mouths to feed and bills to pay so had no alternative but to say yes. In addition, he gave me some good nightclub dates. One was in a club called 'Tito's' in Cardiff with Matt Munroe as the star. We parked our caravan nearby. I presented myself at the club for rehearsal. I did my opening with the band, and then onto a new number I had put in called 'Zorba the Greek' going into 'Hava Nagila'. The rhythm got the audience clapping in time to the music getting faster to the big finale.

When I finished a tall well-built man stepped forward to the stage, which stood about 3 feet high.

"Well played, but you cannot play that."

"Why ever not?" I replied.

"Because the star also features these in his act, and of course he has precedence that's why not, sir." Out of the darkened auditorium, another figure stepped forward. It was Matt Munroe.

"How do you do Lawrie? Listen, you play these very well, so you do them with my blessing," he said smiling. "My manager was just looking out for me."

Matt proved to be an absolute gent and we had a great week together.

He invited me into his dressing room after the first night. "Will you look at all this tat?" he said. The room was festooned with purple velvet and gold braiding and tassels. "It looks like a tart's boudoir. This was Shirley's doing (Shirley Bassey) she always insists on a change of décor." He asked me to join him every night and was very generous with the whisky. I could not resist telling him that we had met some years before. I explained about the Manchester agent's fiasco and that how I had been waiting for about an hour, then he turned up and was shown straight in, whilst I myself went straight out! He apologised most humbly, and I could see he really meant it.

After my act on the Saturday night during the applause, a package containing a bottle of fine expensive whisky was handed up on stage for me. The card read, "Enjoyed your company. Hope we work together again soon. Please accept this by way of an apology for Manchester. Matt."

More venues followed thanks to Eric: a very posh country club, called the Ashton Court, a smaller nightclub called the Palm Court and then a fabulous place called the Music Hall Tavern, all in Bristol. I visited these venues many times again in the future, but my preference was the Music Hall Tavern on the Downs. Terry, the booker and compere always made me very welcome, was an excellent host in his own shows, and the audiences he attracted were never less than fabulous with standing ovations every time.

‚The Ashton Court audiences who were paying huge prices for food and glossy service were very different. They tended to be on the stuffy side, well dressed with many women bedecked in lots of jewellery that rattled as they gave a polite well controlled round of applause. Steve Conway the compere/manager instructed the artistes not to enter the grounds until one hour before our appearance time. Not to venture front of house or mix in any way with the customers, and as soon as we were finished, we were required to leave the premises.

Bristol

Wendy and Tracey enjoyed Bristol. We were able to visit the city and surrounding towns during the day and our caravan not only saved us a lot of money, but Wendy was a great homemaker. She had a knack of creating homeliness. Our caravan was very cosy and comfortable. I loved getting home late from a show to find a home-cooked tasty meal waiting for me. My favourite on a Saturday night was a piping hot stew and crusty bread to dip in to it.

When I finished the last nightclub in Bristol, it was time for me to prepare to fly to Canada. This was the first time my family and I were parted. Six weeks was a long time and I knew I would miss them.

Canada

The cast met at the Prestwick airport, all in requested Highland Dress to show a profile as requested by the manager, Jimmy Warren. The stars, all household names in Scotland, were the Alexander Brothers, Tom and Jack, vocalist Colin Stuart, comedian Billy Rusk, singing duo Joe Gordon and Sally Logan (his wife) and soprano Rae Gordon. Considering Tom Alexander is an excellent accordionist himself, I was flattered to be billed as 'The Wizard of the Accordion'.

Jimmy stood up and made a short speech. "Please do remember that we are all ambassadors representing our lovely country. We expect exemplary behaviour from you, always. I hope you all enjoy your tour. Thank you." He sat down again to a smattering of applause and so commenced our 6-hour gruelling journey.

During the descent to Montreal airport, I became aware of a rumbling sound. An empty whisky bottle rolled merrily down the centre aisle passed our seat.

Jimmy placed his hands over his eyes and groaned, "Oh! My God, it has started already. I know who that will be, Lawrie. When we land, please support Colin and help to rush him across the tarmac and into the waiting limo. Billy will help you."

As the plane taxied to a halt, the doors opened, and two banners roll down from the balcony, a large cheering crowd all waving at us then a Pipe Band struck up, local radio station reporters rushed forwards pushing microphones in our faces.

One said, "Hi Lawrie, we have been playing your Scottish Dance Party Album all this week, welcome to Canada. Have you a few words for our listeners please?"

I garbled a few words as we continued to drag Colin who had an arm round each of our shoulders and his toes were scraping along the ground. He managed to join in with the pipes and drums singing Scotland the Brave all the way to the car.

I said to the reporter. "I'm sorry but he hates flying and he's not very well I'm afraid."

I could hear Jimmy behind us saying, "Hurry up lads, keep movin', quick as yi ken noo."

What an entrance! Canada here we come, your Ambassadors have arrived!

We were whisked away to a huge Park Sheraton Hotel in the city: grander than anywhere I had lived before. We had three days off to recover from jet lag. Getting used to the vastness of Canada took some doing. I asked the doorman where the main shopping street was in the city.

He said, "Right there in front of you, sir."

"Great I'll take a walk along it."

"Right along it, sir?" asked the doorman.

"Yes, will it take me long?"

"I don't think we'll be seeing you again today, sir, it's that long!"

As I started out I soon realised he was correct! I looked at the St. Lawrence River and was fascinated by the huge blocks of ice floating past. Although it was spring it was still very chilly, but it warmed up quite quickly.

In Britain, I had taken the simplest of things for granted such as holding a door open for someone following, or holding a door open for someone who had both hands engaged. Not in Canada! Carrying two heavy cases, I followed a man up some steps. As we reached the entrance, he looked over his shoulder but let the doors slam in my face. I remarked on his rudeness when I staggered through.

He replied, "What di' you think I am, the doorman?"

At the hotel reception desk, I enquired about any mail for me.

The young man glanced round at the pigeonholes and replied in a bored tone, "No."

At my first breakfast in the hotel, I took a seat, looked at the menu and realised that one had to go to the counter to place an order. Workers I presumed, all seated on barstools blocked off the counter were all eating the same type of food: a huge pile of pancakes, over which they poured copious amounts of dark coloured maple syrup from a jug. I was not surprised that the seat they were sitting on was invisible. It looked as if they were balancing on thick chrome poles protruding from their backsides! They all had a huge wobbly kite of a stomach hanging over their belts, but they looked happy enough. Approaching the counter, I asked for a boiled egg and some toast. The waitress gave a smile and said, "Comin' up, sir." I was handed a tall glass which was upside-down with a boiled egg nestling on top of it.

"No egg cups?"

All the customers laughed.

One man said, "Empty the contents of the egg into the glass, put in a knob of butter, salt and pepper, mix it all up. You'll love it."

I did and when I got home and showed it to Tracey, she demanded to have it served in that fashion ever after.

I was being paid such a high salary that I could easily afford to phone Wendy nearly every night. It was a delight to hear her voice. She was staying with her parents in Scunthorpe. I was thrilled to chat with little Tracey and looked forward eagerly to receiving letters from home.

When it was show time, we were ferried to the venues in limos. My heart sank when told we were playing in a gymnasium. However, it was not what I had imagined at all. It had a huge, stage, full theatre lighting and lush velvet tabs. Red plush velvet seating filled the auditorium and we played to a full house.

The show opened with a full Pipe Band and a large company of bedecked Highland Dancers. My spot was received enthusiastically and was over far too quickly.

After the show, we were ferried to a hotel reception where we were royally wined and dined. The first night was a novelty, but repeat evenings became a bit of a chore. I called them Polaroid Parties. As soon as we entered the room, we were asked to pose for photographs with nearly everyone who attended. It was flattering but eventually your mouth goes dry and your jaw starts to ache from grinning and smiling. Apart from that, we were all very hungry and some of the huge spreads called smorgasbord were so tempting, with chefs their knives at the ready to cut any type of meat you chose, which were all succulent. I have never ever seen such a lovely display of food before or since.

After a few weeks of eating like this, I started to balloon up. Jimmy said it was quite common and suggested I go on a diet of 'fillet steak baked potato and black coffee.' This I did and slowly it started to come off and my kilt sat more comfortably upon my waist again!

The tour went right across Canada and back across North America. The views were fantastic. I asked someone how long it would take us to fly across Canada. I was informed that it would take the same amount of time as it did to get from Scotland to Canada, 6 hours! I had a problem getting my head round the vastness of the country compared to little UK.

At 5.30 am one morning, we took a train through the Rockies. The train was wider than British trains and we had a cabin each. I marvelled at the very clever layout. Everything seemed to fold out of the walls, a table, comfortable armchair, and a bed. In the early hours, I woke up and pulled back the curtains. It was dawn and I spotted a wolf gazing at our train trundling past. I felt privileged to have seen it. I could not get back to sleep so decided to make my way to the observation car. This carriage was long with tables and chairs, food and drink served through 24 hours. The ceiling was a green coloured see-through glass or plastic material and the views were stunning. I had a coffee. I had never tasted coffee like the Canadian coffee. I did not mind having it black: I considered putting anything else in it would have spoiled that lovely taste. In England, it was instant coffee and did not compare. The fillet steaks were barbecued and were very tender and tasty.

It was a friendly company although no matter how much praise anyone received, or even glowing press notices, no compliments were ever given to anyone in the cast. This is the way of the Scots.

4 April 1968

There were unforgettable moments, such as the morning when I entered a hotel restaurant. Pausing at the top of the steps, I tried to spot some members of the cast and wondered at the noise. It was like a duck pond at feeding time. Canadian and American women seemed talk loudly and from the back of their throats. A male voice broke into the din.

"Ladies and gentlemen, this is a special announcement. Some hours ago, Doctor Martin Luther King was shot dead on his hotel balcony."

Jimmy Warren appeared behind me and whispered in my ear,

"Well that means we have the night off Lawrie, No Newark and no Detroit either."

"Why not?"

"There will be big riots." He answered.

After playing in many cities and towns, we finally ended up in New York. The highlight was playing in the famous Carnegie Hall. This venue is the American equivalent of our London Palladium. The stage was so huge that the stage manager said to me as I stood in the wings ready to enter,

"Now then Lawrie. Listen to this well. As soon as this act's applause starts, you must begin walking on the stage towards the centre."

I looked at him open-mouthed. "What? Surely not!"

"If you do not, you will find yourself having a very quiet walk all the way to the microphone. Be warned," he said.

I took his advice and thank goodness I did. What an experience to play to this huge audience. It seemed like a football stadium. The audience were fantastic, and my last show of the tour left me with a very satisfied feeling of triumph.

I could not wait to get home. The first thing that struck me was how tiny the cars seemed. Even mine seemed to have shrunk. My wife was waiting for me and my daughter and they looked beautiful. We had a very long cuddle.

Wigan

On my return, Eric my agent booked me into a night club near to home called the King of Clubs. In Wigan! What a comedown. I sat there at the side of the stage.

The compere joined me and said, "Hi Lawrie. How should I introduce you tonight?" He laughed and said, "Well, I never know what to expect. The artist last week was Derek Dene. He said he was on the London Palladium last week. Can you imagine that? I didn't believe him of course. So where were you last week?"

I smiled and replied, "I don't think you are going to believe me either. You see, I was appearing in New York at the famous Carnegie Hall."

Twenty-Nine
The Saga of the Yellow Bath

It was a depressing caravan park on the outskirts of Rotherham and I was not looking forward to doing the 'working men's' clubs in the Sheffield/Doncaster area as I had heard bad reports from various artistes. However, my agent had nothing else to offer and bills had to be paid. Therein lies the difference between the amateur who is free to accept or refuse work, and a professional who is beholden to perform even when feeling his/her talents are being wasted, whether out of financial necessity, or contractual obligation.

It gets worse. The amateur musician only plays music he or she likes personally. The professional cannot afford such luxury but must also please the crowd. In a way, I often consider the professional has to prostitute his talents at times.

One miserable drizzly afternoon when everything looked grey, a knock on the door by a fellow-Scot called Roddy McNeil, heralded an unexpected change in my career. I knew of Roddy, who also worked for Hedley Claxton as a vocalist. Over a cup of tea, he said he had progressed to Entertainment Director on a cruise ship. Roddy told us a couple of funny Scottish jokes. His parting gift was his LP album. Little did I realise how life changing his jokes would prove to be.

I started to pack various things ready to depart for my first club. Wendy opened the caravan door and shouted, "Don't forget to leave me the 'yellow baby bath darling." Obviously, my mind was not entirely on what I was doing. When I arrived at the club, I realised that due to the baby bath episode, I had forgotten to pack my highland costumes. All I had was what I was wearing! I surveyed myself in the cracked dirty mirror. I look a right sight, I thought. A red hand-knitted cardigan, a bit stained and baggy. A pair of baggy checked trousers and suede scuffed shoes. As if that was not bad enough, the organist and drummer came into the tiny dressing room. The organist, an elderly looking grey-haired man wearing a shiny old dinner-suit, was walking carefully behind the drummer resting his left hand on his shoulder. The organist was blind, but I only had to tell him the key I was playing in and he would follow me. The drummer could not read music at all! I was not looking forward to this evening.

The musicians returned to the stage and started to play. They did not sound too bad. All at once, the door swung open. In walked a small stocky man sporting the badge on his lapel, 'Concert Secretary'.

He said, "Right young man, we expect four spots between the bingo games. They are a bit on the hard side here unless they take a liking to you. I will announce you. Right. Let's go."

As I played my opening number and noted the bored looking faces, I decided it might make up for my appearance if I told a joke. The only one I knew was the one Roddy had told some hours ago. Nothing to lose. I expected to be paid-off anyway. They all had long hard expressive faces. I stopped playing then went right into the joke. I was astounded when they all burst out laughing! I decided there and then to tell the only other one I knew after the next piece of music. It was unbelievable, they all laughed again! I received a very good round of applause!

I was still in shock when the concert secretary came bursting in immediately saying, "Hey lad, they didn't say you were a comic. That were reet grand, but they like it a bit spicier than that."

I quickly replied, "Give me an example."

He gave me another four gags that I immediately committed to memory. Next spot, I repeated his gags. As the audience roared with laughter I could hear the con-sec at the back of the room slapping his thigh and exclaiming proudly, "Eee! Ah' told 'im that one ye know."

He repeated this after every joke.

Following me into the dressing room after each spot, he recounted his best jokes and patting me on the back after each spot. I duly repeated them with great success. I was a star!

Never having realised I could make an audience laugh, I was smitten by the wonderful feeling of causing such happiness. I would have to repeat it. Moreover, I did it for the remainder of my show business career. Life is a learning curve.

Next morning, I telephoned a local agent called Sonny Fagin to find out where the other venues were for the week. To my astonishment he said, "Lawrie moy boy! Your agent did not sell you to me as a comedian! You are the only act sent to me so far that received raving reports. Normally the audiences are as hard as nails. He paid off all his acts after their first spot. Well done. You are now top of the bill and I am placing some other acts with you for the rest of your tour. Next time ring me direct and we'll work out a better deal for you."

When I told Wendy she said, "Well, thank goodness I shouted, 'The Yellow Bath!' Now it seems you are a comedian."

I realised I desperately needed more jokes. I listened to anything funny, any radio show with a comic in it, scribbled down anything relevant, and started to build up comedy routines. Later, I bought a set of bagpipes. They proved be a good entrance feature retaining the accordion as a standby. Nothing is wasted in a life I realised. The bagpipe lessons I had as a young boy had come in handy at last.

Plymouth

I had an engagement at the Bird-Cage Night Club in Plymouth for an agent called Ronnie Potter. I was at the bar getting myself a drink when all of a sudden, the doors burst open and in walked what looked like the whole of Her Majesty's Fleet. There were sailors everywhere. The bar man said, "Bloody hell, looks like the Ark Royal has docked again!"

A portly woman called Kinky Katrina was on the same bill. The spotlight hit the stage, the band started to play (Ronnie Potter who was also the organist) the tune 'On the Good Ship Lollypop' into the spotlight danced Kinky dressed as a little schoolgirl with blond pigtails and holding an enormous lollypop.

A great appreciative shout went up from the navy who obviously knew her. As she danced around the floor, she cast off bits of clothing to cheers and shouts, belting out this famous Shirley Temple song. The audience joyfully joined in the singing. She ended up stark naked! A mountain of wobbly pink flesh. She nearly put me off my pork scratchings!

If only my mother could see me now!

I was on next and felt apprehensive facing this large loud boisterous audience but to my amazement, they liked what I did and laughed at my jokes.

A single record

I fancied a try at a single record. As Ronnie and I had hit it off, I asked him if he could tape some specific numbers in my act: I already had an album but there was minimum profit by the time I paid for them to come from the USA. Ronnie agreed and presented me with a tape. I had enough contacts to get 250 singles printed.

I called my label Globe Records. I designed and made the sleeve myself. I put 'Dark Island' on the A-side and a bagpipe medley on the B-side. It was an experiment to test the market.

The result was that the sale of my records during the interval, made more money than I was receiving as a salary! I must have been one of the first artistes to sell their own records direct to the public.

One evening I was appearing at the large British Legion Club in Slough where Adelaide Hall the singing star topped the bill. She had been famous, before my time. The club was packed, and I announced I would be selling my latest record during the interval. I was astounded to go on stage and to be find a queue right up the aisle to the back wall.

As my last customer paid me, he handed me his business card.

"Hi Lawrie, remember me?"

I gasped, "Well! John Keam from Scarborough." I looked at his card and asked, "What is this Triosk Enterprises', John, on Shaftesbury Avenue London?"

"Come and see me on Monday 11 am. I have a great idea you will love." With that, he disappeared into the crowd. Again...you just never know who is watching you.

Triosk Enterprises

On entering a suite of offices on the second floor marked Triosk Enterprises. A young receptionist looked up and greeted me with "Good morning, can I help you?"

I gave her my name and said I had an appointment with the MD John Keam. She buzzed him on her intercom and I heard him say,

"I'll come down." Seconds later there he was looking very smart in a dark grey suit. He was very thin, shorter than I am and had a high-pitched squeaky voice and his hair always looked as if it could do with a good wash. He certainly looked more assertive than when I remembered him at Scarborough.

Coffee and deluxe biscuits were served. His company was engaged in the production of west end shows. He told me how bowled over he was with my act and that I was raking in the money selling my record. He said his company were interested in making me a director of their 'Artistes Recording Department'.

"You must have loads of theatrical artiste's contacts Lawrie, offer them the same deal as you have worked out for yourself, of having their own record to sell direct to their audience. They will buy them from us, and then sell them themselves. Work out the costs, to include a profit margin to suit yourself and us. You take care of the disc and we will take care of the glossy professional sleeve. Are you interested?"

I agreed. He said, "Right, let me show you your office." He showed me a small office looking out on busy Shaftesbury Avenue, and opposite was the famous Globe Theatre.

"The young woman at reception will see to any typing or phoning for you."

I said, "John, I couldn't spend all my time here, I am still an artiste."

"Oh! I understand that Lawrie, come and go as you please. After all, if you are not out selling to your fellow artistes, there will be no records made."

We decided to start with small 45-rpm albums with a glossy picture on the front sleeve and biographical notes on the back sleeve, which I would write. First, I made one for myself but soon three other artistes became interested: a comedian/trumpet player Syd Francis, a top organist called Ron Woodall and a comedian called Steve Collins. All three were very pleased with their records and placed further orders.

Back in the office some weeks later, I had one of my gut feelings. During the staff's lunch hour, I nipped into the main office and went through the accounts where my training of old, via the Co-op, in bookkeeping, balance sheets, trade calculations and accounts came in handy. It came as a shock to realise the company was in financial trouble and I typed out my resignation immediately.

Some weeks later, the Receivers contacted me, informing me that as a director of Triosk Enterprises I was part liable for the company's debts. Mr. Keam had disappeared. I was able to inform them I had resigned prior to the Company's collapse. No case to answer! A narrow escape.

Me the Comedian

Now publicising myself as a comedian it dawned on me that I had to start a fresh career. The only management willing to engage me as a comedian with a summer season was a promoter called 'Bunny Barron Enterprises'. He offered me a season at The Sparrows Nest Theatre, Lowestoft, situated on the east coast, south of Great Yarmouth. The star was Reg Dixon. Reg who had been a huge star in his day. He was the first English artiste to have a hit record with a song called 'Confidentially'. He had also starred in some early black and white feature films.

It was a cosy little theatre and the show did well. The show was a similar standard to the Hedley Claxton Gaytime shows. We enjoyed our season there. Wendy was once again one of the dancers and the caravan life suited Tracey. Finding baby-sitters was a problem but we were usually very fortunate.

Hard times

After the season, we returned once more to our big caravan in Church Minshull. Being billed as a comedian instead of a musical act brought some drawbacks. Bookers were hesitant, and bookings became scarce. Matt McKenzie suggested we might like to team up and try a touring show round the Welsh clubs. We decided to call ourselves 'The Balmorals'. Wendy devised four dance routines, designed, and made the costumes for Matt's wife and herself to wear. I arranged the music and devised the simple programme.

It lasted for about 5 weeks and by the time we divided the cash it was not viable. In fact, we lived on the cheapest dish available, minced beef. I have not been a fan of it ever since! Poor Wendy had stuffed paper in her shoes to stop the rain coming in and her coat was frayed at the cuffs. Nelson Firth in Manchester invited me to appear in his summer show in the Planet Room Blackpool with the black piano star Chester Herriot. It was to be a simple variety show requiring me to perform one 20-minute spot per evening. The money was good, and as we were considering buying a house in Blackpool, it would mean cheaper living.

Thirty
1969 A House of Our Own

We were jolted awake by a loud thumping on our caravan door. I struggled to my feet alerted by revving engines, car doors slamming, dogs barking, shouting and swearing.

On opening the door, I was confronted by a young man who promptly thrust a leaflet into my hand.

"What's going on?" I asked.

"It's all in the leaflet!" he shouted as he hurried off towards the caravan next door.

I noticed blue Land rovers buzzing about. The scene reminded me of a Nazi war movie during a military invasion. Slowly I sat on the edge of the bed as Wendy stirred and rubbed her eyes, as did Tracey. The information in the leaflet quite shocked me. Our caravan site was now the property of Bluebird Caravans Ltd. We had a certain amount of days to consider either moving off the site or purchasing a new Bluebird caravan. I noted the prices and was astounded.

"This is blackmail!" I said.

This news was all we needed to give us the final push into buying a home of our own. We moved the caravan to a big holiday site called 'Ockwells' between Cleveleys and Fleetwood where we lived in it for a few weeks whilst viewing houses for sale in Blackpool.

Cash flow continued from entertainment work in and around the area. We decided to take a mortgage on a terraced house at 94 Manchester Road, in Blackpool. It was a great event to move in to a home of our own. It had no garden to speak off, two large lounges, a fair-sized kitchen, a bathroom and toilet plus three bedrooms.

We left the caravan at Ockwells and did a deal with them to place it on their Holiday Letting scheme. We had paid off the debt on it and so rent would be profit. We would review the situation at the end of that season.

Right away, we started to decorate the house from top to bottom. We had no furniture at all and so beds and other urgent requirements were our priority. We enjoyed choosing paint and wallpaper. We worked together well as a team.

Before long, there was a tap tap at the door and we welcomed in two folks from a few doors away. They introduced themselves as Stan and Ivy Leonards. They became close friends for as long as we lived there and beyond. Ivy was to live to the age of 107.

Rolly, the salesman in a second-hand store about a 10-minute walk from our house, who probably felt sorry for us, kept us aware of bargains. Wendy had a good eye for things and would often say to me, "Darling, Rolly has a lovely settee for us, come and see what you think." With his help, we furnished the whole house.

The time seemed to pass very quickly, mainly down to readying the house. We decided to have a go at enting out two rooms to theatricals during the summer to ring in some extra income.

Canadian/American Tour

Meantime, after negotiating the money I accepted to go on another Canadian/American Tour for Andy Stewart. When I left for Canada, my poor wife was left with the final furnishing and decorating.

I bought an affordable replacement accordion from Bells Accordions in London. They recommended I try an East German make called a 'Worldmaster'. It looked good in black and white mother of pearl, but unfortunately, it proved to be a disaster of a choice.

The company met in a small bar in Scotland. The star was a well-known Scottish recording artiste called Calum Kennedy. A soft-spoken highlander with a lilting voice who could speak and sing in Gaelic.

The comedian was a lovely man called Jack Millroy and wife Mary came with him. Jack had been a big star in Scotland, but at the height of his fame, decided to try his luck in England. The decision proved to be a bad one. When he returned to Scotland, he found it difficult to get work and never regained his original acclaim. Beware of pivotal decisions!

A charming man and wife, Joe Gordon and Sally Logan provided the vocals, while the excellent choice of Ken Haynes the pianist and Bobby Harvey, solo violinist completed the cast.

Unfortunately, in addition to my own act, Calum presumed I would play as part of the accompaniment to his act. Bobby Harvey agreed, but I did not. I had experience of doing this many years previously with the Robert Wilson White Heather Group and did not enjoy it at all. When he argued, I pointed out that this was not part of my contract and if he insisted, I would require quite a hefty fee. He refused to pay a fee. Sadly, for the remainder of the tour he was not over friendly.

I sympathised with Bobby, as he had no choice because Calum would be able to offer him more work. In Scotland, work is scarce, and most artistes end up doing what they are told and agreeing to smaller fees. Thankfully, I had established myself in England. No Scottish management would bully me or dictate what I was paid. I liked the power of negotiation and seemed to be good at it.

The show route and the venues were the same as previous years. I felt on familiar ground, but the new accordion was niggling me. The basses were giving me trouble by sometimes sticking producing a sound like the drone of a bagpipe. My letters of complaint to Forbes generated no response despite making it clear that I would be returning it to them as soon as I arrived in England.

Bobby was just as elated and thrilled to see the sites in Canada as I had been the year before. We had a lunch in a high-tower restaurant, visited Totem-Pole parks and other points of interest. We went up the Empire State Building one sunny morning and it was a great thrill.

One day I had a pleasant surprise. I mentioned to Jimmy Warren the tour manager, my interest in boxing and that I had been involved in the sport as a teenager. I was delighted to find that some of the cast had booked a table in Jack Dempsey's Restaurant in New York. I was gazing in rapture at the huge oil painting of 'Dempsey's World Champion Fight' when I heard a voice saying, "So where are these guys from Scatland?" Jimmy tapped my arm and motioned to the very tall tanned man in an immaculate deep blue suit standing by our table. "Which one is Lawrie Adam?"

"That'll be me," I said. He stuck a huge hand out and said, "Hi there Lawrie, very pleased to meet you. I'm Jack Dempsey."

I was lost for words.

He continued, "I am told you have a pretty little wife and small daughter at home?"

"Why yes, that's quite correct."

"Okay, why don't you give me their address and I'll send them a box containing my famous strawberry cheesecake." I did and cheekily grabbed a menu, which had a copy of the wall mural on the front.

"Jack, I have always been a big fan of yours, would you sign this for me please. No one will believe me when I say I met and spoke with you."

"I certainly will, Lawrie. It's been a real pleasure meeting you."

We shook hands again. When we came to pay the bill the waitress said, "Mr. Dempsey said there is no charge, he loves the Scots folk."

I have treasured that menu ever since.

A week later when I phoned Wendy, she said she had received a huge box of delicious strawberry cheesecake form Jack Dempsey in New York.

One day Ken said to Bobby and me, "It's my birthday tomorrow. I'd like to treat you to an outing tomorrow evening." The first treat was to a cinema to see the launch of Funny Girl starring Barbra Streisand. From there we arrived at a plush cabaret room and had a super meal. The curtains swept back to reveal a large semi-circular stage with feathered dancers on it. After their routine, the stage moved round, and a grand piano came into view. Seated at it was a man called Carmen Cavallaro a big musician star known as the 'Poet of the Piano'. Cavallaro's single best-selling recording was his pop version of Chopin's Polonaise. He was awarded a Star on the Hollywood Walk of Fame at 6301 Hollywood Boulevard in Hollywood. What a truly magical evening. He received standing ovations after every piece.

Soon, it was our turn to face a huge audience at 881 7th Avenue, New York. Steel magnate Andrew Carnegie founded the Carnegie Hall more than a century ago. It continues to draw crowds in droves for classical and contemporary music by the age's greatest musical artists. During my visit the year before, I was overawed by the experience. However, the second time round I was more observant of my surroundings.

As I walked in through the stage door, I was aware of all the large life-sized coloured photographs hanging from the walls on either side. Looking down on me were such stars as Frank Sinatra, Danny Kay, Bob Hope, Bing Crosby, Judy Garland and many more, as if saying, "This place is real special, you had better be the best, yi' here?" To have the honour of playing the Carnegie Hall is a tremendous experience and one that I will never forget, and for a very special reason.

About half an hour before I was due to go on the bases on my new accordion decided to jam! I am not the type who panics, but I must have come near to it then. One hundred and twenty bases sounding like one hundred and twenty cats in pain!

I had the accordion all opened and managed to get the bent 'cheap' East German rods back to where they should be. I made frantic phone calls all over New York to no avail. Ken suggested I place the accordion keyboard grill close to the microphone and concentrate on that whilst he plays heavier on the grand piano bass-notes. "You're a pro, you'll do it," he said with as final pat on my shoulder.

It was like walking on to a football stadium. Approximately 3000 cheering Scottish immigrants clapping and waving. As I started to play, they went wild at the sound of Scottish accordion music. I concentrated hard on the right hand and could hear Ken belting out with his left hand on the piano. I completed my spot, the final one of the tour triumphant. As I walked off, I noticed Ken giving me a grin and a quick thumbs-up.

Gloucester

No sooner was I home than I was down to Gloucester for a week's booking in a nightclub.

Wendy and Tracey came with me. It was lovely to be with my family and I was never parted from them for such a long time ever again.

Wendy had worked hard getting our house completed and had made it very homely. Already theatricals had booked in for the summer season. A soprano from the John Hanson Show at the Winter Gardens, my colleagues from the Canadian tour, Joe and Sally Logan who were appearing on the Central Pier and an old friend called Neil Phelps from our Hedley Claxton days in Paignton who was appearing with Arthur Askey at the Opera House. Their rooms were all self-contained with small cookers and dining facilities etc. The bathroom, however, had to be shared by all.

During a bit of free time, I decided to improve the bath and toilet by giving them a coat of paint, newly invented especially for bathrooms. We chose a turquoise shade. Soon, I was admiring my handiwork as Wendy and Tracey gave their approval.

Our guests arrived: first Joe and Sally followed soon after by Marion the soprano and settled in to their rooms. The front lounge became Neil Phelps' bedroom. We had decided that we could easily cope in the main lounge adjoining the kitchen.

Stan, our neighbour, helped me to fix a drop-down bed in our lounge. Stan was a small chap with a ready grin and a quick humorous quip. When it was all done he stood holding it and said, "Right my son, time for testing, chocks-away!" I removed the bolt.

It was heavier than we had calculated. It fell on top of him! He was unharmed, and we made adjustments punctuated by fits of laughter at the comic situation.

That night as we were having tea, there was a gentle tap on our lounge door. I opened it to find Joe in his dressing gown. He said, in a very calm low voice, "Sorry to disturb you Lawrie, but if you go into the bathroom you will find two white circles in the bath where your paint came off. If you are wondering where they are, they are sticking to my arse. I am going to get Sally to remove them for me." With that, he quietly walked back upstairs.

Almost immediately, we heard a blood-curdling scream coming from upstairs. Wendy and I rushed upstairs to witness Marion dashing out of the bathroom looking very shocked. "Oh! My God, it was awful!

I sat in the bath and it all seemed to rise up and cover me. It was like a horror movie! "A sort of turquoise plastic is clinging to me." She ran into her room.

"So much for the latest inventions!" I thought to myself.

The summer season at the Planet Room within the Winter Gardens complex was a very pleasant show. Instead of hanging about waiting for big finale walk-downs, I was free to go home after I had finished my last appearance. Apart from my pal Syd Francis, I was never involved with any of the other artistes. The star Chester Harriet kept to himself and did not mix. There were no after show parties. It felt strange for a summer season. I was forbidden to sell any of my records. I was not going to be repeating it. The good thing about it was I was with my family at home.

A man approached me from a company called Livingstone Organs. They were a big London based company who made and installed church and theatre organs. They were marketing a brand-new instrument called the Tubon and wondered if I would be willing to feature it in my act. He provided me with one. It is a Swedish built bass-synthesizer invented by Joh Mustad AB in Gothenburg. It was approximately 3 feet long, cylinder shaped with about an octave and a half-piano keyboard, about 6 inches in diameter and looked quite smart in black and chrome. Worn like a guitar, it hung around the neck. I was not impressed by the bass rasping sounds. However, I could imagine Wendy featuring it in my act and playing a simple counter melody. When we had a photograph, he intended featuring us in the Company magazine.

Wendy practised hard and was able to perform some music on it. She certainly looked good, but the instrument was never going to be popular. In addition, it proved very unreliable. After a round of nightclubs in the Bristol area, we decided to dump it. I have never heard of it since. I did not realize it at the time, but this was the world's very first synthesiser keyboard.

The main thing about having a season in Blackpool was the timing. Wendy was pregnant and wanted to have our second baby at home. We had a midwife, Mrs. Patton, who called regularly and kept a careful eye on her. She was a small tubby woman, always ready for a laugh and very agreeable.

The famous Blackpool Illuminations pulled in the crowds as usual. The summer seasons in the town were enjoying an extension. The Winter Gardens show finished first.

Our tenants were ready to say goodbye to us. Marion, who occupied the front flat, had forgiven me for the 'bath-paint episode'. Joe and Sally were in their final weeks at the Central Pier. We still had Neil in the front room who had become part of the family.

Having finished at the Planet room, I was busy doing one-nighters. I did not want to leave Wendy with the baby due any time. The extra cash from our lodgers had come in very handy and we planned to do it again next year. However, we decided to sell the caravan at Ockwells at the end of the season, despite the revenue from holiday lettings. It was sad to visit the site now and see the deterioration in what our first home had been.

On Sunday 12 October, we sat down to a lovely chicken roast dinner in our kitchen with Neil and his friend Roy. I was about to plunge my knife into a steaming plump chicken, when Wendy looked up and exclaimed, "Oh Dear! My waters have broken."

As one, we rose to our feet panicking but as an afterthought, she said calmly,

"Sit down everybody, there's no way I stood cooking all this and then not eating it." We did.

Then it was all hands-on deck. The midwife barked instructions down the telephone and requested we keep her involved in any changes. I had a show booked at a place called Trentham Gardens that evening, an hour's drive away and was getting increasingly anxious about whether to cancel it or not. Wendy kept saying, "It's okay, you go. I'll be fine."

I waited as long as I dared then decided to phone the agent, an ungenerous, unforgiving sort of man called Ronnie Cryer. He ranted and raved, tried blackmail and threats then ended by saying, "Well, Lawrie, I can tell you that you will never ever work for me again." He slammed the phone down. He was wrong, I did but I made sure it cost him! Bad attitudes rarely pay off.

Neil arrived back from his show and said, "Any news?"

I shook my head, "All quiet, you may as well go to bed."

At midnight, Wendy said she had a craving for a bowl of chips that were duly delivered and scoffed.

The drop-down bed was down in the lounge and the house was in a state of quiet slumber. Wendy was lying on the bed, with me kneeling by her side holding her hand as she was experiencing labour pains. She said she wanted me to be there at the birth. The midwife, Mrs. Patton, was hovering around and offering words of encouragement.

Things began to look lively. Wendy was squeezing my hard so hard I could feel tears in my eyes. The midwife glared at me and barked, "What the hell are you groaning at? It's Wendy that's in labour here!"

At precisely 4.25 am on Monday 13 November, I witnessed a miracle. Our little baby daughter was born. There she was all seven pounds of her. I could not take my eyes off her. She had blue eyes, fair hair and was beautiful. I gazed in sheer wonder at her dainty little pink hands, fingers and toes. I felt incredibly proud but at the same time, very humble. Like her sister before her, she grabbed my little finger in her hand and held on surprisingly tight. I felt a tear come to my eyes. What an unforgettable feeling of love. We decided to call her Fiona.

The following morning, Neil came in and said, "Well, I've had some weird digs in my time, but never before did I lie in bed listening to the landlady giving birth in the room next door." Neil and his friend Roy were marvellous helping with cooking and other jobs. We were sad to see them go back to London leaving us to get on with being a family of four. Tracey was thrilled to bits with her new little sister.

I drove down to Eastbourne to appear in a show with Reg Dixon at the Hippodrome Theatre in Eastbourne for a week's variety. It was one of the few remaining grand old theatres still struggling to present variety shows to a diminishing public torn between dressing up and turning out to see a live show or settling down in front of the television. Although the audience responded warmly to Reg and sang along with his former hit 'Confidentially' sadly, it looked like TV was winning the battle for bums on seats.

The following week I was in Birmingham with a star I had long since admired. I first saw him some years back when the cast from our show in a place called Horsham, received an invitation to visit his show. I was indifferent to the show but when he came on, I was in hysterics. He was quite elderly, and his name was Sandy Powell, his catchphrase was 'Can you hear me mother?' Sandy had been a big star of stage, screen and radio. Like Reg Dixon featured in comic strips. His ventriloquist act and his ham magician act were both outstanding. His comedy timing was perfect.

Sandy and his wife were a charming couple and I was sad I did not manage to spend more time in their company. Sandy, like many others was beginning to realise that his generation had all but disappeared and the end was near.

We sat in the tiny dressing room and chatted about the current sad state of our profession. Sandy was not angry or bitter, only sad. He complimented me on my accordion skill and liked my comedy. He said there would be a job for me if I wished on the pier at Eastbourne where he still held a financial interest.

Sadly, our show only lasted three nights before being axed due to the sparsity of audiences. This was the start of a pattern.

He remarked, in his husky voice "I really cannot complain Lawrie. I've had a great run in this business. I've made plenty of money out of it, had tremendous enjoyment, met some lovely people and made some great friends along the way."

I counted it a great honour and a privilege to have spent time with Sandy and his wife and to share a bill with them, even though it was only for a brief time.

On my return home, I was thrilled to be greeted by my enlarged family. There is nothing more pleasurable in the world than to be hugged and loved by your own little family. Even our new baby waved her little pink arms, made gurgling noises and beamed a huge grin at me, which I definitely took as a warm loving greeting saying, "Hi there Dad, glad your home."

After appearing at the big ABC Theatre in Blackpool in 'The Club Acts of the Year', I received an award, Club Act of the Year. An honour to end the year.

Thirty-One
1970 An Increase in Tempo

Realising that our small touring caravan was not going to be big enough for the four of us, we bought the maximum size allowable for touring behind a car.

Unfortunately, my lovely white Mk 2 Jaguar was not going to be powerful enough to pull a fully loaded 18-foot-long Pemberton caravan.

We pushed the boat out and bought an Mk 10 Jaguar. Large cars were available quite cheaply, but the running costs were high to say nothing of repairs. The high mileage demanded a powerful engine. It paid to buy a class car, keep it for two years, and then replace it.

Tracey sat in the back, exclaiming, "Look dad, it even has little drop down tables. I feel like a princess in this car, I love it." They do have a rich aroma about them. It could be the leather upholstery like sitting in a luxurious armchair, or the walnut trim. It was fully automatic and a joy to drive.

We met up with an old pal of mine called Dorothy Holgate who married a Mecca Ballroom manager called Mike Bessie. They lived in Blackpool.

They asked why we had no dog. We explained that we had to find a home for our last dog Dee-Dee. One day they turned up unexpectedly and presented us with a beautiful Alsatian pup from their litter. We named him Jason. The kids were delighted

I enjoyed going for walks with young Tracey to a park close by where she tried to race the dog. Even at that young age, she had focus and always aimed to win. She squealed and laughed as the dog overtook her, executed a quick turn and tripped her up. She ended up in a heap with Jason licking her face.

We introduced her to a Play School run by the Salvation Army in Blackpool, where she had no trouble mixing with the other kids. She was a very perky and bright young thing and easy to love. I treasured it when she took my hand and trotted alongside me.

Wendy's parents, Syd and Freda, were frequent visitors to our house. Now that Syd was retired, they enjoyed spending countless hours with our children.

After the Canadian tour, I continued to complain to the Bell Accordion company and eventually managed a part exchange of accordions. For my next accordion, I decided to spend £400, a small fortune then for a top of the range, hand built Honer Morrino. It was especially musette-tuned to my personal requirements.

The pay as a comedian was more than as a solo accordionist, and it was now not necessary to practise six hours a day. The audience appreciated the accordion, but it became a stand-by rather than a main feature. Is not it typical in life, to be able to obtain things you could have done with earlier?

BBC Radio offered me another show called Take a Bow compered by Bill Gates. Bill was famous for his wartime Workers Playtime broadcasts. The recording took place with a live audience in the Paris Theatre, Lower Regent St. London.

I topped the bills in many cabaret and country clubs up and down the country. Whilst in Plymouth, I made a life-long friend of a fellow comic called Jack Seaton from London. Jack would sit out front when we worked together and make critical notes about my performance and comedy timing but was also very encouraging.

Plymouth agent and musician Ronnie Potter suggested I record a long play album with a live audience at the Forum in the city. The finished album in its colourful red tartan sleeve, entitled Scotland's Lawrie Adam, sold extremely well during the shows. Wendy and I called our label Alpha Records.

A set of bagpipes seemed like a good idea at the beginning of my act and proved a great way to grab attention and work in some visual comedy.

Producer Bunny Barron, offered a summer season at the Knightstone Theatre, Weston-Super-Mare starring Tony Mercer from TV's very popular 'Black and White Minstrel' show. I was booked as second comedian.

The Mk 10 Jaguar pulled the caravan with ease. Wendy, myself, Tracey and Fiona not forgetting Jason the Alsatian eventually turned down a lane heading for the site we had booked. We went over a little hump-back bridge and a few seconds later, Tracey exclaimed, "Daddy, there's a caravan like ours overtaking us!"

I glanced to my right and sure enough, there it was. "Oh my God!" I said, "It is ours!"

It seemed to run along the side of us for ages. I could do nothing but stare at it in disbelief. Eventually it ploughed into the ditch. We got out and examined the damage. We were very fortunate. The jockey wheel had snapped off. Other than that, not even a scratch. I had prepared myself for a write-off. It had bounced off the towing-ball after the bridge. People were very kind and helped us to get it back on the car and we went on our way.

The site was a disappointment, a field with no paths or roads or lighting. However, within a few minutes, the caravan was parked, and Wendy busied herself turning it into the cosy little nest we called home. Food was cooked and eaten. We were all very tired, so it was an early night for us all.

The next morning, we made our way to the theatre to start two weeks rehearsals. It was a very easy show consisting of one show per night at 8pm and two shows on Saturday with no programme changes. In addition to my act, I took part in some sketches and musical scenes. Wendy was one of the dancers. The cast were very friendly.

We brought the kids into the theatre with us until we arranged baby-sitters. It was a stress on Wendy. Dealing with the kids, cooking, feeding, washing and dancing. My job was to collect the baby-sitter then deliver her back to her home again afterwards. During the day, we were able to get out and enjoy the town. Tracey and Fiona loved many of the attractions, especially the model village. They played well together, and Tracey was very loving towards her little sister.

There were still Sunday concerts on offer but as usual, they were miles away from Weston. We did some at the Blackpool Opera House with Dora Bryan, Derek Nimmo and Donald Peers. My mother loved to listen to The Donald Peers radio show and hum along to his big hit 'By a Babbling Brook.' He was flattered when I told him. We also did a couple of concerts at Hastings with the comedian Ted Rogers who had a successful TV show running called Three-Two-One and Impressionist Margo Henderson who did a brilliant Margaret Thatcher.

At the end of the season, Bunny Barron offered me the summer season at Felixstowe, the following year. I accepted. He said, "Well, in that case Lawrie, I'll also offer you a pantomime at the White Rock Pavilion Theatre in Hasting this Christmas. I would like you to play the main starring comedy role of Simple Simon." Again, I agreed.

When we returned to Blackpool, I contacted Jimmy Clitheroe and asked him if he would allow me to store my caravan at his hotel in Knott End. He agreed on condition that I did a cabaret spot free. Thus, was done and indeed Wendy and I spent many happy times in Jimmy's company at his hotel.

On one occasion in the bar when all the customers had gone, leaving only the staff, he said, "Lawrie, I heard you used to be a magician?"

"Yes, I still am Jimmy but only at children's parties for fun," I said.

He looked serious then added, "But I also heard on good authority that you can actually read palms with startling effect?"

"Where did you hear that?"

"From a singer you worked with, in a pantomime in Richmond."

"I remember that instance very well," I said. "We were in a bar after the show when Jean Barrington asked if I could read the palm of a friend of hers. I said, well okay Jean, but only for a laugh. I used to watch my mother do it and she did teacup-readings for the neighbours. Mum told me her Dad, who was Irish, taught her and told her she also had the gift.

Jean's friend placed her hand in mine and I started to utter a stream of information, from where it came, I do not know. I told her she was worried about her husband leaving her and that contrary to her hopes he would not be coming back. That there had been a young road-death, her son in fact, and this was the cause of the gulf between them." She burst into tears and ran out of the room. Everyone had his or her mouth hanging open.

Jean said, "Goodness me Lawrie, that was astounding. How could you possibly know?" I didn't. No one was more surprised than I was."

Jimmy's hotel staff all crowded round me and would not take 'no' for an answer.

I took hold of the hotel manager's hand first. A lovely chubby cheery man called Tommy Trafford. I informed him that he had a yearning to go on the stage as a comedian. (I did not know this). That he would indeed do this, in fact would top bills, and even have a hand in putting on his own shows. Tommy positively beamed at me and said, "I knew it."

The next hand pushed into mine belonged to Derek, the hotel barman. A pleasant very quiet shy type of lad, in his twenties.

I said, "Oh dear! You have a violent temper that can become uncontrollable. You will really have to watch that, or it will get you into very serious trouble."

Jimmy said, "You have that one wrong Lawrie. Derek wouldn't say 'Boo' to a goose!"

Jimmy's secretary, Sally, said, "Right move over Derek, I'm next."

I took Sally's hand and said, "Sally, one day you will be too inquisitive for your own good and you will seriously regret it." The others made a few comments,

"Take extra care in your car." I gave her a long look and did not get a good feeling about her at all.

"Heck, is that it?" she said.

"Yes Sally, I'm done."

I said, "Right, I am now finished, no more."

Jimmy piped up, "Hey! What about me?" I did not want to read Jimmy's hand and refused point blank.

Sometime after this, I learned that most of what I had prophesied that night came true. I was more amazed than anyone else was. Tommy gave up his hotel job up to top the bill in a big pantomime in Southport as comedy dame. He was such a success that he was booked for the following year. He collaborated with a colleague called Ronnie Parnell.

They formed a production company and put shows on themselves. They did this until Tommy's death some years later.

One evening, I was informed, Derek had a disagreement with a customer in the bar. He lost control and leapt over the bar. But for the intervention of other customers, he could have found himself on a murder charge. They found it nearly impossible to haul him off the customer.

Sally, I was very sad to hear, had steamed open Jimmy's will. Consequently, he sacked her. In tears, as she jumped into her small car heading for her parents' home in Leeds. Sally never arrived home that night. She suffered a fatal collision with a large truck.

Regarding Jimmy, that is another sad tale, which I will reveal later in this story. However, I have never read palms since and do not intend to. I do have visions however of happenings that come true. I also catch a look sometimes in a person and can surmise their ending. I can offer no explanation that makes any sense.

It was a very cold morning when we all piled into our car headed for Hastings where I was to appear in pantomime in my first principal role of Simple Simon in Puss in Boots. We decided to book a flat and not take the caravan as the forecast was for a white Christmas.

It was another long trip accompanied by two little voices, this time in unison, repeatedly asking, "Are we nearly there?" Eventually we were.

Hastings by the sea was typical of any resort out of season, cold, wet, windy and uninviting. We were soon unpacked and installed in our flat. It comprised of two bedrooms a lounge/ kitchen and a bathroom with toilet and fitted the description of an 'adequately' furnished holiday flat.

The panto run was quite short. December until early January therefore the accommodation would be fine. The rent was £150 for the run, payable before we left.

The show was quite fun to do and as a principal artiste was kept busy. Alton Douglas played the dame and together we supplied all the comedy input. The script was not brilliant and so we had some fun adding many of our own ideas.

During the last week of the show, the landlord asked if I would perform the cabaret for his Rotary Dinner on New Year's Eve. I informed him the fee would be £150. He agreed that was a fair price. It turned out to be a very successful evening.

When it came time to depart, the landlord appeared at our door and asked for his rent. I said, "There is no point me giving you £150, then asking you to return it for my fee on New Year's Eve."

"Err...err I suppose not. We may as well call it quits then," he replied, looking surprised,

"Exactly.!" I said. We shook hands and we bid him farewell. We never had the pleasure of meeting his wife. As we were packing up the car to leave, I overheard his wife arguing, "What! You bloody fool! You mean they have lived here rent bloody free?" She was not a happy bunny at all. Well, I suppose, that is show business, as they say.

Thirty-Two
1971 The Central Pier Blackpool & a New London Agent.

Mum and Dad kept in touch with us regularly. We sent on press notices, programmes and records requested in their letters. The photograph of their modest bungalow suggested that they had settled into the New Zealand way of life and were enjoying their retirement.

Bill appeared settled in his marriage to Nolene. However, reading between the lines from

Mum, it was clear they did not like her. There had been a few arguments and rifts between the family members. This would not be the first time that Wendy and I looked at each other and said, "What a good thing it was, we didn't emigrate to New Zealand!"

Central Pier Blackpool

The only pier providing theatre attractions in England, not under the control of Trust House Fortes at that time, was the Central Pier in Blackpool. The license holder was Peter Webster who was under pressure to relinquish it but he insisted he would stay until his license ran out.

One morning I received a telephone call from Peter asking me to meet him in the Imperial

Hotel Bar. I took an instant liking to the tall, well-built man sporting a moustache, cigar in one hand and a large scotch in the other. He smiled broadly, as we shook hands, and sat down at a table. Peter was well known in Blackpool and Wendy had many happy childhood memories of 'Uncle Peter Webster'. Every year her parents holidayed at Blackpool, visiting his children's shows and talent competitions.

Peter offered me a summer season at the Central Pier. I knew that he was involved in some sort of partnership with one of the most successful agents in London called Dave Forrester of Forrester George Ltd. If I secured work at the Central Pier Blackpool, Dave would see my act and hopefully like it. Dave had so many big British stars under contract: Ken Dodd, Edmund Hockeridge, Mike Yarwood, Kenneth McKellar, Eddie Calvert and many more. His method was, if you book any of his stars, his supporting acts had to be included as part of the deal. He was a very shrewd operator. His partner was Nancy George and the agency operated from exclusive offices in Park Lane London.

I quibbled at the money Peter offered, as Jimmy Kennedy of Pontin's Holiday Camps had offered me more. However, Peter pointed out advantages such as, I would be working from home, the Central Pier had a 26-week season, the longest running season in the British Isles and a Blackpool season was highly prestigious.

The producer was a former Vaudeville act called Toby Canter. Top of the bill was a new comedy double act from Wales making a name for themselves called Ryan and Ronnie. Second top, was recording star vocalist Clinton Ford, who had enjoyed some hit songs in his time such as 'Fanlight Fanny the Frowsy Nightclub Queen' and 'Old Shep'. I was billed as second comic. That was indeed rapid progress from being an accordionist to a comedian in a Blackpool summer show in such a short time.

The white painted railings on the pier were in true Victorian style, all swirls and curls with benches to match. As I trundled my gear loaded on a trolley I caught glimpses of the churning seawater between the planks making me feel insecure. Rumours came back to me of dressing rooms moving in strong winds as storms bashed against the pier. The strong fresh smell of salt air mixed with seaweed and the squall of the seagulls provided some comfort. I recalled all the famous footsteps that had trundled up these boards before me - George Formby, Gracie Fields, Jimmy Clitheroe, Ken Dodd, Nat Jackley, Jewel and Warris, Norman Evans, Hilda Baker, Joseph Lock, Harry Lauder to name but a few. I felt very honoured and privileged to be walking where they once walked.

I stopped, turned round to face the seashore and stood still for a few moments, surveying the long sandy beach. I realised how long the pier was. It was like being on a ship coming into dock. There before me was the famous Golden Mile that had played host to the millions of holidaymakers down through the ages, mostly from the mill-towns of the north. Blackpool was well loved by many people, especially my fellow Scots, who would arrive in their hundreds.

The cast were welcoming, apart from Ryan and Ronnie who insisted I join them for a chat. Ronnie on my right, Ryan on my left. Ryan enquired what type of comedy I did, as he had never heard of me. I explained,

"Some visual, a couple of impressions, one-liners and by the way, I've never heard of you either."

"Well, let's get one thing straight, Boyo, we are the top of the bill see, and as such, we are telling you that you cannot tell any jokes about politics, weddings, funerals, religion, travelling, holidays, foreign countries, or indeed anything at all that we may do in our act." Ronnie said, "Well, looks like I might be able to say just 'Good Evening'!" With that, I excused myself and went to my dressing room for a hard think.

We had two weeks to rehearse for opening chorus, finale and some musical scenes. The general theme of the show was 'Olde Tyme Music Hall'. The chairman was a very polite man called Alex Pleon from London. Alex had appeared in some prestigious black and white movies in his younger years.

By the time the acts rehearsed with the orchestra, I had worked out a funny comedy routine, which should not offend the top of the bill. They had warmed a bit to me and I realised they were very nervous and conscious of the fact that they were completely unknown in England, although very well known in Wales. They had made a BBC TV series due to be released some weeks ahead. I was sympathetic towards their dilemma.

Rehearsing comedy gags is not easy. Empty seats do not laugh. The comedian tends to explain to the orchestra roughly, what he will be doing. The main elements are music cues and stage direction.

I intended to enter from the back of the stalls playing bagpipes and gradually make my way to the front, then come up on stage. Bearing in mind the restrictions when telling jokes, I intended being very visual. Peter insisted that I wear the kilt as an added attraction for the Scottish visitors.

Peter Webster knocked on my dressing-room door poked his head round and said, "Good luck Lawrie on your opening night. Do remember two things. One, it is 'Landladies night'. They are very critical and not easy to make laugh so don't be too despondent. Two, remember we are twice nightly and so keep strictly to your allocated time, or you will cause an almighty cock-up and I shall not be pleased." With that, he closed the door, leaving me speechless.

The call came through for overture and beginners. I made my way to the stage dressed in my white tie and tails ready for the opening chorus. No one is very chatty on an opening night as each person is hoping to remember everything learned in rehearsals.

The producer, standing at the side of the stage, said in a stage whisper "Good luck everyone."

The orchestra tuned up. I felt a tingle go through me. The stage lights were down to an almost black-out and it went very quiet. The tabs swept aside, the lights came up to full, the music played, and we burst into song and movement evoking as much enthusiasm as we could muster.

There was the applause, the music off, the tabs swept in again and on came the first act as all others scampered off quietly to their dressing rooms to change for their next appearance.

In my own cosy little dressing room, I kept an ear open to the speaker in my room.

As a principal artist had a room all to myself. No more sharing with the vocalist or the dancer.

It was a lot cooler in the dark corridor to the pass door leading to the auditorium.

My heart was thumping. I filled my bagpipes full of air and waited quietly in readiness for my cue - two pipe band type drum rolls then I would once again enter the arena of risk.

My cue! I burst in through the rear of the stalls and made my way down the aisle playing 'Scotland the Brave', accompanied by the orchestra. Slowly the house lights came up revealing a packed audience turning their heads nudging each other and pointing in surprise at my entrance amongst them.

I stuck the pipe chanter in a few ears as I walked causing shrieks and screams mingled with much laughter. On the stage, the house lights dimmed, leaving me in the glare of the spotlight. I stopped playing. The applause had been good so far.

I produced a rubber chicken from the bag, held it up and exclaimed, "Maggie Thatcher doing a streaker." (Streakers were in the news every week). Another big laugh with applause.

Attached to the chicken was a carefully measured piece of elastic thread which should have stopped it short, allowing me to jerk it back with a swanny whistle and drum effect.

As I threw the chicken at a little fat woman on the front row who was drying tears of laughter from her eyes, the thread broke and smacked her in the face. Absolute peals of laughter again. She stood up, swung the chicken round her head, let it fly back catching ME full in the face.

I produced a starting pistol meaning to shoot at the bagpipes, lay them on the floor, stand on the bag and produce a wailing noise. However, when I pulled the trigger, nothing happened but a dull click. A big laugh. Don't they just love it when things go wrong? I looked down the pistol muzzle, tried again and of course, this time it went off with a loud bang! This produced a huge laugh.

I stood on the pipes; they gave a wail, another laugh, especially as all the drones popped out of their sockets and I had to stuff them back in again. I picked up the bagpipes, squeezed the bag to produce a noise like a hoover and appeared to hoover the floor singing the current TV advert 'All the Dirt etc., Hoover sweeps as it beats as it cleans.'

However, it was when I stood over the microphone trap door and it snapped open, that

I received the first belly laughs. As the mike slowly reared its head above the footlights like a submarine periscope and began its journey up my kilt there were peals of laughter. I noticed a little plump woman in the front row topple forward from her seat and end up on her knees on the floor.

As the mike slowly reversed, I felt something leave me. THAT had not been rehearsed.

My shocking pink nylon briefs came into sight causing hysteria. I waved the stage manager to take them back up again which again caused roars of laughter. This went on, up and down until I was sure I had milked it enough. I then stepped out of them and rammed them in to my sporran. Again, hysterical laughter and applause.

Aware that I had exceeded my time, I picked up the bagpipes blew them up and started to play Amazing Grace but owing to the drones having been removed and hurriedly replaced. They sounded like a dozen cats being strangled, which of course raised another loud peal of laughter. I walked off to an ovation.

On reaching the side of the stage, Ryan & Ronnie met me with a barrage of complaints.

The dancers were on their knees at the side as well wiping tears from their eyes and congratulating me on a very funny act. I took two more curtain calls.

Ray the stage manager said, "Great act Lawrie, but you will cop it from Peter for grossly overrunning. I've seen him sack people on the spot for going over their time."

I made my way back to my room with mixed feelings. I was happy that I had gone so well, but dreaded a knock on the door and a reprimand from Peter. I didn't have long to wait.

Bang, bang went the door! I timidly opened it and in came a very long cigar with a small wrinkled faced Jewish man in a dark suit attached to the end of it. Behind him came Peter, but he was smiling and beaming. He said, "Lawrie, meet my colleague Dave Forrester." Dave extended his hand to shake.

He laughed as he said, "That was a great act Lawrie. There is a rumour that I always carry a contract in my pocket. Well, it's quite true, sign there and I'll make things happen for you." I did, and he did make things happen for me.

My relationship with Ryan and Ronnie improved as their TV show eventually hit the screens and people recognised them. They were very funny and talented men. I wrote some sketches and gags for their TV show. When I was working in Wales, Ryan insisted I stay with his family. Sadly, some years later Ryan suffered a fatal heart attack in America.

Regular Sunday concerts paid almost as much as my weekly wage. However, we had to travel again. I did Scarborough Floral Hall with Jimmy Tarbuck, Susan Maughan, Edmund Hockeridge, Roy Castle, Stan Stennet and The Bachelors. They had auditioned for Peter Webster, but he did not like them. The following week they had a big hit with a song called 'Charmaine'.

"He will be kicking himself a bit by now," said Deck, one of the 'Bachelors', "but give him our regards."

The longest haul was to Great Yarmouth to work with the Shadows. The kids and Wendy came with me and apart from the miles, enjoyed looking round the various resorts. Our last one was in Bridlington with David Whitfield.

In Blackpool, during the interval, the stage manager asked if I would see an old work colleague from Lochgelly. In walked my former General Manager at the Co-operative Society, Mr. McEwan. What a wonderful surprise. We had a lovely chat reminiscing old times: sitting the exam for the drapery department, performing magic tricks and playing the accordion in my band. Shortly afterwards, I received a cutting from the 'People's Journal,' a Scottish newspaper with a photograph and details of our meeting up in Blackpool during my show. This season was full of surprises.

Summerland Proposed

At another meeting with Peter, he ushered in two executives from Trust House Forte looking like the Mafia. Both had dark expensive suits, and both wore dark tinted glasses. They wanted me to present the summer show on the Isle of Man the following year. This would be 'my own show'. It would be styled on the current TV Beat the Clock London Palladium show starring Bruce Forsyth. I was not so sure I could fulfil that role, but they insisted that I fly over there at the weekend with my wife and see for myself this huge exciting venue called Summerland. They were sure that once I saw it I would agree.

Peter said after they had gone, "You must do this Lawrie, Dave will get you an excellent salary. You can't really refuse, because they control every pier in the British Isles that's worth having and even recently, they bought the London Hippodrome Theatre in Leicester Square. Please say 'yes' or your career could be over before it has begun."

Wendy and I caught the plane from Blackpool airport for Douglas Isle of Man. It was a bright warm day when we arrived. Memories of our last summer season in 1964 came flooding back. The Palace Theatre with Dickie Valentine. The Douglas seafront had not changed very much, if at all. The horse-pulled trams still trundled along the promenade. The smell of fish and chips still hung in the warm summer air.

We decided to walk along the promenade, as we knew that the venue was right at the end of it.

After some minutes walking, there it was, looking like a huge glass cruise ship berthed on dry land. As we walked closer, it loomed larger, but I cannot say I felt elated at the prospect of working there. In fact, I had a bad feeling about it somehow.

We looked at each other and I said, "Well, what do you think so far?"

Wendy stared at it for a few minutes then said, "Well, let us go in and have a look, before you say no."

As we entered the main large glass doors, a small young stocky man introduced himself as the Assistant Manager. Mr. Delorca the Manager was not available.

"It will be my pleasure to show you both around. It's a very exciting place to work.

We all love it here. This is my second year and I can't wait for it all to get really busy with the famous TT (Tourist Trophy) Week."

"Could you show me exactly where I would be working, and how many might be in the audience please?"

"Of course, Mr. Adam, you would be working from here, up on this stage, follow me."

We mounted a stage area, with drapes behind us and gold drapes in front of the stage that were pulled back.

"Of course, you would be working audience participation on the floor area in front of the stage."

As I stood looking out front, it still reminded me of a cruise ship, but on the inside and laid bare, with all the decks showing.

"We expect an average of five thousand people, except during the TT Week, and then it swells to about 9,000. Pretty impressive, eh? A bit bigger than the Central Pier Blackpool."

Currently appearing were a couple from Blackpool, Des and Julie Owen. Julie, a very pretty blonde woman with a good voice and a charming personality, had worked with me in the past at various venues. I did not know her husband Des.

The manager continued, "Des will be working the upstairs cabaret room next year which will be more to his style. He is more of a holiday camp type entertainer."

We continued the tour, but I had already made up my mind. Definitely Not! I did not get good vibes from the place at all. But, how to tell that to Trust House Forte? Somehow, I would have to think of a way to persuade them to say no to me.

On Monday evening, Peter came into my room and said, "Well, did you like it?"

I gave him a long look and slowly shook my head.

"What? Well, you must like it. They are coming back tonight during the interval and are very keen that you are the one person they want. I do hope you will change your mind. After all, it is only one season. Say yes."

There was a tap on my door. In came the two men once more accompanied by a concerned looking Peter.

"Well, Lawrie, surely you must have been impressed by this new venture. It was built using a new technology called 'Oroglas'. Although it looks smoky and dark on the outside, it always looks warm and like a summer's day on the inside, hence the name Summerland. Give us your opinions?"

"I have considered your very flattering offer most carefully and have a few questions I would like to put to you first, if you don't mind gentlemen."

"Fire away," they replied with broad smiles.

"You mentioned a 'Beat the Clock' type show. That would require large props to be made for the audience participation. Who would supply these?"

"We would Lawrie. We would employ a carpenter to make anything you require."

"Fine and what about prizes?"

"Once again do not worry about that, a mere detail. We will of course be happy to supply all you need."

I then decided to present the 'biggy'. I allowed a thoughtful silence to pass then said, "As I have never ever done anything like this before, I would be putting together a try-out show myself before the season, to make sure I get it right. This would have to be reflected in the salary.

They gave a cautious nod. "How much do you have in mind Lawrie?"

They resembled the broker's men in a pantomime. I thought of a number and doubled it. That should get a refusal. After a moments silence, they turned their backs towards me, huddled together and muttered inaudibly. I glanced at Peter who looked wide-eyed and slowly shook his head.

They turned around and said, "Well, it's rather more than we budgeted for Lawrie, but we agree."

I was flabbergasted, I was sure they would refuse to pay me what I had asked. "That's very good of you gentlemen, but there is one more thing."

"Yes?" they said in unison.

"I visualize this as being a very fast show and I gather you wish me to present a one-hour show on my own to 5,000 people swelling to approximately 9,000?"

"Yes, that is correct. And we are sure you will sail through it Lawrie."

"I will need a hostess like Bruce Forsyth has, who almost knows what I am thinking before I do it."

"You will have six dancers from the cabaret room upstairs. They will do a routine to open your show, bring you on and be your hostesses for part of your show."

"I need a glamorous hostess for the whole of my hour. I would like my wife to perform that role. She is a leading 'Bush-Davies' highly trained dancer."

Peter nodded and said, "Yes, that is quite correct gentlemen, a very beautiful lady."

They started displaying signs of impatience. "Okay, okay, we agree to use your wife."

"And her salary will be?" I asked.

"Oh, come on now Lawrie! This is getting ridiculous, we will pay her a dancer's salary on top of yours. Agreed?"

I had no alternative but to agree.

Peter ushered them out, popped his head round the door and said, "Well, that was some hard dealing you did there pal, well done. Wait 'till I tell Dave. You should be in management."

I still had a bad feeling about it. If only I had been able to read my own palm, I would not have gone. Disaster was in the air.

Mum and Dad wrote to tell me they were coming over for a visit. Could we put them up? We were overjoyed at this news and the period they were coming would mean they could come to the Isle of Man with us.

Meantime, Tracey returned to Devonshire Road School where she was doing very well. Wendy and I were amazed to realize she was seven years old. Fiona at three years old grew cuter every day.

The season finished with a big star-studded show. The Water Rats staged it for charity at the

ABC Theatre in the town. It was amazing to share the stage with so many household names that I had admired. How much longer would some of them be around I wondered. The last greats of a fading profession called Variety.

On the bill that night was Tessie O' Shea, Rod Hull and Emu, The Clark Brothers, Jack

Douglas, Ben Warris, Rostael and Schaefer, Ted Rogers, The Grumbleweeds, Frank Carson, Don Maclean, Duggie Brown, Lovelace Watkins, Joe Loss and my favourite comedian, Ken Dodd. What a night to remember.

The Golden Giveaway Show

Snuggled up on the settee with Tracey and Fiona watching Joe Ninety and puffing away at my pipe filled with Black Cherry tobacco, the peace was interrupted by the doorbell. Wendy dashed to open the door and in walked Jimmy Clitheroe.

He said, "I'm on the cadge Lawrie."

"How much?" I said, laughing, bearing in mind Jimmy was a very wealthy man.

"No, really, I want to borrow five quid for some petrol."

"What! Stars don't borrow from small supporting acts like me. It's the other way around."

"I forgot my wallet and I'm nearly out of petrol." I gave him the fiver.

Noticing some poster proofs advertising a show, he picked one up and read, 'Lawrie Adam Entertainments presents the Golden Giveaway Show'. "What's this?"

I explained about the Summerland season and my intention to get a little show together and tour it for experimental purposes.

"Where are you going to tour it?" He asked.

"Oh! In quiet out of the way places. If it dies a death, then no one will ever know."

"With respect, I know someone who will be a bigger draw than yourself."

"So, do I, loads of them, but it will be an unknown quantity on a tight budget."

He stood up to leave and said, "Look Lawrie, I'll top the bill for you."

I gasped, "But Jimmy, I could never afford your salary, you are a household name. Anyway, these will not be big theatres but social clubs probably in Cumberland, deepest Devon or the Welsh valleys."

"I have fallen out with Sir Bernard Delfont. They have cancelled my TV show and my radio show. All because he wanted me to go to the Winter Gardens Theatre Morecambe for the summer. That theatre is a graveyard and he knows it. He would probably say my pulling-power is failing and that I will have to take less money in future. I refused it. Now, your idea means at least I could keep working in a quiet way.

My price to you would be a secret and I promise you, you will be able to afford it. What do you say?"

"I say, right you are on!"

I made some phone calls and the interest was amazing. In the space of a few days, I had three weeks solidly booked. I found myself embarking upon a new profession, that of impresario. I explained to Jimmy that I needed some prizes. He took Wendy and me to a backstreet warehouse opposite the prison in Manchester, called Pinnacle Stores. We bought a load of great looking stuff.

My car at that time was a Ford Capri. Jimmy said, "You need to invest in a much larger car. Have you considered an American car, good for prestige and they are very comfortable? I will put the word out for you. They are not as expensive as they look."

The Golden Giveaway Show, compered by myself included lots of audience participation. Included in the programme was my pal Dorothy Bessy vocalist, a speciality magic act, Vic Oden and Louise, Wendy, and her friend Audrey who would act as Hostess Girls during the audience participation. Jimmy would be the star finishing the show assisted by his comedy feed Billy Windsor.

Tracey shouted "Dad, Dad, come and see this huge car. It's outside our house, look!" The doorbell rang. It was a car salesman asking if I was interested in the Ford Galaxy.

I felt obliged to have a drive in it but I refused because of the high fuel consumption.

Finally, I settled for a Chevrolet Impala Pillar-less Sedan, Rolls Royce red with a black vinyl roof, black leather upholstery and unusually, a right-hand drive. Fully automatic, it had a V6 economy engine. I clinched the deal when he agreed to accept my Capri in part exchange.

The first booking for the show was over the border in a tiny town called Annan. When I mentioned the fee for the show to the Concert Secretary he said, they could not afford it. By agreeing to take the door entrance money, while he kept the bar takings, we reached an agreement that suited us both.

Vic Oden and Louise travelled from Plymouth in their American car. Wendy and I agreed to put them up in our home for a reduced salary. When the whole cast was assembled we set off. Vic travelled in his own car as he had some bulky magic equipment. He did not ask where we were going.

He just said, "You lead Lawrie and we'll follow you."

We got to Penrith and Jimmy said, "Hey Lawrie, your magic pal is flashing his lights. I think he wants you to stop." I pulled over on the hard shoulder.

Vic said in his thick Brummy accent, "Lawrie, where the hell are we goin'?"

"Just a bit further on Vic, not far." He mumbled and grumbled as he went back to his car. I related the conversation to Jimmy and he was in hysterics laughing.

When we came to a sign that said Carlisle Jimmy said between roars of laughter, "Hey, He's flashing you again."

Vic came running up to my car and said, "Bloody hell Lawrie, bloody Carlisle! How much bloody further can it be?"

"Vic calm down. It's only just a bit further up the road that's all." Once again, he mumbled and grumbled back to his car.

However, when we came to a sign that said, Welcome to Scotland! Vic went berserk, blowing his horn and flashing his lights. Jimmy was on the floor screeching with laughter.

"This is like a comedy sketch. What are you going to tell him this time? 'Just up the road' is getting a bit thin."

I walked back to Vic's car. "Vic I am truly sorry. I didn't realise it was quite this far. I will give you some petrol money, so just bear with me. It really is just up the road I promise you."

Sure enough, we soon arrived at the venue. Wendy and Audrey were organised to take the cash from the eager customers. It was packed, and they were turning people away. The audience participation worked better than I expected, and everyone seemed happy with his or her prizes. Every act received an encore and Jimmy stopped the show. My records sold out during the interval.

At the end of the show, there was a long queue at the dressing room door for Jimmy's autograph. It was quite a small dressing room and the whole cast had to share it. All the coats were on about three hooks behind the door. Eventually, the crowd got impatient and pressed on the old door too hard. As a result, it collapsed and came crashing in.

A large defiant woman stood on the door waving her autograph book screaming, "Where is he, where is Jimmy?"

Dorothy Bessie said, "You're standing on him love, he's underneath all these coats!"

We fished Jimmy out and he just laughed it off and got down to signing the autographs.

On the way home, Jimmy said, "Lawrie that was great. Have we any more like that?"

"Yes Jim, three weeks booked solid."

"Well, I haven't enjoyed myself so much for a long time. Where are we tomorrow?"

"Barrow-in-Furness British Legion Club. A bit nearer to home."

When we arrived at Barrow, there was a long queue right round the building. Jimmy remarked, "Look at that Lawrie, what's going on there do you think?"

"Well, it looks like they are queuing to see 'The Golden Giveaway Show', starring Jimmy Clitheroe." Jimmy was astounded. "Jimmy, you are famous, and these folks here have probably never been to one of your live shows but have watched you on their TV sets and tuned into you on their radio. Now here you are, in the flesh."

It was another big success. Word was getting around and our phone rang from morning 'till night. I had struck a winning formula.

I told Jimmy who said, "Go ahead and book it out, right up until you have to go to the Isle of Man. Pay me what you think is fair." I offered him a chunk of the proceeds, but he said it was too much and wanted less.

To improve the show, I decided to make one or two changes. Reg Daponte the ventriloquist (from my Morecambe days) replaced Vic and Louise and we booked our own organist to be more independent. That worked much better. Retail companies accepted advertising space in exchange for products used as prizes, allowing me to print attractive coloured programmes with biographies of the artistes.

During this very busy time, a typical day would start by waking up Fiona, four and Tracey, eight for their breakfast then fixing Tracey's hair before I walked her to Devonshire Road School, at the top of our road. By the time I returned, Wendy was up. The phone would start to ring about 8.30am with enquiries for The Golden Giveaway Show, but we would try to do a quick shop.

Fiona, strapped in her pushchair, would treat everyone in the supermarket to rousing choruses of 'Where's yer Mamma Gone?' (the latest hit pop-song) whilst she rocked back and forth. When she went quiet she could be found folded over fast asleep. Somehow managing to get her face resting on her legs. We thought she was either going to be a singer or a contortionist. In the afternoon, I collected Tracey while Wendy prepared tea after which I picked up the babysitter. That done, we packed the car with costumes, games, accordion and bagpipes. We kissed the kid's goodbye as Wendy and I jumped in the car and collected the cast to head off to a Social Club somewhere in England. It could be near or as far as Wembley. I gained the reputation of 'King of the One Nighters'! I had never turned over such large amounts of money.

We had a week's booking in Devon, my favourite stomping ground. Folks made us very welcome, especially in the Plymouth and Paignton area. The show drew packed audiences wherever we went and was a roaring success.

Oddly enough, Jimmy was not such a big hit there and became quite depressed and grumbled, "Huh, you don't really need me here, you are going bigger than I am." Nothing we did could change his mood. He seemed to sink in to a deep depression.

That evening, I sat with Jimmy in the bar and tried to cheer him up. I was fond of Jimmy and did not like to see him so depressed, but he seemed in a strange mood.

"To think I have appeared at the London Palladium and been introduced to Her Majesty the Queen and now I've come to this."

"Wherever you are Jimmy, the public love you. You have given hours of laughter and pleasure to millions of people," I said to him patiently. He took a gulp of brandy, got up and left. I had a bad feeling of foreboding as I watched Jimmy walk away from me. Jimmy had decided to stay at the George, a different hotel from the rest of the cast.

Next morning, 23 March, I received a phone call. Jimmy Clitheroe had been found seriously ill in his hotel room. He was rushed to the hospital. Minutes later, all hell broke loose. The press had wind of it and clamoured for news and comments. I told them that Jimmy had been on a strenuous tour of one- nighters and was very tired.

I went to the hospital. The doctor in charge was extremely arrogant and rude. He would not allow me to see Jimmy at any cost. He said, "He is extremely poorly."

Jimmy never realised he was a comedy legend who gave laughter and joy to millions and I would miss him. Sadly, I was never to see him again.

The next barrage of calls I received were from agents and promoters asking what star replacement they were having for their shows that were booked and sold out, reminding me that their contracts had to be honoured. I managed to obtain Reg Dixon for one of the weeks and trumpeter Nat Gonella for the other. Norman Barratt the well-known TV Circus ringmaster with his amazing Budgie act joined us and the show carried on.

Reg Dixon was welcomed until we appeared in Rhyl, North Wales, when he was booed off. They were a tough noisy crowd who had booked to see Jimmy Clitheroe. Although Nat was acceptable, the tour ended after a very stressful time.

The phone still rang, and The Golden Giveaway Show was still in demand even without a star, but I missed Jimmy. He certainly had given us a good start.

Thirty-Three
1973 The Summerland Disaster

It was the usual busy chaos at London Airport when My Mum and Dad arrived. First to greet them was my cousin Janet's family. There was much hand shaking and hugging.

It began again when we arrived, and we just clung on to each other for ages. Dad was close to tears as he hugged Tracey then heard Wendy say to him, "Come on Granddad, you have another grandchild here just dying to meet you." He looked down and melted when he picked up our little blonde three-year-old bundle who said, "Hullo Granddad, I'm Fiona."

Michael, Janet's husband said, "Uncle Wull, there's more." Pointing to two handsome young men. "Our sons Tom and Phil."

We travelled back to Michael and Janet's comfortable home in leafy Little Chalfont for a meal after which the four kids disappeared into the large garden. We wished we could have stayed longer but the road ahead to Blackpool was a long one. We arrived home at 6.30 pm very tired.

We had extended our lounge by making two rooms into one. We had incorporated a smart cocktail bar, which I made myself. An idea I had imported from my Canadian days. Never a pub person, I preferred a drink in the comfort of my own home.

Dad's eyes lit up, "Goodness me, you even have your own bar."

"Help yourself Dad," I said. We enjoyed a good natter and a relaxing drink. It was wonderful to have them back. I had missed them so much. There was much catching up to do.

We enjoyed showing them the town and the area. They marvelled at the prices of goods and remarked that things were more expensive in New Zealand. One of Dad's first requests was for me to play my accordion. I started with a tune he always requested before he could even say it, 'Endearing Young Charms'. It must have meant something special to them as they both went a bit misty eyed. But it was their secret. All too soon, they said they were off to spend some time with our Dundee family and were away for a week. They also made flying visits to other relatives all over Scotland.

Cabaret Theatre Clubs

My new agent Dave Forrester kept me busy with dates in big cabaret theatre clubs with star shows. Wythenshawe Manchester in The Golden Garter nightclub with Roger Whittaker. He was enjoying a hit record 'Durham Town'.

Next, the famous Batley Variety Club with Ken Dodd who attracted an astounding audience. It was a daunting experience facing a huge audience seated at tables dining and drinking. I was required to finish the first half of the show with a 40-minute spot, leaving the audience warmed up and ready to receive the star. I could not go wrong despite lots of movement with waiters buzzing about to and from the bar, which ran almost the whole length on the room.

A sizeable orchestra at the back of the stage played as I took the stage. Following the 'shooting the pipes comedy routine' I was aware of a pale green sparkly silk curtain slowly and silently coming in behind me. This heralded the orchestra moving off to line up at the bar ordering drinks and leaving me entirely on my own on stage with about a thousand pairs of eyes, ears and minds concentrating on me. It was quite a responsibility, but I was well paid, and it was a joy to work with Ken.

He said, "I want you to go really well." Fortunately, I did. Some nights I ran over my time, but he never complained. He was professional right down to his fingertips. He was like a prize-fighter the way he felt out his audience, bobbed, and weaved changing his gags to suit the audience's mood. I learned a great deal observing his brilliant technique. Everything looked off-the-cuff but was carefully planned. Ken did about four to five hours a night, effortlessly, and still the audience screamed for more.

The following week proved to be very different. The Cabaret Theatre Club in Wakefield was smaller than Batley. The TV star impressionist Mike Yarwood topped the bill. In the first half, dancers opened the show. There was a compere, a vocalist, a speciality act then my 40-minute spot just before the interval. This positioning is called the second top of the bill. His brother, who looked like him, managed Mike Yarwood. Mike propped his door open in order to hear what was going on, but he never spoke to any of the other acts. On the first night, I was grateful that my act went an absolute bomb.

However, the resident compere, took me aside and said, "That was great Lawrie, but I'm sad to say you went 'too' well."

"How can I go 'too' well? That's what I am paid for, to warm them up for the star."

He gave a snigger and said, "Yeah! Well not this star. I guarantee you will be opening the show by the end of the week. I have seen it before. Mike cannot stand anyone going as well as you have mate."

He was quite correct. Each night when I arrived I noticed I was billed earlier the show. By Saturday, I opened before the dancers.

I received a phone call from Dave who said Mike was not at all pleased. Dave said I had been earmarked to appear with Mike in London at the Victoria Palace, but he had me replaced by Syd Francis the trumpeter instead. I later learned that Mike Yarwood suffered with nerves and lack of self-confidence. Eventually, turning to alcohol, which ended his career. A sad finale to a truly great talent.

Isle of Man

I was grateful to get back home to my little family, and that coincided with the return of Mum and Dad to Blackpool. We took them with us on a few Golden Giveaway Shows. Some were not too far from base; others meant arriving home in the early hours of the morning. On these occasions, our babysitter slept over. Mum and Dad seemed thrilled with our shows. I was content that I had gained good experience of audience participation and was now confidently looking forward to the Isle of Man summer show.

The first difficulty we encountered was manoeuvring our large American car on to the ferry. Getting off was just as tricky. We headed for our accommodation in a chalet high up overlooking Douglas. Mum and Dad had a room to themselves, Tracey and Fiona shared leaving the other bedroom for Wendy and myself. The weather was warm and encouraging. Just beyond our front door was a lovely view of the whole Douglas seafront. It took the best part of the afternoon to unpack and store everything from the car. The family sat down to a lovely meal cooked by Wendy and my Mum after which, we were keen to visit Summerland.

Summerland was an entertainment complex hailed as one of the greatest in the world when it first opened in 1971. To solve the tricky British weather problem, the visionaries of the Isle of Man created an indoor centre that could cater for holidaymakers all year round. The result was a futuristic playground complete with swimming pools, sports facilities, playgrounds, roller rink, bars, restaurants, amusement arcades, concert rooms, waterfalls, shops and a solarium straight out of a science fiction film. The centre could accommodate around 5,000 people in total.

Underneath the 'Solarium floor', where I would be working, was a fully-operational fairground. Mum and Dad took the kids downstairs as they were champing at the bit to experience the rides. Wendy and I explored the dressing room. It was about 8 feet by 6 feet, stark but contained the bare necessities. The manager told me there would be a carpet fitted before we opened. It never happened. I enquired to the manager about prizes.

"Oh! Yes, well, don't worry you will have prizes before you open do not panic Mr. Adam."

"I would like to meet the carpenter who is to provide the games apparatus."

"I don't know anything about that Mr. Adam. No one has mentioned anything about a carpenter to me."

He seemed in a hurry to be off and a bit edgy. I was suspicious about the whole affair. I met the organist, a young lad who seemed keen and asked what he would be required to do. I explained what I had in mind and he seemed happy with the arrangements.

He said, "I have been told that I will be playing for about half an hour's dancing, then I introduce you to do a warm-up during which you explain what will be happening at nine o' clock, namely, your big show. There will be a break, after which I play again for dancing up to the point when I re-introduce you. I have the music for the cabaret dancer's routine, when they join you on stage. After they exit, it is over to you for your one-hour show."

"Is there a stage manager?"

"Yes! That's him over there that huge six-footer. He is a Manxman and does not care much for us mainlanders. I don't think any of them do, they are a bit of a funny lot."

Approaching the stage manager, I introduced myself, explained my running order for the show and made him aware of my microphone and lighting requirements. I mentioned the possibility of a carpenter making props for the show.

He gave an arrogant snigger, and said, "Oh yeah?" Then walked away. I could tell he was going to be difficult and he certainly was.

In the cabaret room upstairs, I met the cast. The musical act was called the 'Naden Brothers'. Des seemed a bit on the reserved side. I quite understood his feelings as I was taking his job, so he was quite right to feel a bit peeved. However, he mellowed and gave me a few pointers and even suggested some audience games I might try, which was good of him.

The opening night seemed fine. There was a good-sized audience of about three thousand when the organist introduced my warm-up spot. I noticed Mum and Dad seated at a table settling in with their drinks. Tracey and Fiona joined them just before the show. Wendy was in the dressing room sorting out the props for my spot in half an hour. The dancers from upstairs lined up to do their routine behind the tabs. The organist introduced the Golden Giveaway Show and it started. The girls finished, introduced me, and then quickly made their exit to get back upstairs for their other show.

Owing to the vastness of the place and the underpinning buzz of noise, it was hard work getting the gags over. Contrary to a theatre auditorium or even a large nightclub there was movement going on all the time to and from the different levels of the building.

Volunteers came forward willingly to participate in the games. Wendy appeared and assisted me manoeuvring folk into the appropriate spots to perform the tasks asked of them. She looked glamorous in her skin-tight silver floor-length dress. The experience gained from the touring show beforehand was paying off now.

There was a good atmosphere and the laughs were there. However, when it came to give out the prizes I was astounded. They had provided me with packets of crisps and packets of marshmallows.

"Cheapskates!" I thought. "We handed out better quality prizes than this in our own shows."

I asked for a couple of children to join me on stage. They performed a song or a poem. Little Fiona appeared by my side. She looked so dainty but beautiful. I placed her on a stool. Her blonde hair was done up in a bun on top of her head. She sang 'Twinkle Twinkle Little Star' and brought the house down.

She won the prize of a Teddy Bear, which she seemed pleased about and said, "Oh! Thank you, Daddy." This got another huge laugh.

My only managerial point of reference was Mr. Delorca the manager. His experience was limited. He had been a catering manager for Fortes before he came to Summerland. He was often in an excited state displaying an air of general confusion. I complained about the prizes.

He just shrugged and mumbled, "That's all I have to give you." then disappeared.

I phoned London to complain about the empty promises made. They agreed that I could have a small budget to visit a warehouse in Douglas and purchase some better prizes.

At the warehouse with the family in tow, the girls discovered a gorgeous tiny white kitten that did not want to leave them. The warehouseman asked if we wanted to take it with us. The girls looked with pleading eyes, so the kitten came back to the chalet with us. We called him Twinkle. He snuggled up to everyone in turn and we fell in love with him.

Tracey had to attend some weeks enrolled in a school in Douglas where she made many friends and was a good communicator. Before the school broke up for the summer holidays, we took part in the sports day. Wendy was in the egg and spoon race and I did my best in the sack race. It was good fun and good publicity for the show as it happened.

We delighted in touring the island with Mum and Dad and admiring the sights. They loved spending time with their grandchildren playing games with them and going for walks. It was heart-warming to see Fiona taking Dad's hand and chatting away to him.

However, all too soon it was time for them to leave us and start on their homeward journey for New

Zealand. They were going back to cousin Janet's and she saw them off on their flight home. I felt incredibly sad when we said goodbye thinking I would never see them again. I was correct for it was indeed the last time we would enjoy each other's company.

The TT Week arrived. There were motorbikes and holiday visitors in abundance and an air of excitement. Summerland was packed every night. The volunteers for audience participation were in the main motor-bikers who were mostly inebriated. I could not do any games that demanded any degree of concentration, so I did a 'Yard of Ale' competition. A yard glass is a thin tube of glass approximately a yard long with a bulb shape at the bottom and a mouthpiece shaped like a trumpet. When filled with ale (about 2 pints) the contestant is required to drink from the glass as quickly as possible. There is a trick to it, but most of them ended up with the ale pouring all over themselves. They took it in extremely good humour and it looked hilariously good fun.

That evening Fiona's babysitter arrived. Tracey accompanied us on certain evenings and enjoyed playing with Des and Julie's young son who was about Tracey's age. She understood that she had to check in with us periodically and was good at remembering to do so. Summerland was deemed safe enough to allow your kids to wander anywhere.

As we set off for work, the weather on the evening of Tuesday, 2nd August 1973 was unsettled with drizzly rain and heavy cloud laden skies. The loud haunting lonely sound of the fog siren was heard all over the island for hours. It sounded like the eerie call of the Banshee. As we drove past the hotels that line Douglas promenade, it occurred to me that holidaymakers having their roast beef and two veg must be wondering what they could do on such a miserable night. Many would be able to see Summerland from their dining room window and its bright lights and attractions may have seemed a perfect way to spend the evening, I hoped.

By 7.30 pm, there were around 3,000 people inside Summerland. When I did my warm-up spot, I would tell the audience that they could expect a rousing show at 9 pm and so book seats in plenty time. I asked someone standing alongside me to go and investigate the slight smell of smoke and report back to me as soon as possible.

Outside near the mini golf course, three boys from Liverpool were looking for a place to have a smoke. The two 12-year olds and a 14-year-old managed to break a lock on an empty kiosk nearby. A discarded match from one of the three started a fire in the kiosk that they could not control. In fear of being reprimanded for the fire, the three boys fled. However, the only security was in the form of one elderly man with a serious stomach complaint. One punch and he would have been rendered useless.

The kiosk was situated near the sidewall of the complex - a wall covered in a highly combustible material called Galbestos and another glass like material called Oroglas. The kiosk fell against this wall and the fire quickly spread, initially between a gap in the inner and outer walls, hungrily making its way up to the roof barely noticed.

People smelled smoke, but nobody did anything nor did any alarms sound. The design did not incorporate sprinklers and none of us had received training in fire drills.

The organist introduced me and as I stepped onto the stage I could see some smoke at the back, it appeared to be in the kitchen area.

I noticed some slightly concerned faces looking backward and so I joked, "The chef's set fire to the chip pan again. Never mind perhaps our organist can play, Swanee River, and we can all dive in."

Everyone laughed and calmed down. However, the situation became horrifically worse in seconds.

A massive explosion burst from the Oroglas wall.

Flames shot up the walls like a waterfall in reverse but with fire, which produced a roaring sound. The fire raced towards me like an inferno.

I glanced to my right and was amazed to see the tall bearded ticket seller still admitting people and at the same time, people were desperately trying to get out!

I shouted for people to get out and directed them to a stairwell on the left. Then my microphone went dead.

The worst affected people I realized would be the ones on the three floors above this level. Everyone from every floor and above our floor (the Solarium) had to descend one main set of stairs. Directly above us was the Marquee Show bar and above that was the

Leisure Floor and right at the top the Cruise Deck floor.

The amusement arcade fire took hold at the exact point where the stairs came down. Sheets of flame shot between the open steps on the stairway. The Oroglas roof began to melt and molten balls of fire fell onto the people below. It looked like a disaster movie.

People were running about with their heads on fire and their clothes in flames and everything happened at super-fast speed.

Now very anxious about Wendy and Tracey, I joined the crowds pouring down the staircase. They were unusually quiet and leaving in an orderly fashion. Even young children holding on to their parent's hands were silent and looking down concentrating upon the grey concrete steps.

I burst into the dressing room startling Wendy and Tracey

"The building is on fire. Follow me out NOW! Leave everything. Just get out."

We joined the mass of people still crowding down the stairway heading for the fairground area. The lights were still on. It was surprisingly quiet. There were no signs of panic down here like there was upstairs. We headed for the exit and stood outside with crowds of people. We turned to look at the building and saw Summerland in a sheet of high flames from end to end.

Through the thick billowing smoke, a still sad little blackened figure could be seen clinging to the remnants of what looked like a high walkway.

A woman nearby exclaimed, "Oh! My God, that's a person up there."

Later it became clear, to my shock and horror, that no fire services were called from the Summerland complex. The first calls to the emergency services came from a passing taxi driver and from the captain of a ship two miles out at sea who reported, "It looks like the whole of the island is on fire."

The padlocked fire escape doors further exacerbated the situation: meant to prevent people entering without paying, they blocked the essential ability to exit.

The following morning, everyone was summonsed to meet in a hotel for a head-count. A smartly dressed member of the management stood on a small stage in an expressionless voice calling out names from a list.

I heard Wendy's name and mine. "Here," we replied.

Sometimes there would be no reply, only a silence, followed by some stifled sobs, or the sudden scrape of a chair as someone fainted against it. Friends were heard offering words of comfort.

Some three years later, I learned that Don Taylor, the organist who had his own trio, had become trapped trying to get out of a fire door which would not open, jammed shut by a staff member's car backed up against it. He was found underneath about eleven dead bodies on a stairwell. He suffered lung damage.

We were in a state of shock. It was hard to realize that only a short time ago we were presenting entertainment to happy holidaymakers in one of the foremost and new leisure centres in Europe. I recalled the convincing publicity portraying Summerland as a safe place to bring your family.

"Turn the kids loose. There is no traffic in here, no danger in Summerland. The place is fireproof. If there was a fire, it is designed to be contained immediately. Why, there are exit doors everywhere!"

HOWEVER, there was no mention of them being locked and some even padlocked. What an absolute irresponsible disgrace. What an absolute betrayal of public trust!

A member of Fortes staff took me aside to speak to me confidentially in a quiet sombre tone. If approached by a member of the press, I was not to say anything. If I conducted myself in a respectful manner, there would be work for me on the mainland. Words and looks implied, should I not comply, things could be difficult for me!

What an honourable company to work for, I thought.

As we emerged from the hotel ballroom onto the promenade the first thing I noticed as I walked hand in hand with Wendy towards our car, how very quiet people were as they moved about the town. No one spoke. An eerie silence had descended upon Douglas. As I looked into the faces that walked past me, I could tell some of them were still living with the awful memory of the night before. For many of them, that would be the day that they would never forget for the rest of their lives. I knew I would not.

The death toll from this tragedy was the worst involving a fire in Britain since 1927 when 71 children died in a cinema in Paisley Scotland. All told, 50 people died in the Summerland disaster, 48 were found dead in the building and two women died later in hospital. One family lost five of its members. Many others lost members of their family that night, children lost their parents, parents lost their children. Seven married couples died, and 17 children lost one or both parents. Most of the dead came from the north of England (27) not surprising when you consider that this part of the country accounted for 63per cent of visitors.

On 17th September 1973, three Liverpool boys – two of them 12 years and the other 14 years – appeared before Douglas Juvenile Court and admitted wilfully and unlawfully damaging the lock of a plastic kiosk next to Summerland. They were each fined £3 and ordered to pay 33 pence compensation and 15 pence costs (Liverpool Echo 17 July 2013). The media coverage from outside of the island soon fastened on to the fact that Summerland could never have been built under the planning laws in the United Kingdom - the hint being that everyone wanted this project so much that a few corners were cut.

All the telephone lines were blocked and communication with my parents or Wendy's were impossible. We knew they would be very worried and that this disaster would be broadcast internationally.

Four years later, when my father sent me a gift of his diaries I gleaned the event from their point of view.

Quote:

The nine o'clock news came on and the first word we heard was "Catastrophe! In Douglas Isle of Man! Fire has gutted the new two and a half million-pound Summerland Theatre and Amusement Centre. Hundreds of people dead and injured as flames engulf the building.

"My God!" were the first words that passed our lips. "Lawrie is there!"

I looked at Fay. Her face had gone deathly pale. She was shivering and quivering. We were both shocked into silence. I could feel the blood drain from my head and face and arms to flood the heart, which was pounding like someone using a fourteen-pound hammer on a solid oak door. The sensation was awful.

He goes on to explain about frantic phone calls to the TV station the Police, the press etc., and dispatched a telegram. Eventually they received a telegram from cousin Janet and Michael informing them that we were all safe and accounted for.

We were in a bit of a predicament. We desperately wanted to get off the island and back to England, but we had no home to go back to, it was let out to theatricals until the end of September and we had no work.

When lines of communications were restored, agent Ronnie Potter phoned from Plymouth to say he had at least three weeks work for me. My family were welcome to live with them. Only one proviso, no pets as they had a dog. What a lovely kind gesture.

Fortunately, the only loss in the fire was a new amplifier that was on stage. My accordion costumes and props were all in the dressing room below the main floor and the dressing room was virtually a windowless concrete box.

As we stood on the ferry deck watching the shore recede we felt relieved to be leaving finally. I thought, "I will not be in any hurry to return to the Isle of Man, if ever."

We dropped of our little kitten Twinkle in a cattery then made our way down to Devon. Unfortunately, Twinkle stared at the cage opening, refused to eat or drink, and died of a broken heart. The kids were grief-stricken when they heard. The cattery did give us a replacement cat on our return, which we nicknamed The Duchess. Her character was very different from Twinkle's and eventually went off with the next-door neighbour who had been secretly feeding her on best salmon.

Thirty-Four
1973-74 Out of the Ashes

Ronnie and his family were very welcoming, and he kept me supplied with work. I even managed to make another long-playing album at one of my favourite venues, the Forum, in Plymouth, with a live enthusiastic audience.

Out of the ashes of Summerland, a new type of career opened for me. Restaurants and hotels approached me to put on floorshows for them. Artistes were asking me to represent their acts and be their agent including a folk group called The Haughton Weavers. I was able to get them out of the small club type circuits and introduced them to bigger venues. The first one was the Floral Hall theatre Southport. They packed the place with their fans and impressed the boss, who was not easy to impress. They went on to make records and appear on BBC2 in their own show. The group obtained prestigious bookings including the North and South Piers in Blackpool amongst others through my agency while I continued to do my own act. However, having reached a comfortable position, I was able to choose where I worked and accepted bookings only if I knew I would enjoy them.

An agent friend of mine asked me to manage a show for him in South Wales and appear myself. The star was Emile Ford That was funny as the last time I met Emile was when I was a struggling act working in Lewis's in Manchester. (We theatricals call it, 'resting'). He was appearing in a 'Top of the Pops' show in the store and requested a transistor radio in lieu of a fee. I reminded him of this event and we had a good laugh about it.

We were in the same digs in Wales and I grew to know him well. He was a smash hit in the touring one-night show for the two-week run. He sold his records during the interval at 50p each. I was selling mine at £1 each. No matter how many he sold, I made twice as much, which amazed him. He was working for only £35 a show, which was too low a fee in my opinion.

At the end of that week, he asked if I would be his sole agent. Others had exploited him very badly. I agreed and shook hands on it instead of a binding contract. Emile had been in Sweden for quite a while. He told me he had fallen foul of the Lew Grade organisation and as a result could get no work in England. Through my guidance within 6 months, he was earning approximately £400 per night. He made a record on our Alpha Records label that sold very well. He arrived at the front door one day in a lovely racing green Rolls Royce. He said, "Thank you Lawrie, this is all down to you." He started doing silly things like doing the odd appearance for £50 during a Bingo session around the corner from where he was booked in cabaret at a big fee for the week. As a result, his show was cancelled.

KTell Records made him an offer to fly him out to Nashville Tennessee to make records for them. He was stupid and difficult about it. Next, a silly little blonde teenager arrived announcing that she was

Emile's new manager and all deals would go through her. I realised why Lew Grade had dumped him, so I did likewise. Shame, I really liked Emile.

He was a nice man with a huge gift of talent but possessed an illogical thought process.

Our two flats were full of winter lets and we were, for the first time, seeing savings in the bank. Wendy suggested that now would be a good time to consider moving to a larger house and was sure we could afford it. She had spotted a property in Warbreck Drive. Blackpool. We had a look at it, fell in love with it, and arranged to move in. It had a square entrance hall and a large lounge with a bay window. The kitchen was a good size and a dining room almost as big as the lounge. A wide staircase led up to a big landing off which were three bedrooms and a toilet/bathroom. We had great fun decorating the whole house ourselves.

The only problem was St. Stephen's Church across the road. It was of the high Anglo- Catholic tradition, which meant Sunday bell ringing from 8 am, then 10am and again at 6.30 pm, plus bells at funerals and weddings. One day I opened the door to find a priest on my doorstep. He welcomed us to his parish and hoped we may come to his church. I was a bit curt with him. I told him we were not churchgoers. Could he do something about those dreadful bells going off all day, please? I did not invite him in. We would meet again some years later in different circumstances.

Dave Forrester invited me to come down to London as he had a proposition for me. I had appeared at the Southport Floral Hall theatre for him with Ken Dodd. I tried to grill Nancy George, Dave's business partner, but Nancy gave very little away and although always polite was not overly gifted in the communications department.

Dave's offices were within a swanky suite on Park Lane and impressive. However, I was astounded to note that his desk was small and bare except for a telephone, a silver biro and a small silver covered notebook. No in/out trays, no piles of letters or photographs. He asked if I was interested in putting together a summer show for him in Bridlington to be in two parts: the early summer show to be a classy well costumed 'Old Time Music Hall Show', for six weeks. I could top the bill myself or share with someone else. He would decide which. I said I could do that.

He threw the notebook and pen across the desk and said, "Okay, let's see you cost it out for me."

I replied in a state of some surprise, "What, this minute?"

"Yes, right now," he said smiling.

By this time, I had experience to draw on and within a few minutes threw the notebook back to him.

He studied my proposal, nodded and said, "Okay, lad, the show's yours. Keep me posted as to who is to be in it and keep to the budget you have here."

My first summer season for Dave and I could produce it. I could not wait to get started on it. I booked artistes right away.

The Horseshoe Show bar was interested in staging a Golden Giveaway show in at the famous Blackpool Pleasure Beach for a one-night Saturday trial. They were a strange management to work for. My point of contact was the General Manager called Roger. He was a tubby pleasant man in his forties, who did not really have a clue about show business. I got the impression that he viewed me with suspicion. The story he gave was that the owner, Leonard Thomson, had been producing all the shows but was getting a bit frail. I gathered business was also faltering and they were looking round for new people and new ideas.

The venue, upon inspection, was very interesting. An art-deco building built in the nineteen thirties, circular in design. It overlooked the south promenade situated before the actual pleasure beach amusement park. The interior was very clever and must have been ahead of its day in design. The dance floor served also as a sizeable stage able to rise to approximately four feet. Red velvet house drapes swept round to enclose the stage, which had full stage lighting. The wings were on the small side. Parked at the side of the stage, was the 'Astral Stage', a circular smaller stage holding up to four dancers. It was fixed to a crane jib arm that could sweep out over the audience, similar to the one in Las Vegas.

All the seating looked comfortable and arranged around tables in such a way that no one had their back to the stage. Running almost the length along the outside wall was a balcony with more tables and chairs. Drinks and meals were served throughout the evening. To the right of the stage was a long bar. The room design incorporated floor to ceiling shutters, mounted upon tracks that opened up to enlarge the room if required. Standing on the stage, felt very comfortable. It had a good feeling.

The young musicians, called the 'John Peate Trio', had been there for some years. They were excellent playing for both the dancing sessions and accompanying the shows. They were at the rear of the stage. To the left of the stage, surrounded by bar stools on ground level was a circular bar, in the middle of which, was a grand piano played by Eddie Nelson.

My theatre training and large cabaret club experience would be useful here. We were booked for many Saturday evening cabaret shows. Gradually they became more popular even though attracting an audience in any seaside town during the winter season was not easy. Therefore, Wendy and I booked many different acts in the various shows and it was good fun and right on our doorstep.

Thirty-Five
1974 Bridlington beckons

Folk passing by our house on Warbreck Drive Blackpool paused to listen, as our old piano rang out most of the day as I tried out various permutations of possible musical numbers for our forthcoming summer show at Bridlington. By the time I had worked out the opening chorus, the kids knew the words to every song. This caused many a giggle, as the tunes were not of their generation. As they did their homework, they could be heard singing, 'There's something about a Soldier' then 'Goodbye Dolly I Must Leave You', and 'Casey would dance with the strawberry blonde and the band played on'. They might come dancing into the dining room/office singing at the top of their voices a rousing rendition of 'Oh! Knees up Mother Brown'!" Sometimes Tracey or little Fiona sat beside me on the piano stool and sang happily along with me playing - work alongside family quality time.

Soon I had all the acts booked, the scenery and costumes booked, and the musical scores written up. Dave suggested Wendy and I take a trip to Bridlington to have a look at the stage and have a chat with the Borough Council Entertainments Director, a Mr. Brian Myford.

He said, "I want this show to be a success Lawrie because I want it next year as well."

Mr. Myford was pleasant enough to deal with but Council Entertainment Directors seemed to roll off the same conveyor belt from the same factory. I did not dare tell him this was my first job as a theatre producer. I was nervous, but also excited at the possibilities before me. His conversation was guarded and so was mine.

The Blackpool Pleasure Beach asked us to put on more shows for them. John Peate, the resident organist there, told us the only time the place was busy was when our shows were on otherwise it was a bit of a graveyard!

Our last show for the Pleasure Beach before we departed for our summer season was an idea I had for a 'Rock and Roll' night. An organiser for Rock 'n Roll clubs operating all over the country agreed it should be a huge success. I booked a Rock & Roll DJ and provided advertising. The cost was a lot cheaper than putting on a show.

In reaching an agreement with the Pleasure Beach, I stipulated to General Manager Roger Wilcock that we would keep the admission takings and they would have the bar. There would be no cost to them at all. I would manage the proceedings including compering. For the show, the staff would be dressed in rock and roll outfits. The show publicity asked the audience to dress in the same mode.

Roger turned his nose up at this saying, "Very well Mr. Adam, but our security staff will be prominent."

I replied, "I do hope not. Have them there but surely not in everyone's face as they enter."

I reminded him that the bar agreement was to run until midnight. As I never completely trusted their agreements, I had taken the trouble to put in a clause regarding insurance in the small print. He signed the agreement. I had no law degree but was red hot when devising contracts.

Wendy and her friend Audrey, who had also been in our Golden Giveaway shows with Jimmy Clitheroe plus my friend Harry Buttress, made up the staff. Harry was my Road Manager. The opening night arrived. We stood at the door welcoming the Rock and Roll audience. The outfits were amazing, the girls in flared colourful skirts, the men in electric coloured jackets with velvet collars and string bow ties. The women had their hair arranged in bouffant style while the men had the Tony Curtis haircut. The staff including myself were similarly dressed. All except the security men, who wore sombre suits, were six feet tall (ex-policemen) and had haughty grim expressions displaying the unnerving policeman's stare.

The night went incredibly well and everyone was having a great time.

Peter May, the bar manager approached me and said, "Please announce Lawrie that the bars will be closing in half an hour."

I glanced at my watch, "But that will be half past ten!"

"Correct," he said.

"They bought tickets in good faith, which constitutes a contract and states that the bar will be open until midnight."

"Sorry about that, but I have changed my mind and they will close."

I turned to Harry and said in a loud voice, "Harry, here are the keys to the car. Please collect our folk, install them in the car, park it at the foot of the fire-escape stair round the back and leave the passenger door open with the engine running. I will be with you very shortly."

Mr. May laughed and retorted, "Lawrie, if that's meant to frighten me you are joking."

"Very well, here we go then. On your head, be it."

We had just concluded an exciting Jive Competition after which I apologised to the folk and made the bar closure announcement. The room went deathly quiet. Then all hell broke loose. I took my exit as planned, jumping in the car, which took off. As it turned the corner onto the promenade, we watched various items of furniture crashing through the lofty large Horseshoe Bar windows. A huge upholstered chair seemed to hover in the air, then crash onto the promenade.

The next morning when I went in to collect my takings from the previous evening, I was met with a stony silence. Young Mr. Thomson walked in.

I smiled "Good morning." He completely ignored me. I remarked to Mr. Wilcock, "That's a bit rude isn't it."

He replied, "Oh! Mr. Thompson never ever speaks to concessionaires. I am afraid there is nothing for you here Mr. Adam. In fact, we will be sending you a bill for damages."

"Please study the paragraph regarding insurance on you contract, then you can pay me please," I said.

He stared at it, "Well I'll be damned!" He gasped.

Mr. Thompson, grabbed the contract, looked at it open-mouthed and then glared at his general manager saying curtly, "Pay him!" then marched out.

As I left with my large cheque the thought entered my mind, "Well that's the last I'll hear from them." But it was not.

We booked an apartment in an art-deco type building overlooking the beach a few miles out of Bridlington. The girls shared a bedroom. We had extended an invitation to our friend Jack Seaton, to bunk in with us, as there was plenty of room. He had agreed to play the part of Music Hall Chairman. Even the cat came with us. The girls soon made friends with the family across the road who ran a pig farm who encouraged them to get familiar with the animals. They loved it. In addition to the many pigs and piglets, they had a couple of donkeys one of which was pregnant. Fiona aged five would don her Wellington boots and we always knew where to find her. She just loved animals and still does to this day. Tracey was more of a beach and water type.

One day Tracey came shouting and screaming in through the door telling us to come quick. Fiona ignored the warning not to go near the donkey as it was pregnant. She received a hard kick on the forehead. When we saw her, her blonde hair was crimson with blood. Our hearts nearly stopped. Fortunately, it was a superficial cut and she was okay.

We rehearsed the initial show for one week before we opened and ran for six weeks. Following which, it was replaced by the big show starring Ronnie Hilton, Norman Collier, Sheila Buxton, Lennie the Lion and myself. The same dancers and the same speciality act 'Skeletons Alive' remained. I produced the show and acted as Company Manager.

It was hard work staging the early show within a week. Fortunately, in forward planning, I had sent to the cast in advance, the words of musical numbers to learn. The scenery arrived was erected and looked magnificent. The costumes looked very glamorous. I had ordered duplicate costume-leotards for the men to match up for a comedy high kick dance routine we would do with the girls.

All the music worked well. Jack helped me to prepare a few comedy tricks and gimmicks. We rehearsed from ten in the morning until ten at night. The cast were conscientious and hard working. John Stanley and Margo Lloyd the singing duo were brilliant. The speciality act, Dumart and Denzer, presented an ultra violet skeleton act. The stage was blacked out and many illuminated skeletons appeared and danced to music then suddenly came right out over the audience's heads to excited screams from the delighted crowd.

There was a problem with the dancers who had been booked by Dave from a Manchester agency. They came with routines of their own and were reluctant to make any changes. On the Friday at a final dress rehearsal, the dancers were noticeably slacking and letting the team down. I was fully aware, that the following evening, opening night, the Forrester George Agency from London, would be sitting on the front row, judging whether their faith in me had been justified. I stopped the rehearsal and called the dancers down to the footlights. I decided to let them have it. My choice of language could have been better, but my verbal surgery was having an effect. So much so that I felt a gentle squeeze on my arm.

It was Wendy who whispered, "Steady darling, that's enough. They've got the message." One of them started to shed a tear and apologise. I heard a sharp intake of breath behind me.

I turned around to find a clergyman staring at me with his mouth hanging open.

"Well, Mr. Adam, I did come here to introduce myself and welcome you to the town. However, after that disgraceful display of abuse, I am going home to pray for you." With that, he turned on his heels and swiftly departed. He should have realised I was being cruel to be kind.

The show opened to a packed theatre and everything went even better than I imagined. The finale of the first half was a tribute to Music Hall artistes of the past with Jack saying after each act, "But we still had those lovely 'Tiller Girls'." Whereupon the girls would come out in a line doing high kicks right across the stage and off the other side. However, after the last act, Jack once more announced the girls and by this time, the audience joined in with him. The girls once more high-kicked across the stage but there was a huge roar of laughter when four men from the cast (myself included) all dressed the same as the girls tagged on the end of the line. When they went into the 'wheel', the men could hardly keep up with them. I caught hold of the curtain at the back of the stage, which appeared to collapse, and dropped down, revealing four stage hands seated at a card table drinking beer and playing cards. They scattered leaving various moving bumps grovelling under the large velvet drapes attempting to find a way off. Cue the house curtains. The audience were in an uproar. It had taken them by surprise. I learned from my Blackpool Central Pier days, that they just love it when it looks like things have gone wrong. When the second half opened, the audience were still laughing!

Everything went exceedingly well, and Dave was so pleased with the show he said, "Lawrie, I want you to put in another show for me next year."

"Great, what about a Roaring Twenties' show?"

"Agreed, get on it."

We had a great run and the coaches rolled in from Hull and as far away as Leeds. We were packed every night with the House Full 'signs up on the pavement. After the run, the show changed over and welcomed in the Big Show for the summer. Ronnie Hilton and Norman Collier registered with the audiences very well. Sheila Buxton kept to herself and sadly had a drink problem. Lennie the Lion a well-known TV ventriloquist act was a private person, and an excellent act.

During the season, I received a visit from the same clergyman that I had caused offence to during the rehearsals. He waved aside my apology and said he wanted to invite my company to a special service for all the entertainers in the area. After the service, there were refreshments laid on for us. He approached me and asked my opinion of the service. I told him religious-wise it meant absolutely nothing at all to me. The hymns were boring, the seats were uncomfortable, and everyone had an expression of their face as if they had been told they had a terminal illness. Once more, he said he would pray for me.

The Bridlington Lady Mayoress requested advice on entertainment at her hotel, which was opposite the theatre. I explained to her that the audience were not warming to her organist and soprano singing songs from the shows. All she required was a young piano player, playing a variety of sing-along music. I booked a young man from Newcastle who was an instant hit and her bar was packed.

The same woman approached me again. She said her son was the barman and was not happy with the piano player.

"He comes swanning in here, sits at the piano, people buy him drinks all night, make a big fuss of him then he swans off again to big rounds of applause. He gets more money than I do, and I work harder and longer. It's not right," he said.

"I'm afraid the hard facts are that given 15 minutes the piano player could do your job. However, given the rest of your life you could not do his," I explained.

"Sack him Mr. Adam and get me someone else. I would like a female piano player," his mother said.

I explained that it would be difficult to find a good one in the middle of the summer but would try.

I found a lass from Birmingham who agreed to come. I shall just say her name was Althea. Althea was around the fortyish mark, quite portly and bore a strong resemblance to the actress Margaret Rutherford. She carried a huge handbag stuffed with music, wore her hair in a bun that threatened to come loose. She wore a string of large beads, had thick-lensed glasses resting on her nose and looked as if she had been poured into a baggy multi-floral ankle-length dress. However, she had a lovely smile and was very jovial.

On the evening I introduced Althea, Ronnie Hilton and Norman Collier stood at the bar with pints in their hands. The bar was packed. In sailed Althea. First, she clobbered a stout man with his pint up to his mouth with her handbag, knocking him sideways and the whole table full of drinks went everywhere. She apologised, carried on towards the piano ignoring the few giggles. She sat down at the upright piano, produced sheets of music, and looked round for the microphone, which was on a boom stand. As she swung it towards her, it hit her in the face and starred her glasses. By this time, the giggles were loud bursts of laughter. She was undaunted and started to sing in a very loud screechy voice, "My Boy Lollipop, who-hoo-hoo-hoo." That did it. There followed howls of laughter. I glanced at Ronnie and Norman. They were on their hands and knees in hysterics and making for the door. The crowd loved her, and she received a standing ovation. That night the hotel burned down! No one was injured.

Dave Forrester's son Tony invited Wendy and I to join him for a meal. He said he was a merchant banker. During the conversation, he said that his father had asked him to sound me out regarding putting the Bridlington show in at the Central Pier Blackpool the following year.

I was agreeable until he said, "However, Lawrie, I am afraid that you would have to be willing to allow the current producer, Terry Cantor, to take the credit as his contract still has some time to run yet. Would that bother you?"

"I am afraid it would my friend."

"So that's a no then?"

"Yes, it is. I don't see why someone else should take all the credit for my hard work and vision."

He replied. "That is what I told my father you would say."

The winter saw us very busy touring the Golden Giveaway Show all over the country with a larger cast including the 'White Heather Pipes and Drums'. I had managed to secure some very good sponsorships thanks to my contacts at the Isle of Man season. As a result, we were able to give out some worthwhile prizes.

Surprisingly, the Blackpool Pleasure Beach asked me to put in a Christmas show. I engaged my old mate from the White Heather Canadian tour, recording star, Colin Stuart. He did an excellent show for us and he and his charming partner Ruth stayed with us.

What a truly great memorable year it had been for us.

Thirty-Six
1975 The Accelerated Years

As I was ushered into the board meeting at the Blackpool Pleasure Beach, I was reminded of my first interview for a job in the Lochgelly Co-operative.

Leonard Thomson had died, his son Geoffrey fresh out of university, had succeeded him. He sat at the far end of the long boardroom table. My seat was at the opposite end, facing him. My chair was lower than everyone else's was, and I was facing a large bright sunlit window: an old ploy for which I could easily compensate. Other board members sat along the sides of the table. Roger Wilcock was seated near Geoffrey.

Roger had contacted me to ask if I would be interested in pitching for the oncoming summer season show. Forewarned, I had come prepared to do a positive deal. I wasted no time in offering to stage a different show each night, seven nights a week under the banner of 'Lawrie Adam and his Golden Giveaway Show.' They looked quite stunned and asked me to explain.

I outlined a Saturday Spectacular, a 'Hawaiian Carnival' night, Music Hall Cabaret, a Believe it or Not Show featuring hypnotism, a Cabaret Circus Night, a Golden Giveaway Show and concluded with a Caribbean Carnival. In addition to myself hosting the shows, they would feature glamorous dancers, a beautiful girl vocalist and speciality acts. In addition, there would be audience participation with exciting sponsored prizes.

Geoffrey smiled patronisingly at me and replied, "Of course Mr. Adam, you must realise we have in fact had many offers from other promoters. Bearing this in mind, how much would you be charging us for this?"

I returned his smile and said, "Absolutely nothing!"

Immediately, they looked up from their piles of papers in front of them and said together, "Nothing?"

"That is quite correct. I am so confident of my offer that I would be happy to share a percentage of the door take. You would have all the takings from the bar and the meals. I would in fact be concessioning the room from you."

They muttered amongst themselves and Geoffrey said, "Well, you certainly have our interest Mr. Adam, but obviously we will have to discuss this and let you know in due course."

"Sorry Mr. Thompson, that's not how I work. You have my offer and I require the deal be completed either now or not at all. When I leave you here, I will be going to London to discuss other summer shows featuring stars such as The Kay Sisters and Joe 'Mr. Piano' Henderson. They will require positive dates and details from me." I felt 'I had the ping pong ball' as they say.

"Very well Mr. Adam. It would be good to get this tied up I suppose."

I continued, "As I am taking a huge risk here, I suggest a percentage of 80/20?"

Roger beamed and said, "Are you sure you could manage on 20 per cent Lawrie?"

"Of course, not Roger, you would have the 20 per cent," I replied.

"No, no. Perhaps 60/40 might be workable?" He said.

"No sorry, 75/25 is my final offer to you," I said quickly.

They accepted. I carried on,

"Your store of used Ice Rink costumes are of a very high quality, I would be very pleased to keep your standards up by using these on my dancers."

Mr. Thompson said, "Yes I agree. They are good costumes and they are just sitting there in storage."

"Also, I doubt whether I could find better musicians than you already have and so would be happy to use them as well."

Roger said, "Well, we did have trouble in finding them and it would be a pity to release them, so I would say yes." They nodded in agreement.

I said, "Finally, publicity. I am sure you would rather control the look and design of this and so I would be happy to leave this to your graphic designers."

Again, they nodded in agreement.

"Send me the contract, gentlemen, and I will begin preparations immediately." I walked out thinking, "What a great deal I have." I could hardly believe it. No costumes to hire, no band to pay, no expensive publicity to generate and I have 75 per cent of the door.

Wendy and I started auditioning at the Pleasure Beach not only for artistes and dancers in the Blackpool show, but for the Bridlington show as well. Back at the piano, I worked on the opening choruses and scenes for the 'Roaring Twenties Ragtime Revue'. Steve Colins would be the comedian plus a strong supporting cast.

For Bridlington, I hired the appropriate costumes from the Blackpool Pleasure Beach at a reasonable price. The Bridlington show started before the Blackpool one, with only a week to rehearse and stage. Wendy's choreography was second-to-none. It seemed strange producing a show but not being in it myself.

Once again, we had a hit show for which Dave paid a lump sum. The agreement included returning to produce the star show, which took over from the original show and starred the Kay Sisters and Joe 'Mr. Piano' Henderson.

We returned to Blackpool with two weeks to rehearse and stage the show to open in June. My only concern was that we were starting the show on the early side, as visitors to Blackpool were not expected in any great numbers until July.

Suppliers were keen to sell their products in to the Pleasure Beach, so sponsorship deals had gone very well. One day a brewery truck arrived packed full Colt 45 lager. Peter May, the bar manager told them he did not order such a quantity.

They replied, "It is not for you it's for a Mr. Lawrie Adam."

We packed a dressing room from floor to ceiling with the lager. Galois cigarettes from France, plus high-quality tee shirts. Crates of Jamaica rum appeared. Kronenburg lager donated attractive, large, green ashtrays. I prepared a large stock of my records for selling and Wendy made Hawaiian garlands and roses. We did not miss a trick!

My apprehension about audience numbers proved correct as trade was on the thin side. I was soon down to my last £5! In desperation, I contacted a Scottish reporter from a national Sunday paper who was touring England and giving opinions about what was on offer around the English seaside resorts. I pleaded with him on the telephone to come to Blackpool to give me a 'leg-up'. When he arrived, we toured round a few of our competitors. He gave them bad reports but praised us saying our show was the best value without a doubt and as a result, the show proved to be a great success with packed audiences most nights.

Mr. Thompson appeared one evening and said we would have to strike another deal. He realised he had made a mistake and wanted a bigger percentage of the take. I was very diplomatic about it, but my answer was "not on your life." I could tell he was used to getting his own way. He had met his match and did not like it.

The highlights were the Hawaiian Carnival Show, and the 'Golden Giveaway Show'. Wendy and I had never earned as much money. The Hawaiian music, the grass skirted dancers, Wendy's excellent choreography, the support artistes, the very funny audience participation and the prizes the contestants were loaded up with, everything contributed to a wonderful night out for holidaymakers.

The Cabaret Circus night featured our glamorous dancers, our vocalist Janice Loren, professional clowns and daring circus acts. We even featured live animals (not big ones) and snakes.

For 'The Believe It or Not Show', I did a deal with Ripley's Believe It or Not Museum on the golden mile, featuring their unusual exhibits. The audience had to guess what they were and received a prize if they guessed correctly. The second half was in the hands of a once famous hypnotist whom I discovered working as a Security man for the Pleasure Beach. His name was Richard Payne. I auditioned him and persuaded him to work under the name of 'Lord Payne'. Richard was a top-class attraction and very soon became a big draw.

The summer season concluded with the Blackpool Illuminations. The town was packed and so were we. The room dividing shutters were fully open every night and people queued to get a seat. Bookings were coming in to take the show on tour.

We had a family holiday in London. Not many theatricals managed a holiday, owing to the rules of the game, 'No work, no pay'. Until then, a summer season was regarded as the holiday. We had a great time and the kids loved it.

As soon as we returned home, I put together a Hawaiian Carnival Show Tour. I followed a similar route of the former Jimmy Clitheroe tour venues and the bookings came flooding in again. Although the show was entirely self-sufficient, this time the clubs paid a fee. It did mean however a return to the old routine of driving miles to venues, doing a show then returning home in the early hours. Having to cope with all the elements thrown at us, driving rain and fog were the worst. I found it very tiring as I had to drive, do the bulk of the show then drive home again.

I booked a more talented Hawaiian guitarist by the name of Ray Kirkwood. He was a lovely man and a brilliant musician. Ray and his wife Ruth travelled in their own little van. We took the dancers, who on the way to the venue, made attractive garlands (leis) and colourful roses for the women's hair. The girls received a percentage of those that sold.

A London agent telephoned to ask if we could do a one-night Hawaiian show in a five-star hotel in Lytham St. Annes for £1,000. I realised we were the only such show in the UK. The agent advised me not to say that we lived up the road in Blackpool and that the dancers should not speak to any one and to avoid giving away their Lancashire accents. When the hotel manager moved on to another venue, he suggested engaging us for the following summer season.

He said, "Give me a month then come to inspect the venue. It will require some theatrical additions to be purchased upon your advice." Meanwhile, we organised another 'Rock 'n 'Roll' night at a caravan holiday resort in Fleetwood managed by a star-name of the past called Ben Warris of Jimmy Jewel and Ben Warris fame. Again, the venue was packed. This time the bars honoured the deal, and everyone was happy.

I was pleased to accept the part of Idle Jack in the pantomime Dick Whittington at Southport Civic Theatre. The Dame was an old friend of ours from the Jimmy Clitheroe days, Tommy Trafford. When I met Tommy for rehearsals he said, "Well Lawrie, you did tell me that I would be topping bills in theatres, and here we are." The last time I had met Tommy was at Jimmy's hotel where he was a Chef.

The producer was Ronnie Parnell. I remembered Ronnie from my schooldays when my mother took me to a local Lochgelly club to see a concert called 'The Sunnysiders'. It was Ronnie's show. The pantomime had an excellent run, which I enjoyed, and the good thing was I was able to commute each night from home.

Wendy's Mum, Dad, and her brother John visited us for Christmas. It was perfect being at home having a normal Christmas Day like everyone else. It was wonderful to hear the screams of delight from the kids as they opened their presents, the delicious smells emanating from the kitchen of cooked turkey and all the trimmings. We hold these special, quality times in our memory store forever.

Thirty-Seven
1976 The Conversion

I launched a show, which we named 'The Golden Opportunity Show'. The various venues were responsible for publicising forms in their local newspaper, inviting all comers to apply to enter our talent show. Winners would receive appealing prizes at a big final show to be held at the Horseshoe Show-Bar at the Blackpool Pleasure Beach. Soon the show was booked to tour as far south as Devon and Cornwall. The posters were very attractive showing glamorous dancers called 'The Jet Set', exotic belly dancer Nayana, The John Peate band, renamed 'Tandem' and a vocal guitarist. I acted as host and did my act. It looked good on paper.

Unfortunately, when we opened in Plymouth the dancers I booked were not available. A double dancing act from London called the 'Pett Sisters', who looked good in the book Show-Call were free to appear. Their agent assured me they did a very lively can-can plus other routines.

We arrived at the venue and the boss said, "I hope this is up to your usual standard Lawrie, we are sold out tonight. Your leggie dancers look gorgeous on the poster."

My stomach had a sinking feeling, which did not improve when John Peate, our organist, who had a dry but very funny sense of humour remarked, "Hey Lawrie, looks like the cleaners have arrived."

Two portly middle-aged women dressed in moth-eaten looking fur coats approached me.

"We are the Pett Sisters Louwie," said in a broad cockney accent.

"Bloody Hell! You look nothing like your pictures."

"Oh! Please do not send us home Louwie. We are ever sow good 'onest."

I replied, "Well, for a start the can-can costumes are designed for showgirls. I doubt you will get your thigh in the waist!"

"No worries Louwie, we have our own and they are beautiful." There was no alternative but to agree to engage them.

In came the audience and we were soon filled to capacity. Galoise Cigarettes had provided their own girls dressed in powder blue mini-skirts, very pretty, tall with long blonde hair. They caused a stir just giving out free cigarettes.

I opened the show and after a warm-up announced, "Ladies and Gentlemen, from Paris France, please welcome our Glamorous Jet Set Girls" The music went into a rousing can-can and down the centre aisle they thundered, the very floor shook underneath them. They were screaming as they ran and went into their routine.

The first reaction from the men was, "Bloody hell, look at the state of that!"

The women in the audience clapped and cheered. The girls went a bomb! They received a standing ovation. I could not believe it.

The boss said, "Good ploy that Lawrie. The wives loved it, but it could easily have backfired."

The rest of the show went like a rocket. The local talent appeared, and we selected by applause, one act to appear in the finals in Blackpool.

The tour continued and enjoyed a successful sell-out everywhere we went. We had a slight problem when we played a night in a small place called Tonypandy in Wales. Nayana, a very attractive and lovely natured woman very slender, tanned with long black hair, danced to a tape recording of lively Arabic music. In the middle of her act, she would invite three men up to try to dance with her. That always produced huge laughs. Her act lasted for 40 minutes and was good value. However, on this particular evening, the tape for some reason went into double speed.

She kept shouting, "Switch it off...Switch it off!"

We were in hysterics and so was the audience. Her 40-minute act finished in about three minutes and she was exhausted when she staggered off collapsing into a chair!

The finals in Blackpool played to packed crowds drawn from the towns where we had performed. A young man from the Lake District won the prize.

Jimmy Kennedy, who booked for Pontins Holiday Camps, apologised to me that he had not been able to participate in the show. To make up for it, would my family like to fly to Torremolinos in Spain for two weeks. Everything would be paid for and I would be required to perform my act only once each week.

Off we went and had a great time. I never performed even once however. April weather meant it rained quite consistently and heavy. I was told that being Easter it was 'The tears of Christ' and there would be no entertainment.' The kids had a ball. They kept the red sombreros we bought them for years. It was sheer delight to see them having such great fun in the Spanish sunshine.

When we got home, Jimmy phoned again and apologised that I did not get to perform. To make up for this would we like another holiday, same deal but in Yugoslavia in September.

I did a week's cabaret in the New Bond Street Night Club in London's West End.

After my rehearsal with the band the manager, who seemed to have taken a shine to me, gave me a few tips. "We have had royalty in here you know," he said. "Not just from this country but from all over. Before you go on, make sure you sit over there with the hostess girls. They are nice lasses but get offended when some of the acts look down their noses at them. They can make the difference between you going well or dying the death." I took the trouble to sit with them and have a chat. They were very friendly. Some were from up north.

The show started with the Pamela Davies Dancers. Very glamorous in plumes and feathers. Not as good as my Wendy though. I intended making my entrance from the door playing bagpipes. As I passed the bar heading for a big table with men in dinner suits and their wives, I presumed, the manager grabbed me and steered me in an opposite direction. My act went well enough, but they were not my usual kind of northern audience. Afterwards I marched over to the manager and asked him what he thought he was doing?

"You were heading for a coming out party. If you had stuck your pipes in their ears or sat on their wives knees we wouldn't be having this conversation."

"A coming out party? Coming out from where?"

"A long stretch in prison!" he said. "Have a closer look at their jackets and notice the slight bulge. They have guns. Welcome to the big wicked city son."

I was amazed at what I saw. Nothing was served in a glass just in the bottle - whisky at horrendous prices and the champagne cost a fortune. I noticed a hostess girl would screw up an empty cigarette packet and looking at her customer with pleading eyes who would then order more for her, always a packet of 20 and again at a cost. It was usual to hear a curse from a young man when presented with a huge bill for the night. As soon as he looked like causing a disturbance, tall security men in dinner suits surrounded him. They took him aside out of hearing and... convinced him to pay. This was about as contrasting from my home town of Lochgelly as I could get. A different planet!

Back home with my little family in Blackpool we were busy booking out package shows. The Haughton Weavers were doing very well. We were all set to open with Hawaiian Nights at the Trafalgar Hotel for the summer. We filled up coaches from Blackpool hotels and ferried them out to the Trafalgar Hotel. Our show was the best Hawaiian ever. We had a four-piece group, starring singer Beverly, who had a warm sounding voice. The five dancers including Wendy plus Ray Kirkwood Hawaiian Guitar were ace. I acted as host and performed my act. It was a glamorous fast-paced floorshow with the band on a small stage behind. After the show there was food galore and dancing to our band and then it finished off with two glamorous girl DJ's. For a modest sum, the audiences had on offer a very attractive array of food and were invited to eat as much as they liked. On entry, they were given a glass of Hawaiian Punch.

Wendy had to take one of the dancers aside and suggest she say to the men "Would you like a garland, sir?" Not "Good evening sir, would you like a lei?"

A phone call from Dave Forrester suggested I appear at the Villa Marina with Ken Dodd on the Isle of Man.

"When Dave? I am fully committed now, and I have enough on without catching a plane to that island of all places. I don't think so Dave."

"Ken has asked specially for you Lawrie. He doesn't want a mucky club comic going on before him."

"How much are you thinking of paying me?"

When he told me I said, "Dave, I can earn £100 when I book the Haughton Weavers for a night and I don't even have to leave my desk!"

There was a long pause then he said, "I was good to you when you needed it Lawrie. You should not forget that. Come on, do me this favour."

I considered what he had said. "Okay, Dave, I'll do it as a favour for you."

"Great, please wear your kilt as there will be lots of Glasgow folk there."

It seemed strange to be in Douglas again. I made my way to the Villa Marina. After the rehearsal with the orchestra, I needed to book a hotel for the night. I tried to get as close to the theatre as possible and so turned up Broadway.

All the bed and breakfasts had groups of loud Glasgow-voiced girls sitting on the doorsteps. Some shouting, "Hey, Jimmy, come in here, ye'll hae a great time wi' us yins."

I wanted peace and quiet, so I walked further down and decided to try a hotel called the Odeon. However, I noticed a plaque on the wall beside the door it said, 'Christian Hotel'.

The door opened, and a man appeared in a white apron.

"Looking to book?" he said.

"Yes, but I am not a Christian," I replied.

"That's okay," he laughed, "We take anyone. I only have one room left. You are very lucky. Douglas is jam packed this weekend."

It was a small upstairs room containing a bed, a wardrobe, a chair and a bedside cabinet. There was a window looking on to Broadway.

On the way to the theatre, I bought a bundle of newspapers. I always found it difficult to sleep away from home and generally read myself to sleep.

The stage door keeper said, "Lawrie Adam?"

"Yes, that's me."

"A phone call for you," he said.

It was the organist from Summerland. He had seen my name on the show bills. He invited me to his home for some food before the show. He said he would collect me in five minutes.

We had a great chat and a super meal, which his wife had prepared. He explained that he had been buried under about eleven dead bodies at the foot of a stair well. The door had been locked. The unfortunate people on top of him had somehow filtered the poisonous fumes. Unfortunately, he now had serious lung damage.

The Villa Marina was packed with happy Scottish holidaymakers. It was always a pleasure to work with Ken. In my books, he was the best comedian in the UK. I enjoyed the show, but the venue was more akin to a ballroom than theatre.

After the show, it was not until I reached my room that I realised I had left my newspapers in the organist's car. I had nothing to read. I got into bed and glanced at the bedside cabinet seeing the Gideon Bible. I picked it up and started to read. I did not realise it then, but it was the King James translation written in ye olde English and full of 'thous', 'thys', 'henceforths' and 'begets'.

I said "Yuck," and chucked it back on the table. I just sat there, looking round the small room. The window was open as it was a hot sticky night. I heard the revellers coming back from the pubs singing at the top of their voices and the clicking of stiletto heels on the concrete pavements. "I'm never going to get to sleep," I thought.

I heard a slurred woman's voice saying, "Here Jenny, that wis a great nicht we hid eh? Whit a cracker."

I decided to do a desperate check on the shelf in the bedside cabinet. I reached right along. Nothing. I did another sweep right at the back, and my hand rested on something...a book! I was thrilled to bits. I brought it into view. It looked a very old book. The title was Good News for the Modern Man. It was quite thick with a faded grey and blue designed cover.

I thought, "Well this looks boring, but I don't care, I am going to read it."

I opened it up and the page edges had turned pale yellow with age.

I started to read and realised, "Oh! No, this is a religious book." I read on, The Gospel of St. Matthew. It was written in plain easy to read English and I was soon devouring every word. Funny the noises outside did not intrude any more, the room was still and quiet.

When I reached page eight entitled The Sermon on the Mount, I could picture the scene quite easily. Crowds of people, the heat, even the smell of the grass, the flowers and the odd chirping of birds in flight as the people eagerly listened to the words that fell from the lips of Jesus. The words rang home and touched my heart. Then something strange happened to me.

As I read on and on, certain words seemed to leap out at me

436

'I chose you, you did not choose me.'

'Seek and you will find'

I was being spoken to, I did not feel alone.

'Knock and the door will be opened to you'. Then, 'Follow me.'

By this time, I had tears running down my cheeks. Me, well known as a cynic who questioned everything. I realised I could have lived a better life than I had been doing and felt some remorse.

Suddenly, everything was reversed, and I felt an almighty sweep of joy go right through me. I was in tears again but they were tears of joy. I gently replaced the book on the cabinet and enjoyed the most peaceful and deepest sleep in my life.

The following morning, I awoke to the sounds of hymn singing from below. I remembered this was a Christian Hotel. I dressed, went downstairs, and sat down at my place in the crowded dining room. There was a bowl of corn flakes in front of me, so I poured on the milk and started to eat with gusto. I came to an embarrassed halt as the landlord, unnoticed, had entered the room and was saying grace.

As I paid the bill, I said to the landlord. "I know this is probably a strange request, but I read a book last night and wondered if I could buy it please?"

He looked surprised, "The Gideon Bible?"

"No, it was called Good News for The Modern Man."

He laughed, "Goodness me I thought we had cleared these out ages ago. We must have missed that one. I'm afraid I can't sell it to you, sir." My heart sank.

"That's a great pity," I said

He smiled as he said, "I'll give it to you as a gift." He called the waitress and asked her to bring it to me. It felt like receiving a precious block of gold as she placed the book into my open eager hands

I stood at the hotel door waiting on my friend, the Summerland organist, who said he would collect me and run me to the airport.

As I climbed in, he remarked. "Well you look very fresh Lawrie."

"Fresh?"

"Yes, your face is shining like the sun."

"I had a great night."

He looked at me again and said, "Hey, you are not on drugs, are you?"

"Certainly not," I replied.

We chatted, said our farewells then I was aboard the plane. I realised that something special had happened and could not wait to tell Wendy. I knew that a different man was flying out, from the one who had flown in. I did not realise that an old discarded book was about to change the whole direction of my life and that of my family.

Thirty-Eight
1977 As One Door Closes

I sat Wendy down and told her about my Isle of Man experience. I expected her to say something like, "That's just unbelievable. Surely you must have imagined it." However, I could not have been more wrong.

After regarding me with a long studious look she said calmly, "Well, how wonderful darling. I'm very happy for you."

I might have known she would understand right away and knew more than I realised at that time. We had a long conversation about religious faith. She had been a Christian as long as she could remember and was a member of the Church of England. She had never mentioned it because I had never mentioned it. However, now she was glad I had. During the three years she studied ballet at Bush Davies in East Grindstead, she attended church every Sunday and was confirmed there.

For a few days afterwards, each time I walked past St. Stephens on the Cliffs Church, just around the corner from our house, I experienced a slight pull as if I was walking past a magnetic field.

One evening at our family meal I said, "How does everyone feel about going to the church this Sunday?"

SILENCE! The kids stopped eating and gaped at me.

Wendy said, "Well, I think it would be a good idea, why not?" The kids looked at each other, said nothing, and carried on eating.

I continued, "What about the evening service?" They kept on eating and nodded.

That Sunday evening, we entered the door of the church. There were quite a few people there. We sat at the back. It was called a 'Book of Common Prayer Evensong'. I could not make head nor tail of the book. It seemed so thick and contained so many wafer-thin pages. I enjoyed the hymns. The sermon was interesting, but I experienced no feelings of great ecstasy. The kids were not amused but behaved very well.

As we left the church the vicar, a kindly smiling-faced well-spoken elderly man with wispy grey hair, shook our hands and said, "How do you do, it's lovely to see you all. Why don't you come next time to the morning family service, I'm sure you will enjoy that much better?"

During the week, it was back to business selling our shows. We had the Hawaiian Show, still selling well, Cabaret Parisian, The Ronnie Hilton Show and even a touring Pantomime managed by my old friend from Arbroath days, Ronnie Wayne, Goldilocks and the Three Bears. In addition, I was booking out the Haughton Weavers who were very popular.

On Sunday, we attended church again as a family but this time to the morning service. A woman appeared at the side of our pew and asked if the children would like to go with her to their Sunday

\School. They looked relieved and escaped. Everyone was very friendly. We had decided to sit halfway back. I was immediately aware of a strange smell.

"It's incense," Wendy said.

"Incense? What for?" I asked.

"This is an Anglo-Catholic Church," she replied.

"Catholic! Not Church of England then?" I said.

"Yes, it is Church of England. It is not Roman Catholic. It is called High Church."

It made no sense at all to me. Although, I did feel more at home this time than I did on my visit to the church in Bridlington.

I had not been aware of the chatter surrounding me until a bell sounded and suddenly it went very quiet. A bell tolled three sets of three bongs and then I counted nine. To my theatrical senses this was tantamount to the orchestra tuning up, the house lights slowly dipping, indicating that the show was about to start. Everyone stood. The organist situated high up in his loft struck up the introduction to a hymn. In walked a tall young fair-haired man dressed in colourful robes carrying an ornate silver cross, held high before him on a long pole. Behind him, all robed in bright blue and white came a choir of approximately 20 men and boys singing the hymn. What a glorious sound I thought, and what an unexpected spectacle.

Following the choir, was a man with his hand upon a very small boy's shoulder, as if kindly reassuring and guiding him, as he swung a contraption like a silver bowl emitting smoke and suspended by long chains. Behind them, another three men appeared wearing ancient Roman looking robes. Two men in smart suits each carried a wooden staff with some sort of metal emblem on top preceded the clergyman we had seen at the evening service now dressed in a long gold elaborate cloak. Everyone obviously had appointed places. The two men in suits split to the side of the steps allowing the vicar to walk through. As he reached the last step, he turned to face the congregation and the hymn ended. Perfect timing, I thought. It was all very smart and professional, and very theatrically pleasing to my producer's eye. I do not know what I had expected but it certainly was not this.

The service proceeded with readings from the Bible, hymns, a sermon and then a very wordy sung portion, which implied great importance. A bell tolled. Folk crossed themselves. The air was thick with incense swirling around the main players. I looked up and thought that it resembled a classic old oil painting. There was a feeling of Holiness in the atmosphere. I was full of questions, but who to ask? Just then, the vicar announced in the notices that he was having a six weeks' session in the vicarage on a certain evening and anyone was welcome.

"I'd like to go to that," I said to Wendy.

"Then we will," she said.

Wendy and I attended the first session and were warmly welcomed into the cosy lounge. The vicar spoke about Christian faith and then invited questions. I was full of them! We made friends with a woman with a very educated accent. I remember thinking, 'She's a bit posh.' Her name was Doctor. Valerie Davis. The vicar asked us all if we had been baptised. Wendy said she had.

"I don't really know vicar, but I'm sure I probably have been," I stammered.

He smiled, "Ask your parents, you may be surprised."

I received a letter from my mother in New Zealand informing me that my dad was not very well I telephoned them, and it was so wonderful to hear their voices.

Dad said, "Oh! It's nothing Lawrie, just a wee blip. Dinna worry son. I'm fine, really."

I asked if I had been baptised.

There was a pause and then he said, "No. We decided to leave that decision to yersel. Why di ye ask anyway?"

"No particular reason," I replied.

I had decided not to do a summer season as we were busy enough booking shows and artistes and we didn't want to uproot the girls any more than necessary from their schools. A local agent booked me to do a spot in Morecambe called The Harbour Band Arena every Wednesday afternoon to an audience seated in deckchairs.

One dull cool windy summer's day I received a telegram from my mother informing me that my Dad had died. I was struck dumb. Wendy suggested going into the church and that I might find some comfort from prayer. I went and did indeed find it a calming help. I realised however, I still had to put in an appearance in Morecambe. Whatever happens, 'The Show Must Always Go On.'

Wendy went with me. There was very little atmosphere within the Harbour Band Arena. A microphone, a stage, an organist and me with a twenty-minute spot to do to an audience trying to cope with the gusty wind huddled up in coats on deckchairs. The empty ones (and there were many) were billowing like ships sails. After I did my very best to entertain them I picked up the accordion and went into some sing-along choruses. When I had finished they cheered and shouted for more.

I said, "Okay, one more request, what will it be?"

It went quiet then a voice shouted "Play 'Endearing Young Charms'."

I gasped for breath for a few seconds. The only person who had ever asked me to play that particular melody was my dear Dad.

I started to play, I glanced off stage and Wendy had her little hand up to her mouth and was in tears. By the time I finished the number, I too had tears rolling down my cheeks. It was as if he had come for a final visit to say farewell.

Thirty-Nine
1977 Many Searching Church Questions

"Champagne on draught," said the brightly lit sign at Yates's Wine Lodge'. Suddenly, some movement caught my eye. I stopped and found myself looking with some amusement, and some sadness, as four small puppies tried their hardest to attract my attention in the Pet Shop window. They were clambering over each other, pawing at the glass and looking up at me. I came out five minutes later with a small cute black pup nestled in my arm.

I placed him on the passenger seat of our black Mercedes, but as soon as I started to drive, he crawled over and sat in my lap with his tiny paws on the bottom of the steering wheel. We drove home together, and he seemed to enjoy the experience thoroughly.

I rang the doorbell. Tracey answered. As soon as she saw the small puppy, she let out a scream of delight and grabbed him from me. Fiona was soon on the scene and they were both thrilled. We decided to call him Shep: he was a mongrel, black with a white cross on his chest and he was to live with us for the next 12 years.

Both girls went to the same Norbreck Primary School, which was a tram stop away. Every morning Shep had to come with us as we ran up the street to the tram stop, which was high above the North Shore promenade at Bispham. We usually caught the tram by the skin of our teeth every morning. Fiona's little thin

7-year-old legs had a job keeping up with Tracey who was a very athletic 11-year-old. Shep and I did our best.

Wendy and I drove to the school to collect the girls at home time. Fiona was always out first and then some minutes later out would saunter Tracey. Some evenings they went to dancing lessons'.

As the vicar's evening classes continued, Wendy and I made some good friends. Soon we were being invited to small dinner parties which we reciprocated and had lots of fun. This side of life was new to us. We realised that our show business life was rather insular.

Two favourite people of ours were Doctor. Val and her husband Kopel Davis. They had two charming daughters and apart from Kopel, who was a Jew, were what was called a 'big church family.' Val became our doctor and I enjoyed playing accordion at barn dances for Kopel who was a skilled caller.

There was a service on a Thursday morning in the side chapel, called the 'Lady Chapel'. It had quite a grand statue of the Virgin Mary with a plaque underneath stating that it was a gift to the church from the show business star, Tessie O'Shea.

The curate, a young man called Reverend. Michael Harman who was married to a school teacher called Jane, took the service. Jane was very easy to talk to and had a good sense of humour. I was always pumping her for answers to my many questions. I was still reading my 'Good News for The Modern Man' book.

One day she said to me, "Oh dear, Lawrie, questions questions. Look, I have a proposition to put to you. How about I take you for an O-Level course on Religious Studies. I will give you information and homework. At the end, you can even sit the exam. What do you say?" She certainly kept me busy and satisfied many questions I was having about Christianity.

Bearing in mind my 15 years in a hard very pushy business, I decided I would not volunteer for anything in the church but would always wait to be invited or asked. After a Thursday morning service, Michael took me aside and said, "Lawrie, as you seem to be a regular attender, I would appreciate some help. Would you consider assisting me on a Thursday morning?" He outlined what I would be expected of me.

"Me! Wear a what, a cassock? And give out the wine?"

Eventually I agreed, and he gave me a quick rehearsal.

That first Thursday morning when we knelt together at the altar rail and prayed together, I had a strange feeling of a weight being lifted from my shoulders. I felt very humble and privileged to be assisting Michael.

I was still experiencing some strange events that were verging on the comical. One Sunday morning I stood up at the side of the pew ready to go up to the main altar rail. Wendy could receive communion, but I could only receive a blessing, as I was not confirmed. I was still trying to make sense of that one. Suddenly, a large woman resembling the TV character Mrs. Bucket, but pronounced bouquet, materialised right in front of me. She wore a large hat and dressed in a silk bright royal blue outfit with a very wide accordion pleated skirt. The whole lot descended onto my lap. She stood up abruptly, glared at me and said, "Sorry, I was genuflecting!"

I thought, "What the hell does that mean?"

Later I saw another large woman come to a sudden halt just before a doorway and genuflect very graciously, cross herself, then walk away.

I called after her, "Excuse me," I said, "I'm new here and trying to make some sense of many things. Could you tell me why you just did that please?"

She glared at me, went slightly pink and muttered, "Oh, yes, I have heard about you. I think it's to the war memorial." Then she marched off indignantly. I looked upwards. Above the door was a plaster cast of a soldier leaning on his rifle.

I asked Michael later and he smiled as he said, "Poor woman. She has seen the priests genuflect at that spot. If you look to your right, you will see a small light above a tiny velvet curtain on the wall. We keep the Holy Sacrament in there in readiness to take to the sick or housebound." I did not have a clue what he was talking about.

I said, "What exactly is the Holy Sacrament?"

"What! You don't even know what that is? Well, during a celebration of Holy Communion, a number of wafers are dipped in consecrated wine and placed in a ciborium which is then placed in the Ombre."

I drew a breath to ask what a ciborium was, but he said, "Please no more questions for the moment. You are giving me a headache!"

I enjoyed my sessions with Jane and no sooner had she given me some homework to do than it was done and back with her for marking.

Michael would pop in to see us almost every week and have a coffee with us. Sometimes he would appear in the middle of me selling a show and would settle himself in the important client's black armchair. Lower than my seat and facing the sun! He said it was interesting to hear my sales patter but when I mentioned money, his jaw dropped.

The Hawaiian Show was still selling well and now included two local dancers who had jobs in a bank during the day. The conversations in the car went up a notch or two from the norm.

Eventually Wendy declared that she would like to retire from the long-haul package tours, as the kids were getting older now. I understood and agreed but missed having her with me.

Eventually the vicar's evening classes concluded, and he took down names for those who wished to be confirmed.

Wendy nudged me as he looked at me and so I said "Yes." I also admitted that I had not in fact been baptised.

He grinned and said, "Ah ha! I told you so. No problem, we will do it privately during the week."

And so I was duly baptised. Two Sundays later, I was confirmed and took my first Holy Communion. Slowly things were dropping into place but I still had a hunger for knowledge.

I had a bizarre experience at church one Sunday, which shook me up a bit. I looked up at the vicar at the end of a service as they were processing towards the door and suddenly I saw 'my head on his body.' It seemed to last for some seconds.

Wendy said, "What's up? You okay, you look like you have seen a ghost!"

"I'll tell you later," I said.

When I did she said, "I'm sure you have some Irish Gypsy blood in you."

"Well, maybe I have. My mother's side has always been an unknown mystery to me."

Forty
1977-78 A Strong Calling is Tested

It was very sad for Wendy and myself to note the pain of bereavement in my mother's voice as we chatted to her on the telephone. I wished I could have placed my arm around her little shoulders and try to offer some comfort as she struggled to find the words of how heartbroken she was at losing my father. She said her world had ended. She felt as if the sun had set and would never rise again. I knew how devoted they had been to each other. They were always a pair and now she was on her own. She told me that Dad had been asking about us right to the end. She was sending me two diaries he had written and wanted me to have them. I knew my brother Ronnie and his family would look her after. They had spent a great deal of time together since they emigrated. Dad told me of the New Year parties and the holidays they shared. My brother Bill however, was now an unknown quantity as there had been a falling out.

I had just finished assisting the curate Michael at a Thursday morning service when in walked the vicar. Most of the congregation had left to make their way to the small hall for coffee and biscuits. Wendy was chatting to our friend and doctor, Val, and a couple of others.

The vicar said, "What do you think of my new suit?" Val and Wendy gave a complimentary reply.

He looked at me and said, "And what do you think Lawrie?"

I replied, "Well, quite frankly, for someone who purports to represent the Good News it's a bit on the sombre side. Sorry if it's not what you expected to hear, but when asked for my opinion, I always give it." He gave a grunt followed by a curt nod and departed.

Val said, "Lawrie, when the Archdeacon of Lancaster asks you for an opinion, I suggest you adopt a more kindly and diplomatic approach."

I entered the vestry and Michael was putting away the vestments in a large drawer.

"I didn't realise that the vicar was the Archdeacon of Lancaster," I said.

Michael nodded and replied, "Yes, the Venerable Geoffrey Gower Jones is certainly that."

"Well I think I have just upset him."

Michael said, "Really? Well he has just asked me to train you up to assist him at a special afternoon service next week, if you are free and agreeable?"

I nodded, "Certainly if you can answer a question for me? That garment you are placing in the drawer, what do you call it and why does it have an elaborated 'Y' shaped braiding on the front and back?"

"Ah! Here we go again, more questions. Well, it's called a chasuble. Originally, it was a Roman garment. As to the Y shaped braiding that would signify our Lord hanging on the cross."

I purchased a book to assist me in unravelling many of the mysteries surrounding the sacramental nature of this new faith. I looked this one up and was surprised to note that my wise curate guru had it wrong. A chasuble is similar to a poncho and made in sections. The braiding covers up the unsightly stitching. I realised that not only was some teaching required amongst the people in the pews, but also the teachers!

I continued to enjoy growing in the faith and learn the ecclesiastical terms of the church.

As one of the altar serving team, I enjoyed the new experience. I exchanged the long black cassock for a long white cotton Alb (which symbolises innocence and purity), worn with an amice (a collar-like cloth).

Michael rehearsed the Sunday services very carefully, as Father Geoffrey did not tolerate mistakes, and accepted only perfection. I too was a perfectionist and so this was to my liking.

Michael said, "If Father Geoffrey is not pleased he will give a loud sniff! Beware of the sniff!"

At the end of the High School term Jane organised my attendance to sit the O-Level exam and take my place alongside a classroom full of schoolgirls. Admittedly, there were a few strange looks and the odd snigger, but I completed the paper. I was amazed when Jane presented me with a B pass certificate and her congratulations.

She said, "You know, I didn't think you would stay the course, well done."

One morning in the vestry, I confided to Michael that I had been carrying around a great weight these last weeks and just had to talk about it. He invited me to do so.

I said, with much difficulty, "Well, I have this deep feeling that God wants me to do more. I wonder if he is calling me to the priesthood, but surely, he cannot be. Not me. Not with my background and my cynicism."

Michael smiled, placed his hand upon my shoulder and said, "But hasn't it taken a long time Lawrie. We have watched you grow in faith. Father Geoffey said to me some time ago, 'You know Michael, I do believe that man is destined for the priesthood, but do not say anything. It will have to come from himself or not at all.' "

"So, Lawrie, do you want to take things further and test your calling?"

"I think I'll have to, so that I can have some peace," I replied.

Some days later, I had a chat with the vicar who explained the long road of testing I would have to travel. He said, "I'll fix up an appointment for you and Wendy to see the Bishop. If he is satisfied, you will be invited to see the Director of Ordinands, who is a very shrewd, knowledgeable and wise man. If he is content, he will recommend you attend a conference of the 'Church of England Advisory Council for Church Ministry (ACCM)'. You will reside there for three days and be studied closely and questioned by five people. If they agree you do have a true calling, then they will recommend you for theological educational training. This would last for three years. The whole journey takes seven years and can be terminated at any time. So, there you are Lawrie, it would be a long road ahead of you. Do you still wish to proceed?"

I said, "Yes, I need to know whether it is all in my mind, or if I am truly being called."

He replied with a kindly smile, "All you have to do is be absolutely truthful and answer all questions put to you honestly."

"The truth is, I just cannot imagine myself as a priest and actually have no burning desire to be one!"

He chuckled and said, "Well, that is a good honest attitude for a start. Let the journey begin. I will make an appointment with the Bishop for you."

Wendy and I had never met a bishop before and so we asked Michael for some advice. He told us to give a slight bow and just say, 'Good morning, My Lord'. "He will do the rest. Just answer all his questions with honesty. Do not worry. He's a very nice man really."

We received a phone call from the Bishop's secretary giving us an appointment. I parked our gleaming black Mercedes Benz on his drive. We stood on the doorstep facing the large front door of his palace, looked at each other, took a deep breath then rang the doorbell. We were both a bit surprised when the bishop himself opened the door as we expected a housekeeper to perform that task.

We both bowed from the waist and said together, "Good morning, My Lord!"

We felt like two munchkins from the Wizard of Oz!

He grinned, looked over our shoulders and remarked, "I say, is that your car over there?"

I replied, "Yes, it is."

"Well if you go forward that will be the first thing to go! Come on in."

He asked us both a barrage of questions. He asked Wendy her feelings about a possible change of lifestyle. He said if I was recommended for training, it would mean the diocese was committed to invest a large four-figure sum in my education and training. He ended the conversation by saying if he felt I had a calling I would hear from his Director of Ordinands, who would then wish to interview me. We left it at that and took our leave.

Morecambe

Bob Brierly, Morecambe Entertainments Director, asked me to consider featuring our Hawaiian Show for one hour per day throughout the summer in their brand new open-air leisure park. He showed me round. It consisted of a large pool with some smaller pools joined together by pathways and islands. It was attractive, but of all places, poor old cold, windy, Morecambe.

I recalled my old pal Colin Crompton saying, "In Morecambe, they don't bury their dead - they just stand them up in bus shelters!" The resort did have that sort of look about it.

Bob said he would be able to supply eight attractive Hawaiian Dancers and musical backing. I had to produce it, present it, and perform some audience participation and provide a pretty vocalist.

We negotiated a fee, which I felt was a bit on the low side but Morecambe was always strapped for cash and had little vision. He tried to sweeten the deal by saying he could put the show in on certain evenings at what used to be the old Alhambra Theatre, (where I had previously played a summer season with Johnny Victory and Robert Earl) now renamed The Inn on The Bay and refurbished. I agreed.

I found myself in the Law Court every month suing musicians and artistes for money owing to us. They did not seem to care that I also had bills to pay and a family to feed.

This did trouble me, as it seemed contradictory to my understanding of Jesus saying, "If your brother wants your shirt, give him your coat also."

ACCM Conference

I presented myself to a Reverend Canon Neil Pritchard who was the diocesan Director of Ordinands. The Bishop felt I might have a calling and this was the next step along the way. Canon Pritchard and I talked at great length. Finally, he said he was recommending me to attend an ACCM conference where my calling would be scrutinised, and a decision made.

Some weeks later, I received a letter to attend a retreat house for three days to take part in an ACCM conference.

"This would be it then." I thought. "At least someone will now tell me if my calling is genuine or not."

About 30 men and women were sitting on upright chairs along the walls of a hall staring at each other for what seemed ages. A bishop entered, introducing himself as 'The Bishop of Birkenhead'. He stood in the middle, welcomed everyone, and then explained roughly, what would be happening over the course of the next three days.

"But first, let us introduce ourselves to each other. Please stand up, state your name, where you are from and in what occupation you are currently engaged. Can we start with you first please?" he said pointing to a tall man at the end of my line.

I was amazed at variety of occupations and the geographical whereabouts of each person. There was an abundance of teachers, a public-school headmaster, a brewery executive, a steelworker from Sheffield, a farm labourer, a solicitor, an accountant and a variety of others.

As everyone supplied his or her intriguing information, it occurred to me that it was like finding yourself on a space ship having been beamed up and mystified as to how exactly you got there!

At the evening meal, I sat next to a man from Fleetwood. He wanted passionately to be a priest and was aghast when I told him I was not bothered one way or the other. I just wanted someone to tell me whether I was truly called or not, so that I could get on with my life.

That evening we were all gathered in a small lounge, given a slip of paper with a subject written upon and asked to stand up and talk with authority on this subject, whether we were conversant with it or not. We must be prepared to speak with confidence and without hesitation for two minutes.

I did not find it too difficult to speak about atomic energy, although I knew absolutely nothing at all about it! Others had some difficulties with their subjects.

In the days that followed we were questioned by our five interrogators one at a time – 30 minutes each person.

The middle-aged woman from a department of education, (who reminded me of the actress Margaret Rutherford) had been chosen to determine whether I could cope with three years of intensive studies. Another man was there to decide whether he could imagine me as his vicar.

I had an interesting time with the Bishop of Birkenhead who, after a short silence and staring intensely at me from behind a large desk, drew in a sharp breath and said, "Lawrie, tell me why you want to be a priest."

There was a long pause: I did not know what to say.

He carried on "I must have an answer from you, I'm afraid."

I replied, "Probably for the same reason you wanted to be a bishop." I noticed he was stumped.

He said, "Err thank you that will be all."

My last interview was designed to test my spirituality. The Rev. Ian Harland, a clergyman from Doncaster, was spellbound when I related my conversion experience. This interview was terminated by a loud knocking on the door. He glanced at his watch and said, "Good grief! We have gone well over our time. You have been here for an hour instead of 30 minutes."

Eventually, it was over. After we departed, the five questioners would meet and discuss each candidate one by one. The candidates would be informed of the conclusions by letter.

Before I left, I had a conversation with the Fleetwood man and he said, "Keep in touch Lawrie, it would be good to know if we have been accepted."

I was astounded some two weeks later to receive a letter stating that I was being recommended for training. I felt sure it must have been a mistake and probably my letter was intended for the man in Fleetwood. I phone him up. He sounded very sad because he had been turned down. He said they did not make mistakes with letter mix-ups and congratulated me. I was in a daze. I had been positive I would be turned down. I recalled something Father Geoffrey had said as he showed me out his door.

"If God wants you Lawrie, no power on earth will stop Him."

I received another invitation from the Director of Ordinands. He explained that I had two choices open to me. A residential Theological College, or a new idea which was only 12 years old but proving very successful. It was similar to the Open University in that I would continue to live at home and earn my living, but also attend lectures in Manchester once a week.

Added to this, I would be required to attend a long weekend, once a month, which would be residential, and a 12-day summer school residence. This would continue for three years. There were no examinations as such, but continual assessment. I would be required to compile essays and theses up to about six thousand words. These would be monitored by college staff and sent to external examiners for marking.

I decided to opt for the Open University type studies, as I did not want to leave my family if at all possible.

I was required to attend two further interviews. The first one was with the Principal Hugh Melinsky of the Northern Ordination Course of the Baptist College Rusholme in Manchester. He would decide whether I was a suitable candidate. If accepted, I would commence studies the following year.

However, it was the Reverend. John A. White, Director of Spirituality who would deliver the final decision.

Forty-One
The Rookie Student

The principal the Reverend Canon Hugh Melinsky was a tall quietly spoken sophisticated man, dressed in a dark blue velvet jacket with dark penetrating eyes. He had jet-black hair, greying at the temples and his skin had an expensive tanned appearance. As he outlined what would be expected from me should I be acceptable, I experienced feelings of growing irritation.

"Of course, Lawrence…"

"I prefer to be called Lawrie, Mr. Melinsky," I interjected.

"As you wish, er, Lawrie. I was going to say that you might find it difficult for the first few months for one reason or another. Especially bearing in mind your lack of academic background. I note that you attended Primary School, and Junior Secondary School. No mention of high school, grammar school or a college?" He said looking up over his glasses.

"I did sit exams from the Co-operative College in Loughborough and in fact was awarded a bursary to attend there as a residential student."

"Ah! Yes," he said placing his fingertips together and glancing down at some sheets of paper in front of him.

"Let me see now, you gained certificates in the following subjects, Trade Calculations and Accounts, Co-operation stage 1, Salesmanship and Commodities Non-Foodstuffs, Arithmetic stage 1, Book-Keeping stage 1 and stage 2. I am afraid they may not prove to be of much use to you, should you embark on three years of ordination training. I should also add that you will be sitting alongside men and women holding university degrees and some with a long history of higher education."

There was a long pause, and then he looked at me directly and said, "So, Lawrie, how do you feel about that?"

I looked him in the eye and said, "Due to my God-given talent and skills, I have been self-employed in one of the most difficult businesses in existence, in this country and abroad. I have had my own record label, I have produced sizeable theatre shows for London managements, and indeed at this very moment, have my own shows on tour all over England. I am a member of the 'University of Life'. I must possess leadership skills and business skills to say nothing of communication skills. Will, I wonder, the men and women I sit and study with, have as many skills at *their* fingertips, sir?"

He smiled, stood up, reached out and shook my hand warmly as he said, "I will fix up an appointment with the Reverend John White for you. I personally would welcome you to the course. Thank you for coming. It has been good to talk to you."

In response to a phone call from the Reverend John White, I presented myself at his small, very tidy bungalow on the outskirts of Manchester. John was about my height and build, dressed in a casual sweater and open neck shirt. He had short-cropped sandy coloured hair, and a well-clipped small beard and moustache. I was aware I was being interviewed by a very skilled and shrewd academic, but with a sharp sense of humour and wit. He was very interested in the show business side of my life in fact he displayed an aura of the entertainer himself. John invited himself to my home saying he would love to meet Wendy and the girls. A date was fixed.

Meanwhile, Wendy and I were still very much engaged in our showbiz pursuits. We arranged 'Show-Case' evenings. Artistes were invited to display their talents. The intention being that agents were invited to watch and would book them for summer seasons and shows. We had to keep a very sharp eye out for poachers, bookers who took advantage of our hospitality (drinks and meals) but tried discretely to do a deal with the artistes themselves, thus cutting us out of the equation to save themselves a fee. I was never surprised by the dishonestly of some people and was often reminded that it was a very competitive tough and ruthless business.

I remembered a conversation I had with Father Geoffrey in the quiet of St. Stephen's Church one evening. He was showing me the beautiful work surrounding the altar in the Actor's Chapel. At first glance, it looked like robed apostle figures gathered together in a row. However, it became most intriguing when he pointed to some of the faces based on famous show business people. He remarked that in times gone by they used to have a big service for all the entertainers in the resort. Circus people and show people would gather here together. He related how he had in fact conducted the marriage ceremony of the famous comedy star of stage and screen, Nat Jackley.

I asked him if he admired the show business folk.

He replied, "Sadly, no Lawrie. I could never understand the awful things they would do to each other."

When the Reverend John White arrived at our Blackpool home, he received a royal welcome. He hit it off with the kids straight away and established a lifetime friendship with Tracey.

Having been accepted for training and given a starting date, I was warned to keep everything under wraps. Training could be ended for one reason or another at any time. There was never any guarantee that I would be ordained.

He said, "Remember, many are called, but few are chosen."

Forty-Two
1978 A Familiar Door Closes as Another Opens

The final curtain on my show business life was slowly but assuredly falling. Summer seasons away from home and driving up and down the country, appearing in cabaret shows or pantomimes, ended.

From this point on, my routine changed to allow me to attend lectures and compose essays.

However, shows within striking distance from home, plus booking out our package shows and artistes allowed me to earn enough money to provide for my family. The Christmas season was financially fruitful. My own experience working as an artiste provided the knowledge, which enabled me to book cabaret artistes into many of the Blackpool front hotels for the festive duration. Meticulous planning was required to ensure all the artistes arrived exactly on time at the correct venue each evening.

During the same period, we enjoyed our involvement in the many church services. I delighted in being at home more often and taking a greater role in family life. It was lovely going to see Tracey and Fiona performing in their dancing shows, running them back and forth to guitar lessons, and attending school concerts.

True, there were times, when listening to a class of nervous recorder players, that I felt I was losing the will to live, but in the main, Wendy and I were thrilled to watch them.

Although our income had declined, life was more organized and less stressful.

I produced a version of our Hawaiian show for a summer season in a Bridlington holiday camp. A double act called Cornell & Day booked me for a cabaret summer season in the Kings Arms Hotel Morecambe. Wendy and I had lunched there as a treat when appearing at the Palace Theatre during a summer season some years ago. It was a feasible proposition, as I was only required to do one spot and appear in a finale.

Fiona pleaded to come with me. She had studied her Mum very carefully and suggested she could do any little bits that Mum did. We were amazed that Wendy's silver tight-fitting dress fitted her and agreed a trial.

She proved to be excellent. My bagpipes were all prepared every night. She arrived on cue with a bell to ring during an arrangement of a very fast accordion number called The Flying Scotsman. When I had finished she had everything all packed away in the proper order.

There was only one request she made... to stop on the way home for fish and chips. We journeyed the rest of the way home singing bawdy ballads, which she roared and laughed at.

I would say, "Do not tell your mother I taught you that song."

As soon as we walked through the front door, she immediately burst into the songs! I learned that confidentiality was never to be one of my young daughter's gifts.

We holidayed on a canal boat on the Lancaster Canal. It was one of the most memorable of our family holidays.

However, it was eventful. Shep ended up in the canal. A plastic fertilizer bag got itself tangled round the propeller. To free it, I ended up in the canal.

One morning, we ran aground. Athletic Tracey said, "Leave it to me Dad!" as she reached up for a branch on a nearby tree to hang on to, whilst she pushed with her feet, causing the craft to move forwards. Unfortunately, the boat moved away more quickly than she bargained for leaving her hanging on the branch. She too ended up in the canal!

We enjoyed mooring up and exploring the local shops. Antique and charity shops were the favourites with the girls. I was very curious about a purchase Wendy made for 10 pence. It was a small old rusty 'Oxo' tin. She said it reminded her of her childhood. We did not realise it at the time, but this small purchase would lead to us running a 44-seater tearoom and museum plus end up buying our retirement bungalow. It was a holiday full of laughter and quality family time.

Northern Ordination Course

With much trepidation, I attended my first Northern Ordination Course (NOC) lecture held in the Polytechnic College on Oxford Road in Manchester. I travelled by train from Poulton to Manchester's Victoria station.

Manchester held many memories for me as I stood on the platform: my bubble car days when, due to dense fog I ended up on a platform. As I emerged from the station, I saw the spot where the examiner informed me I had passed my road test. I passed Lewis's store where I worked as a salesman. From the station, it was a smart 20-minute walk through the city.

John White welcomed the 30 plus students to the lecture room. John used many long words I had never encountered before. I thought, "This is not going to be easy. I'm going to require a dictionary."

He outlined the contents of the course. "You will be required to study the Old Testament, the New Testament, Christian Doctrine, Church History, Christian Worship, Christian Ethics, Pastoral Studies, and New Testament Greek. We will during these subjects, touch on Philosophy and Psychology. You will be given lists of books you will require, and some of these may be borrowed from the Baptist College library."

We broke for coffee. I was in a dazed state of shock as John White walked alongside me and said, "Well Lawrie, what do you think of your first lecture?"

I stopped walking, turned and looked at him and replied, speaking very quickly,

"Well, you did labour under the exuberances of your own verbosity, which was an exactitude after I had concluded my ablutions!"

His jaw dropped, and he stared at me. "I'm sorry! I don't understand what you just said!"

"Exactly. Now you know how I felt during your lecture. Ease up a little on the long academic wordage," I replied.

He laughed loudly, "Well put. I certainly will."

The weekly lectures took place on a Monday. I took copious notes and read them up on the way home on the train. One evening a strange thing happened. A middle-aged woman entered my carriage and sat opposite me at the other end. I was busy looking through my notes when she said, "Excuse me, did you know you have a very pronounced blue aura surrounding you. I've never seen anything quite like it before."

"Really, not something I've ever been aware of'," I replied.

"My name is Doris Stokes, I'm a medium. Are you a religious man?"

I considered the question then said, "Yes, I suppose I am."

"Ah! I thought so," she said. She never spoke another word but remained staring at me.

I was glad when she got off at her station. Sometime later, I learned she was well known, in her line of work as a spiritual medium.

Morecambe

Bob Brierley the Entertainments Director, asked as I was in Morecambe, please would I compère a Bathing Beauty Competition and look after the celebrity judges. I was required to escort them to the Midland Hotel, have lunch with them and make sure they had all they needed.

"Who are they?" I asked.

"The two girls from the 'Liver Birds' TV series.

I enjoyed my duties and the girls were charming.

An event called the 'Kendal Gathering' asked if I could possibly get the services of the TV Coronation Street Star Pat Phoenix (who played Elsie Tanner) to sit in a horse-drawn coach, open the proceedings then take part in the procession through the town. In addition, could I put on a variety show in the town hall?

The variety show part was easy. Pat was trickier. At that time, she was living with the Prime Minister Tony Blair's future father in law, actor Tony Booth. I had worked with Pat as a 'walk-on' on an episode of Coronation Street when I played the part of a doorman bouncer and had to throw her down stairs, three times! Pat was blunt, outspoken and a notorious chain-smoker. Nevertheless, like Elsie Tanner, she had a heart of gold and inspired affection in everybody. She also enjoyed a tipple. After many phone calls and the promise of a four-figure sum, she agreed but turned up about an hour late and gave my organiser friend ulcers. I was not far behind him. However, she was a big success and as a result, I had this job on an annual basis providing star names and putting on shows.

NOC Weekend

I turned up at the Manchester Baptist College for my first NOC weekend. We were allocated the bedrooms vacated by residential theological students who were away for the weekends. They were warm and comfortable. We had visiting lecturers in addition to the NOC staff. The staff included a woman called Wendy Bracegirdle who taught Old Testament studies and was very pleasant, easy on the ear and informative. A vicar from Moss-Side was a regular lecturer, but for the life of me, I did not have a clue what he was endeavouring to impart. I was not alone!

I sent him a letter requesting that he might like to send me his lecture on a post-card to save me the trouble of coming in. I had just travelled by moped, in pouring rain as the trains were off. I considered his content as worthless. He was not amused, and neither was the principal, who insisted I apologise, otherwise I would be asked to leave the course.

Hugh Melinsky announced during one lecture, that we were going to learn Greek and we should purchase a Greek translation of the New Testament.

I thought, "I can hardly speak English never mind Greek."

This worried me very much. So much so, that on that Sunday after the service had finished, I was still on my knees in the pew.

"Well, Almighty God, you got me into this mess. How on earth am I going to cope with Greek?" I asked.

I finished praying and was aware of a tall figure in black standing by my side. I looked up and saw an elderly gentleman, wearing a clergy collar looking down at me and smiling.

I stood up. He shook my hand and said in a soft cultured voice,

"How do you do. My name is John Fawcett I am a retired priest and I have been informed that you have started ordination training?"

"That is correct, I have," I replied.

"Well, I am a classical Greek scholar, and it occurred to me that you may need my help?"

"You are indeed an answer to my prayers. When can I start?"

I visited him every week and he taught me many things. He was without a doubt the wisest man I ever had the privilege of meeting. We became great friends and his counsel was always greatly valued for the remainder of my life.

He had many tales to tell. He had been an army chaplain during the war. He was with the first liberation party inside the infamous Nazi Belsen Concentration Camp. He was present when Heinrich Himmler was captured and was outside the office door when he allegedly committed suicide. When asked to conduct the burial, he refused.

I was excused from the Greek classes, as I was having personal tuition. Some weeks later, at a lecture taken by the principal he said, "Now, gentlemen, I wish to see where you are all up to with your Greek. Please take out your Greek bibles. I think we shall start with you Lawrie?"

Everyone stared at me. The principal had a look of amusement. I got the impression he expected me to stumble through the passage. I opened the book and started to read St. Mark's Gospel. John Fawcett had taught me well and I read many verses in perfect Greek to the astonishment of all. Hugh Melinsky said, "Well, I suppose that speaks highly for personal tuition. Well done Lawrie." I realised my tutor was a star and that my prayers had been answered. 'Ask and it shall be given unto to you.' (Matthew 7.7.)

Our friends the Harmans announced they were leaving and moving to Plymouth where Michael would take up duties as a Royal Navy Chaplain. A young parishioner and I assisted them in their hired furniture van, to move to their new home. We missed them.

Gerald Field and a second curate called Keith Sillis replaced Michael. We became close friends with both them and their wives. Keith had come via NOC, so we had much to discuss and he was always very supportive. Eventually, he moved to look after a daughter church in a nearby housing estate. Gerald was married to a teacher, but we did not see much of her.

I was very impressed with Gerald's guitar playing and he proved very popular in the parish. He possessed a good folk type singing voice and was talented at composing some of his own songs. I persuaded him to appear in one of my shows in Southport at the Floral Hall, where I put in a one-night show each week. He went down very well indeed and appreciated the fee

BBC Play

In addition to studying and writing essays, I was fortunate in gaining a useful contact in Manchester who ran her own television artiste's agency. She was able to pass on to me various television bits for myself and for other artistes on my booking list.

Wendy and I appeared in a BBC Henrik Ibsen play, a film about the Bronte Sisters and a film called Bill (short Love Amongst the Artistes. When for Willemina) the agent, saw Wendy walking down a long staircase in a yellow crinoline dress she clutched my arm and said, "Who the hell is that?"

I replied, "That Bill, is my wife, Wendy."

"Well, she is gorgeous. I'm going to do a lot for her."

"No, you won't I'm afraid, she says this is her last time, as she gets bored out of her tree with television!"

"Oh! What a pity."

We did do another programme together when we played judges in a detective series called Inspector Crib. In a Victorian walking race scene (when a murder took place) I was required to walk arm in arm with the leading lady, who was dressed in a bright canary yellow dress, large hat and parasol. The crowds lined up alongside the racetrack.

As part of the action, I unhooked a heavy chain, about six feet long, threw it aside and with a flowery gesture, allowed the actress to pass across the track into a tent situated in the middle of the course.

The first time I did it, the director screamed, "Cut, Cut! For God's sake man, really throw the bloody chain, do not just lay it down. Now, Action!"

I did as he requested. Unfortunately, it struck one of the actors between the legs and he slowly sank to his knees holding his crotch with his eyes crossed.

The actress doubled up laughing as the director shouted "Oh! Cut! Cut! Bloody cut!" And so, the whole thing had to be filmed again. Mind you, I did notice a smile flickering across the director's face.

The essays came thick and fast. Quickly, I became knee deep in books. John Fawcett taught me how to pluck the information from a book without having to read it cover to cover.

The weekends were hard work but made interesting by John White's clever Sunday Spectaculars. Usually, I was hauled into that one way or another and each one was a learning curve.

He grabbed me one Sunday evening and said, "Lawrie, you are taking evensong tonight."

I replied in astonishment, "What? I've never done that in my life."

"Well you start tonight"

"I haven't got a cassock."

"Really? Charles!" he shouted to a very tall thin student, "Lend Lawrie your cassock and cincture."

He did, but it was far too long for me. I felt like Dopey from the seven Dwarfs. He wrapped the cincture round my waist. This is a black cummerbund with two tails hanging down. It was a bit on the loose side to say the least.

John said, "Right, there is the book, on you go."

I walked through the college chapel doors heading for a lectern on top of three steps. It was quite a long walk. Students were kneeling on either side of me as I traversed the aisle. One of them, who was to become a lifelong friend, Dick Swindle, had his hands over his face. I noted he was shaking as I drew nearer to him then he pitched forward as if worshipping Allah! I thought he was crying.

As I walked, I felt something slowly slipping down over my waist. 'That damn cincture' I thought.

I reached the first step, but as I raised my foot, it caught somehow in my cassock. I raised the second foot and realised I was in fact now walking up the inside of my cassock. As I walked, the front of the cassock went down, taking me with it until I had to grab the lectern throwing all the papers and books on the floor in the process. I sorted myself out, turned around and the whole chapel was in bedlam. My friend Dick was prostrate on the floor in hysterics. The remainder of the students were rolling about with laughter. I looked at John White and the Principal. They just glared at me and slowly shook their heads. I carried on.

A young male vocalist called Dave Paris popped in to see me. He had driven up in a huge black Mercedes Benz.

"Dave, you have been through a real struggling time but now are just beginning to show a profit. You are too early with the big limo," I said.

"I promised myself one like yours," he replied.

Sadly, he went off to perform at some late nightclubs and suffered a head-on collision on his way home. We received a phone call from his wife Julie informing us of his death. We drove straight over to their terraced house in Blackburn. Julie was a nurse and had just had a baby. The house was in a mess. Dave had started to knock a wall down and do alterations. She had very little money.

A New House

She said, "I just want to sell up and go back home to New Zealand. There is nothing here for me anymore. A Pakistani man has offered to buy the house. I'm sure it's worth more than he wants to pay." She told us how much. We doubled it and bought it. It felt good being able to help Julie and her baby out and it turned out to be a good investment in the end. The altering and decorating provided a welcome distraction from the stress of making a living and studying.

All the way through the theology studies, I felt the power of Jesus by my side.

Wendy typed out my hand-written essays. We gave John White some good laughs. One sentence was intended to read, 'He became known as the Prince of Israel.' Unfortunately, there was a slip of Wendy's finger and it read, 'He became known as Prick of Israel.'

Another said, 'When he got home, he sat down and decided to explore all around his base.'

John White's comments in red exclaimed, "Oh! Surely not!"

One morning, when he gave out the topics he said, "Ah! Lawrie, you can have some interesting fun with this one. Pornography in the 80's"

I certainly did, but I made sure he became part of the joke. First, I researched what pornography was being marketed, then who was buying it and their reasons. I had to read the Lord Longford report. It certainly proved an interesting project.

I put the word our discretely and was astounded to have a brown envelope pushed through my door containing magazines with very pornographic images. I was curious, as I knew from whom they came: a very pretty, quietly spoken young married woman living around the corner. When I questioned her, she said they belonged to her husband and she was glad to get rid of them and did not want them back.

In fact, she had some videos that I could look at in her home, but she did not want to be there when they were viewed. The two curates agreed to come with me on that occasion just in case I was in danger of corruption. We all sat on her settee and started to watch.

The woman in the movie said to the actor, "I'll just go and get the cookies...you prepare yourself."

My two curate friends were sitting there in their dog collars, eyes wide open, and jaws dropped, with cups of tea balanced on saucers A sudden squeaking noise interrupted our concentration, it was the window cleaner. I quickly hit the remote and there we were apparently watching Noddy in Toyland! The window cleaner had a look of amused bewilderment.

John White travelled to London most weeks and I took advantage of this fact. I was also aware that he marked essays on the train and travelled in his dog collar.

He related to me on the Friday at a weekend gathering that what I did was quite unforgivable! I asked why. He replied. "I took my seat on the train which was quite busy. A young woman and three children asked if I minded if they shared the table with me. I beamed at them and invited them to join me. I explained I was a lecturer and did my marking of student essays as I travelled. This was politely accepted.

After about three essays, I arrived at yours. I turned over a couple of pages and was aware of a sharp intake of breath from the young woman sitting opposite me. I glanced down and there in glorious technicolour was an A4 glossy sheet from a magazine of a pornographic nature! I very quickly tuned over but was acutely aware of some bewildered stares from the woman and some stifled sniggers from the children. I felt my face burning. Then, I could not believe it. I turned over another page and there was yet another one! The woman mentioned another seat had come free, took her children and left. How could you do this to me?"

I will say this for John, he never held a grudge and I always counted him as a friend.

There followed another topic he wished me to pursue to be called, 'God in the Media'. This involved visiting the producer of Songs of Praise at the BBC TV studios in Manchester who was very helpful. I spent time with religious radio broadcasters. I met a Suffragan Bishop (a sort of assistant to the diocesan bishop) in Manchester called Stewart Cross. He was involved in religious television and very interested in my project. He proved very helpful. He also proved very encouraging after I was ordained and later when I became involved in media projects. After my second visit to the BBC in Manchester, the producer invited me to join him for lunch in the canteen. This felt odd, as I had been there before but as an act. We sat down; another producer called Barney Colehan MBE joined us who was well known for his famous TV programme from the City Varieties Theatre in Leeds called The Good Old Days. He took his seat opposite me and kept staring at me.

Finally, he said, "You are a turn, aren't you?"

"No" I replied," I am an Ordinand."

"Well, I never forget a face, and I see you playing an accordion."

My producer friend said, "Barney, he is studying and preparing for the priesthood, he's not a turn. You have that one wrong."

"Well, he has a clone then."

I decided not to put him right.

The Retreat

One weekend took the form of a retreat and was in a convent where the nuns looked after us. The visiting lecturer was a clergyman from Cleveleys called a Reverend Eric Flood. Eric made a point of seeking me out and asking me when it came to my placement if I would like to spend it in his parish. I was aware that when the course was nearing its end, the students were required to spend six weeks in a parish different from their own local one. This would include Sundays and some mid-week time. I agreed, especially as Cleveleys was only up the road from my home.

My six weeks covered the Christmas period and the experience was very valuable to me. Eric and I got on very well. The parishioners were very welcoming. Eric had been a curate at St. Stephens on the Cliffs and held the vicar Geoffrey Gower Jones in high regard. He asked if I would be interested in becoming his curate when my studies concluded. I talked it over with Wendy and we agreed.

Father Geoffrey (as he liked to be called) stopped me one Sunday and said, "Lawrie, would you do me a great favour today?"

"Certainly, if I can," I replied.

"We have been providing the Sunday service at the Butlin's Metropole Hotel in Blackpool. However, the curate who usually does it is ill. Would you do it? It's not a communion service just what we call a hymn sandwich with prayers and a short sermon, off the cuff."

I said, "Certainly, it will be a valuable experience."

However, I was unprepared for the reaction. I put on my cassock and surplus and as I strode on to the platform in the ballroom, the organist started to play Scotland the Brave, the signature tune for my act.

He said, "Well, when they said you would be taking the service I thought it proper."

There was a group of men drinking at the bar. They turned around and gave me their whole attention. I really enjoyed it and it seemed to go very well.

Afterwards the organist said, "Hey! Lawrie that is the best that has gone in ages. They are usually bored to tears and ignore the whole thing."

Many things were crowding into our lives as the course ended. The vicar retired and a new one came in place very quickly. The final essays were heavy going. I was in the middle of writing a six thousand-word thesis on Isaiah when the phone rang. It was a colleague called John Stirling whom I was assisting. We had Marty Caine, a comedienne appearing in Sheffield.

"Lawrie," John said, "if Marty doesn't get paid right now she will not go on!"

I put down my pen and I dare not put into print my instructions, but the last word ended in 'off!'

I went back to Isaiah. Wendy popped her head round the door and said in a calm voice, "And this is the man who might one day be a vicar?"

I found the Northern Ordination Course on the one hand, a very gruelling experience, but on the other, a most rewarding three year where I had made good friends and acquired much knowledge. Every time someone was dropped from the course for one reason or another, I always had the feeling that I would be next.

Every year we held a student's concert after summer school. I compered the first one. I thought it had gone very well. The laughter was raucous. The applause was loud and appreciative. Yet, the Principal sent for me and I was told off. He had received complaints, especially from some clergy wives about the tone and content of my humour.

One had said, "Really, Principal, is this the sort of man we want to turn out as a vicar?"

I promised it would not happen again.

He said, "Lawrie, most of you all arrive here as rough iron ore. We attempt to refine you all into high quality steel and turn you all out as gentlemen, gentle, men."

A TV drama

My TV agent friend Bill phoned to ask if I could do a week on a big TV drama starring Sir Laurence

Olivier, Dorothy Tutin, Diana Rigg, Robert Lindsay and John Hurt.

"Wow!" I said. "This will be my last one for you Bill. I am leaving show business at the end of that week. What am I doing in it?"

"You will be the grooms-man for King Lear. You know, looking after his horse. And by the way, I don't believe you will ever leave the business." She was right in a way of course. A few years into the future. I ended up by producing, directing and presenting a religious series of TV programmes for Granada TV,

So, there I was in this huge studio-based production, holding on to Laurence Olivier's horse. He was quite ill when he did this and had to keep having breaks. He also had great difficulty remembering his lines. I remember Dorothy Tutin saying, "Poor Larry, he really shouldn't be doing this, he looks quite ill."

Diana Rigg ignored everyone. I had a bet on that I could get her to say at least, 'Good Morning' to me before the end of the week. I lost the bet.

I was in the canteen having lunch when John Hurt walked in and said, "Do you mind if I join you?" We had a lovely chat. What a charming man he was.

Some of the filming was quite hairy. I had to run around and round this huge spacey studio which resembled a forest, hanging on to Larry's horse with him in the saddle. Other horses and runners were alongside me plus some huge Irish Wolfhounds barking and snarling. There were simulated ditches and I had the occasional bucket of dirty water thrown in my face as we ran around finally arriving at large stockade type doors.

We stopped to be challenged by the gatekeeper. I think it was Roy Kinnear. Three times Larry forgot his one line and we had to run around the studio again! I managed to have a brief chat with him during a lull. I told him this was my last effort as I was going into the priesthood.

He exclaimed, "Really? Do you know I seriously considered that road myself at one time in my life?"

"Why do you still do this?" I asked him.

"Because I need the money old boy!"

'Knock and the door will be opened to you' (Matthew 7.7)

Everything started happening very fast. The final summer school ended. We attended a Commendation Service in Manchester Cathedral where we were presented with a Preachers Stole (a wide black silk scarf) and a NOC Hood in the colours black, red and silver grey. Someone said to me, "I bet you didn't think you would end up with a degree in theology." Wendy and our girls attended the ceremony. It had been a long hard haul for all of us. John White said, "I expect you will be having a holiday to celebrate?"

"No, afraid not John. We have not managed to sell our house and the cash is not rolling in any more. I started out with a black Mercedes Benz and through the kindness of one of the students, I am now running a car I bought from him for £40."

"Oh! Yes. I wondered to whom that wreck belonged. That fawn thing with a cream driver's door and all hanging with rust. It's nicknamed Adam's chocolate éclair."

"Yep, that's the one alright. The seats also gone, and I now drive side-saddle."

"Well, I have been appointed as a Canon at Windsor Castle. I have been given very nice apartments and so you and the family will come and have a holiday there with me."

I said, "What, THE Royal Windsor Castle?"

"The very same."

It was difficult to believe that the police were escorting us through the gate of the castle. John was waiting for us. We had a great time and visited everywhere. There was a large Madam Tussaud's Waxworks Exhibition inside the railway station simulating the visit of King Edward the fifth and Queen Mary. It was amazing. We took John to a play in the theatre (where Wendy had danced in pantomime some years earlier) to see our pal Bryan Burdon who had a part in it. Afterwards he was thrilled to sit with the cast in the bar.

One morning John invited me to go with him to a small chapel situated above the main St. Georges Chapel called Queen Victoria's Chapel. I felt very privileged to be invited to read the lesson.

I happened to remark to John as we were leaving that he had some very weird ornaments doted about his apartments. He said, "Students give me things and I feel obliged to display them."

With that in mind some days later, we were attending a car boot sale and Wendy spotted a little chalk budgie. It appeared boss-eyed, had half a beak and needed a re-paint. We bought it and sent it to John with a note, 'Students give me things and I feel obliged to display them.'

John placed it centre on his birdbath on his small patio. One morning he heard peals of laughter. Upon investigation, he discovered it was Her Majesty the Queen. She was looking over his wall and pointing to the budgie and was in hysterics. He explained to her, that it was a gift from some weird student from 'ooop north' Ma'am.

The local Blackpool Gazette got hold of the story that I was to be ordained and serve as a curate at Christ Church Thornton Cleveleys. The reporter Robin Dukes said in print, "I was gobsmacked!" Some other newspapers also carried the story.

BBC TV asked me to appear in a programme telling my story.

An invitation followed: to be interviewed by well-known TV broadcaster Martin Bashir (of Princess Diana fame) who was curious as to my conversion story.

After-dinner talks came rolling in and invitations to preach in various churches. All this and I was not yet even ordained!

Although the house was up for sale, we had to keep dropping the price, as the housing market was not healthy. We moved into a new house on an estate in Thornton Cleveleys. Everyone there seemed to be first-time buyers and friendly. All apart from the next-door people, Derek and Edwina. The neighbours said they had nicknamed them 'Doe-doe and Deadwina'! They did give us a bit of needless trouble and were never helpful but extremely awkward.

It was a much smaller house than Warbreck Drive. When the girls saw their reduced spaced bedrooms, Tracey just slid down the wall saying, "How could you do this to us Dad?" I felt like a criminal. Fiona was quite happy and excited at the new prospect.

Wendy, logical and practical as ever said, "Well, it's smaller than we have been used to, but I am looking forward to a new type of life. I know the money is much less than we have known, but at least it will be regular for a change and I will know exactly where I am with things." I never thought of that.

No sooner were we all settling in than I was on a silent retreat for a week before ordination in Whalley Abbey. This quiet time was spent in meditation, prayer and preparation for a big change in culture. We were warned that people would react to us differently. Even the wearing of a dog collar would produce various effects and reactions.

On the morning of the ordination, I noticed my name along with some others on the notice board. The Bishop wanted to see us. My name was last on the list. I had a strong feeling about this. At the appointed time, I knocked on the heavy oak door. A voice bid me enter. There was Bishop Stewart Cross, silhouetted and sitting by the window. He looked very serious and had a concerned frown on his face, which was usually peaceful. He was without a doubt, the gentlest and deeply spiritual man I would ever meet. It always felt uplifting to have been in his presence. He truly was a man of God.

There was a long silence. He looked at me in a very concerned way as if not sure how to break some news to me.

I took a deep breath and said in an even voice, "Bishop, I know you are struggling to tell me that it has all been a mistake and that I will not be ordained today. I do not want you to worry about it. I really do understand. It is quite all right. Do not be upset. I have been expecting this."

He looked stunned then burst out laughing. "I say Lawrie, it's a bit late in the day for that isn't it?" He said a prayer with me, congratulated me on my three-year studies and in coming through them and arriving at this day.

In the car park, I just could not get my old banger of a car to fire up. I was very frustrated. Today of all days. As I tried this and that, cursing and resorting to the odd swearing, when I heard a calm voice behind me saying gently,

"Now then Lawrie, later today you will be acquiring the title of Reverend. You should be praying not swearing."

"Oh! Sorry Bishop. I will say a prayer." Which I did. Pressed the starter and it fired up!

"Well, I'll be damned," said the Bishop as he walked away chuckling to himself.

490

Introduction

We filed into Blackburn Cathedral where a packed congregation sang at the top of their voices Crown Him with Many Crowns. I noticed that all the candidates wore brand new cream or white stoles (silk scarves). Mine was obviously quite old, faded and worn, but I was so proud to be wearing it in honour of my Classical Greek Scholar mentor. He wore the stole in the Belsen Concentration Camp when he took communion with the survivors. It was my way of saying a big thank you to him. I noticed a tear in his eye as I passed his pew.

As I knelt down, I am sure I was aware of all the Angels in Heaven celebrating over one saved sinner. The Bishop placed his hands gently upon my head and said, "Send down your Holy Spirit on Lawrence, ordained Deacon."

After some months, I knew I would be back here again to be ordained a priest.

And so, we emerged into the bright sunshine surrounded by well-wishers sharing in our joy. Wendy took my arm and my lovely daughters gathered close. We were looking forward to a new journey and a new chapter which was to prove even more exciting than show business. Little did I realise not only would I become a vicar within four years but also be producing and directing documentary video programmes up and down Britain and presenting network TV and satellite programmes nationwide.

However, dear reader, that adventure will be in my next book. Hallelujah! Amen.

Blackburn Cathedral

Wendy and her new Curate

Our lovely family

Tracey and John

One of the most exciting days of my life and the start of a new chapter in our lives.

Fiona our youngest

1982. Ordained Deacon at Blackburn Cathedral